"Kardong is America's foremost scholar on monasticism in general and on monastic rules in particular. To his much-acclaimed translation of and commentary on the Rule of Saint Benedict, Kardong can now add his translation of the Rule of Monks, the Cenobitic Rule, the Penitential Rule, and the Rule Walbert. Kardong's translation, based on both French and English sources, as well as on his own prodigious knowledge of Latin, is first rate. Especially helpful is his introduction and copious footnotes. In both, we see Kardong's wit and scholarship at their best. A must-have for anyone interested in monastic studies."

> —Fr. Benedict M. Guevin, OSB
> St. Anselm Abbey

"Columban was a force to be reckoned with and his story becomes even more compelling as presented by Terrence G. Kardong. While having some things in common with the Rule of Benedict, the Rule of Columban presents a fascinating view of another type of monasticism that existed shortly after the time of Benedict. Kardong presents it in a clear contemporary translation, accompanied by interesting and detailed commentary. While its penal code may seem harsh to modern sensibilities, many of the faults it deals with will be no stranger to readers. Kardong points out that Columban's penitential actually paved the way for the sacrament of confession as we now know it. Although it appears last in this volume, those interested in rules for women's communities will certainly not want to miss the rule that Columban's successor Walbert wrote for nuns."

> —Sr. Colleen Maura McGrane, OSB
> Benedictine Sisters of Perpetual Adoration

"The productiveness of Fr. Terrence Kardong is astounding and from it we have all benefited. Here, once again, he makes accessible to us a literary monument of the ancient monastic tradition, this time the Rule of Columban, written not more than fifty or sixty years after the Rule of St. Benedict. With the meticulousness and erudition and wit that we have come to expect from him, Fr. Terrence provides fresh and lively translations of this historically significant Rule and one of its epigones, the Rule of Walbert. What a wealth of fascinating—and strange—material one finds in these texts!"

—Mark DelCogliano
Assistant Professor of Theology
University of St. Thomas

CISTERCIAN STUDIES SERIES: NUMBER TWO HUNDRED SEVENTY

Saint Columban

His Life, Rule, and Legacy

Translated and Introduced by

Terrence G. Kardong, OSB

α

Cistercian Publications
www.cistercianpublications.org

LITURGICAL PRESS
Collegeville, Minnesota
www.litpress.org

A Cistercian Publications title published by Liturgical Press

BR
1720
-C624
A25

2017

Cistercian Publications
Editorial Offices
161 Grosvenor Street
Athens, Ohio 45701
www.cistercianpublications.org

The three rules by Columban are based on the critical edition by G. S. M. Walker, *Sancti Columban: Opera* (Dublin: Dublin Institute for Advanced Studies, 1970). The Rule of Walbert is based on *Regula Cuiusdam Patris ad Virgines*, PL 87:1011–46.

Unless otherwise noted, Scripture texts in this work are translated by its author.

1   2   3   4   5   6   7   8   9

Library of Congress Control Number: 2017028030

ISBN 978-0-87907-270-4   ISBN 978-0-87907-170-7 (ebook)

Contents

Abbreviations

Coen	*Coenobitic Rule of Columban*
Conf	Cassian, *Conferences*
CSEL	Corpus Scriptorum Ecclesiasticorum Latinorum
CSQ	*Cistercian Studies Quarterly*
De eccl dogm	Gennadius, *De ecclesiasticis dogmatibus*
DHGE	*Dictionnaire d'histoire et de géographie ecclésiastiques*. Paris, 1912– .
Dial	*Dialogues*, Gregory the Great
DialSul	*Dialogues*, Sulpicius Severus
Enchir	*Enchiridion*, Sextus
Ep(p)	Epistolae, Augustine; Jerome
Inst	Cassian, *Institutes*
Instr	Instructions, Columban
Liber Davidis	*Excerpta Davidis*
MGH	Monumenta Germanica Historia
Mir	*Miracula*, Gregory of Tours
Mor	*Moralia in Iob*, Gregory the Great
NAB	New American Bible
OLD	*Oxford Latin Dictionary*

OT	Old Testament
Paen	*Paenitentiale*, Columban
Pen Bigotianum	*Paenitentiale quod dicitur Bigotianum*
PenF	*Paenitentiale*, Finnian of Clonard
Penit	*Penitentiale*, Theodore
Pr	*Praecepta*, Pachomius
Praec	*Praeceptum*, Augustine
Praef Gildas	*Praefatio Gildae de Paenitentia*
RB	Rule of Saint Benedict
RBasil	Basil, *Regula*
RCes	Caesarius, *Regula*
RDon	Donatus, *Regula*
Reg	*Rule of Monks*, Columban
Reg Virg	*Regula sanctarum virginum*, Caesarius of Arles
RM	Rule of the Master
RM ThP	Rule of the Master Thema Pater (commentary on the Lord's Prayer)
RSV	Revised Standard Version
S	*Sermo*
SBo	Sahidic-Bohairic
VC	*Vita Sancti Columbani*, Jonas of Bobbio
VMart	*Vita S. Martini*, Sulpicius Severus
Wal	*Rule of Walbert*

Preface

A reasonable opening question to introduce this study of the Rule of Columban might be simply: why? The Rule of Columban is not a very attractive body of early monastic literature, at least to the modern sensibility, as is suggested by the fact that the last, and only, English translation appeared forty-three years ago: *Sancti Columbani Opera*, edited by G. S. M. Walker, Scriptores Latini Hiberniae (Dublin: Dublin Institute for Advanced Studies, 1970). The reason behind this lack of interest is revealed by a cursory glance at the pages. This Rule is, by our current standards, quite harsh. Of course, that might be said of almost every ancient monastic Rule. Yet the Rule of Columban is an extreme case, for it is largely composed of penalties. In fact, two of its three sections (*Regula Coenobialis* and *Paenitentiale*) are entirely made up of faults and their punishment.

Still, this Rule from about AD 600 is well worth another look. At least one of the greatest experts on early monasticism, Adalbert de Vogüé, thought so. He devoted two entire volumes in the Bellefontaine series *Vie Monastique* 19–20 to the life of Columban and to his Rule. Vogüé also included about two hundred pages of commentary on the Columbanian texts in his monumental *Histoire Littéraire du Mouvement Monastique dans l'Antiquité* 10–11 (Paris: Éditions du Cerf, 2006–2007). Although Vogüé's work can intimidate any scholar coming after him, his obvious respect for this material certainly recommends it.

So, then, what is the positive value of this literature? For a Benedictine monk like me, the Columbanian material has important connections to the Rule of Benedict. For one thing, the Rule of Columban was written not more than fifty to sixty years after the Rule of Benedict and therefore provides a rare glimpse into a rather murky period of monastic and medieval church history. Columban was an immigrant to continental Europe from Ireland, but he was well read, and that reading included the Rule of Benedict (see Adalbert de Vogüé, ed. and trans., *Règles et pénitentiels monastiques*). Columban does not quote the Rule of Benedict directly, but the mere fact that it influenced him is significant, for it suggests that Benedict's Rule was known north of the Alps by AD 600.

This possibility becomes a probability when we consider that by ca. 630–640 Columban's successors were *supplementing* the Rule of Columban with the Rule of Benedict. Both Abbot Walbert of Luxeuil and Bishop Donatus of Besançon, a former monk of Luxeuil, wrote Rules for nuns in which they included parts of these two Rules, plus others. The reason they created these "mixed" rules was probably that the Rule of Columban is not sufficiently comprehensive. There are many aspects of community life that it simply does not cover.

This being the case, we might say that the Rule of Columban was the vehicle, as it were, that carried the Rule of Benedict over the Alps. If we wonder why the Rule of Benedict needed help for this to happen, I think the probable answer is the Lombards. They were the latest, and fiercest, Germanic tribe to invade Italy, and they destroyed Benedict's own monastery of Monte Cassino in about 568. But the Lombards did much more damage than that; they were aggressive Arians who crippled the Catholic Church in northern Italy for a whole century. Anyone who reads the correspondence of Pope Gregory the Great gets a vivid idea of how grievously the Lombards wounded the church in the sixth century.

Therefore it is not surprising that Benedictine monasticism only slowly spread north. Yet the reverse was not true: Columbanian monasticism soon spread south when the saint himself crossed the Alps and in the last years of his life founded the monastery of Bobbio. I find it baffling that these Irish Catholics were allowed to settle within a few miles of the Lombard capital of Milan-Pavia, for Columban was staunchly anti-Arian. Lest anyone think this fact shows that Columban had mellowed in his old age, his biographer, Jonas, in *Vita Sancti Columbani* assures us he had not! But Jonas also says that by the year 610 the Lombard kings were looking for accommodation with Rome. Perhaps Columban and his monks helped further this process.

Aside from its role as a vehicle of and partner with Benedict's Rule, is Columban's Rule of much intrinsic interest to us today? As far as I know, no modern religious order claims to follow it, so why should we bother to study it? The first reason is that it was and is one of the foundational documents of early monasticism. As such, it is worth our attention if we wish to understand the mind-set and customs of the pioneers of an important movement in the history of the Roman Catholic Church.

When we read and study the Rule of Columban, it is well to remember that it is an *Irish* Rule, transmitting the Christian vision of a non-Roman church. A glance at the map of Europe shows plainly that Ireland is on the edge. At the time of Columban, people thought Ireland was virtually the end of the world, *finis terrae*. But even if Ireland was peripheral, it was not marginal. Indeed, it was the home of a vibrant and self-assured Christian community. It was a long way from Rome, both geographically and temperamentally, and so it tended to make the European church nervous. Where the customs differed, the temptation was to bully the Irish back into line. A man like Columban, however, was not easily pushed around. He would lecture the pope himself if he thought the sovereign pontiff needed it (see his Letter 1 to Gregory the Great). As such, Columban stands as a healthy symbolic antidote to Roman Catholic centralization and Ultramontanism, which has become especially strong in our own day.

As we have seen, the Rule of Columban is loaded with penalties. From the standpoint of general monastic history, we might say that it is *overloaded* with penalties. Did monks ever live that way? They certainly do not today! I have lived in a typical American monastery for fifty years, but rarely have I seen a monk publicly punished. Maybe some of us should have been, but we were not. Moreover, it does not look as if Saint Benedict was nearly so preoccupied with punishment as was Columban. True, there are about a dozen short chapters of the Rule of Benedict devoted to penalties, but that is well below the Columbanian standard.

In this regard, we might ask whether the monks of Columban actually lived under such a penal system. Perhaps it was just one of those ascetic ideals that were more theoretical than practical? No: they put it into practice, as is suggested by the fact that the Rule (Coen I) begins with the requirement that "we make confession before meat or entering our beds." That is, the monks confessed their faults to the superior every day. What is more, when this Rule was adapted for women, e.g., by Walbert for Eboriac, the nuns were urged to confess their faults *three times a day!* See *Regula Cuiusdam Patris* VI; French version: Lazare Seilhac and M. Bernard Saïd, trans.,"Règle de saint Donat, ou Règle pour les vierges," in *Règles Monastiques au Féminin: dans la tradition de Benoît et Columban*, Vie monastique, série monachisme ancien, 33 (Bégrolles-en-Mauges: Abbaye de Bellefontaine, 1996), 57–95, here 69–71. When a nun was experiencing a hard death, the "Miracles of Eboriac" (see part 2 of the *Vita Columbani*) assumes that it is because she has not confessed her faults and sins to the abbess.

It is often pointed out that the penitential transaction between monks and nuns and their superiors was not sacramental. Probably not, but it does seem that it had a definite effect on the history of the Catholic sacrament of penance. Before the sixth or seventh century, penance was a public affair, involving only very serious sins and resulting in long, severe penances. The upshot was that many people deferred confession until their deathbed. Because of the influence of the Irish missionaries like Columban, the Catholic Church developed a more humane practice of private confession that has now been in effect for 1,500 years (see *Oxford Dictionary of the Christian Church*, ed. F. L. Cross and E. A. Livingstone, s.v. *penance*). Still, it does seem that the Columbanian Rule was preoccupied with the element of penance. For the penitential practice to have a long-term monastic future, it had to be modified.

The same could be said for the Divine Office. Modern nuns or monks who read this legislation for the first time will probably wonder how they could possibly have said so many psalms together. To our way of thinking, their horarium was as grossly unbalanced as was that of Cluny a few centuries later. So this feature also had to be modified in subsequent generations. But Columban was not alone on this point. Not only was Irish monasticism noted for its enormously long Offices, but so was the practice of the Frankish monks and nuns. For his part, Vogüé never missed a chance to complain about the overly long Offices in ancient Gaul. He knew that such practices had a deleterious effect on general monastic health. But the Irish felt right at home.

Yet it does not make sense to dwell too much on the weaknesses of the Rule of Columban. Even though it did not prove to be an adequate pattern for long-term cenobitic excellence, it nevertheless contains a wealth of detail concerning early medieval monastic life. When a person examines the text minutely, as I like to do, many curious aspects of everyday life come into focus. As L. P. Hartley said in *The Go-Between*, "The past is a foreign country. They do things different there." They do indeed, but our tendency is to read our own culture and mind-set back into the past. We can only avoid this by practicing careful exegesis: trying to grasp what the ancient text is actually saying. The hermeneutical question comes only second: How should we respond to it?

One of the great attractions of the Rule of Columban is the happy fact that we know quite a lot about the author and his circumstances. Unlike most early monastic legislators, we have a good *vita* of Columban and his followers. Therefore I thought it helpful to include a fairly detailed summary of Jonas's work, although the text itself is too long to be included. Of course, Jonas's *vita* is not a modern biography with all the warts, but it rings much truer to real life than, say, Gregory's *Dialogue II* on Benedict. Here too there is a wealth of detail, which would repay a close commentary.

Not only was the Rule of Columban important in its own right, but it also had a significant effect on posterity. Two of Columban's own disciples from Luxeuil, Walbert and Donatus, wrote monastic Rules for nuns. These Rules use parts of the Rule of Columban plus materials from other monastic Rules, especially those of Benedict and Caesarius of Arles. For my purposes here I consider the Rule of Walbert (*Regula Cuiusdam Patris ad Virgines*) more interesting. Therefore I have included a translation of and commentary on it in my book, following the three parts of Columban's rule: *Regula Monachorum* (Reg), *Regula Coenobialis* (Coen), and *Paenitentiale* (Paen).

But we have even more than a Rule and Life for Columban. We also have some of his letters and some of his sermons. I have not studied these in any depth, but at least I can say that we know more about Columban than about most ancient monastic writers and founders. I plan to expand my research, and I hope others will join me.

Assumption Abbey
Richardton, North Dakota
Spring 2014

Introduction
Columban and His Posterity

Columban[1] was an Irish monk who nevertheless spent his last twenty-five years on the European continent. In fact, his self-imposed exile from Ireland to Europe established a pattern for Irish monks that continued throughout the Middle Ages, with important consequences for European Catholicism. This tradition of pilgrimage (*peregrinatio*) was seen by the Irish monks as penitential because of their love of their beloved homeland. But it also had a missionary thrust: Columban went to Gaul to convert the Gauls.

Columban was born in Leinster, a county in eastern Ireland, in about 540.[2] Regarding his early life, his biographer, Jonas,

---

[1] Columban is often confused with Columba, another great Irish saint of the same period (521–597), who also left the Emerald Isle to evangelize, in his case, Scotland. In fact, their names are identical in Irish: Colum Cille. What is more, Columban calls himself Columba (*vilis Columba*: a poor dove) in a letter to Pope Gregory I (Letter 1, AD 600). *Columbanus* is simply the adjectival form of *Columba*.

[2] Jonas Elnonensis, *Vita Sancti Columbani Abbatis* (*Life of Columban* = VC) 1.9. Jonas does not offer a date for Columban's birth. In fact, he seems to know rather little about Columban's Irish days. That is not surprising, since Jonas never met Columban in person. He became a monk of Bobbio in 617, two years after Columban's death. The Latin original of Jonas's *Vita Columbani* is found in PL 87:1011–46A. The only English I was able to consult appeared in an old series called *Translations and Reprints from the Original Sources of European History*, ed. Dana Carleton Munro, vol. 2, no. 7 (Philadelphia: Department of History, the University of Pennsylvania, 1899), 1–36. This book contains only the first book of Jonas's *Life*. My quotations of the *Life* come from this book.

relies on some rather blatant hagiographical clichés: While his mother was pregnant with him, she dreamt that a sun rose from her bosom and shone over the whole world (VC 1.6). The boy Columban began learning grammar[3] and also became aware of lustful attractions. He consulted a holy woman, who urged him to flee the world. To do so, he had to step over the body of his mother blocking the door (VC 1.8). He then went to study the Bible with the holy man Senilis, who pressed his students to live out what they were learning (VC 1.9).

Columban's next move was to Bangor, a monastery in the far north of Ireland where the famous Comgall was abbot. Jonas does not present any particular motivation for this move, which seems like a logical one for a pious young man. In fact, the Irish church in the sixth century was heavily monastic, so much so that some historians have claimed that abbots, not bishops, ruled it.[4] Whether that was strictly true or not, it

---

[3] In "The Career of Columbanus," in *Columbanus: Studies of the Latin Writings*, ed. Michael Lapidge (Woodbridge, UK: Boydell, 1997), 1–28, here 3, Donald Bullough says that Columban got a decent education and was quite literate before he went to Bangor. But even though Columban occasionally quotes classic authors, Bullough thinks those passages are mainly from memorized copybooks and not from any deep classical learning. Still, Columban writes good Latin and can vary his style depending on his purpose. The standard version of Columban's works in Latin and English is found in *Sancti Columbani Opera*, ed. and trans. G. S. M. Walker (Dublin: The Dublin Institute for Advanced Studies, 1970); the manuscript history of the three rules translated in this volume, explaining the long and short versions of each, appears in Walker, xliv–lv. Vogüé discusses the long text of the *Coenobitic Rule* in Saint Colomban, *Régles et pénitentiels monastiques*, trans. Adalbert de Vogüé with Pierre Sangiani and Jean-Baptiste Juglar, Aux sources du monachisme colombanien vol. 2, Vie monastique 20 (Bégrolles-en-Mauges, France: Abbaye de Bellefontaine, 1989), 94–115. Wherever I depart from Walker, the translation is my own.

[4] The *Oxford Dictionary of the Christian Church*, ed. F. L. Cross and E. A. Livingstone (Oxford: Oxford University Press, 2005), s.v. "Ireland," puts the matter nicely: "Until the 12th cent., the Irish Church retained a

probably colored Columban's later conflicts with the bishops in Gaul.[5]

Jonas does not tell us much about Columban's life at Bangor, except that he had been in the cloister "many years" when he left for Gaul in 590–591 (VC 1.9). Yet Jonas also says that Columban was about thirty when he left Ireland (VC 1.10).[6] The main experts on Columban, namely G. S. M. Walker and Adalbert de Vogüé,[7] think that he was in fact closer to fifty when he left. Moreover, Walker thinks he was the chief teacher at Bangor for many years.[8]

Because Columban was one of Comgall's main collaborators, Comgall only reluctantly granted him permission to depart for Gaul, and all the more reluctantly since he was taking with him a dozen brethren. But what was Columban's real reason for making this decisive change in his life? Certainly it was not to get away from Comgall and his monastic customs!

---

structure that lacked metropolitan jurisdiction and remained unaffected by the developments which in the 9th and 10th cents. elsewhere established the boundaries between pastoral and monastic churches."

[5] Walker, *Sancti Columbani Opera*, xvi.

[6] Walker, *Sancti Columbani Opera*, xi. Thirty was considered a perfect age because Christ was thought to have begun his ministry at that age.

[7] Jonas, *Vie de Saint Columban et de ses disciples*, trans. Adalbert de Vogüé with Pierre Sangiani, Aux sources du monachisme colombanien vol. 1, Vie monastique 19 (Bégrolles-en-Mauges, France: Abbaye de Bellefontaine, 1988), 43 (cited below as *Vie de Saint Columban*). Columban's three rules translated below appear in Saint Colomban, *Règles et pénitentiels monastiques*, trans. Adalbert de Vogüé with Pierre Sangiani and Jean-Baptiste Juglar, Aux sources du monachisme colombanien vol. 2, Vie monastique 20 (Bégrolles-en-Mauges, France: Abbaye de Bellefontaine, 1989). Cited in the notes to the Rules as Vogüé, Règles.

[8] Walker, *Sancti Columbani Opera*, xviii, gets this information from the Life of Saint Gall; Saint Gall was one of Columban's companions in Europe. See Wettinus, *Vita S. Galli*, in *Passiones vitaeque sanctorum aevi Merovingici (II)*, ed. Bruno Krusch, Repertorium Fontium 11, *Monumenta Germaniae Historiae. Scriptorum Rerum Merovingiarum* IV, 256–80, here 257.

Columban never lost his love for Irish ecclesiastical and monastic usages. We can assume that his Rule is largely what he learned at Bangor from Comgall. And his troubles with the French bishops were largely due to his stubborn adherence to the Irish date for Easter.

But then what was Columban's motivation? According to Jonas, he was driven overseas by the famous text of Genesis 12:1, where God commands Abraham, "Go from your country and your kindred and your father's house to the land that I will show you." Of course, that explanation still leaves open the question of exactly where God was sending those Irish monastic pilgrims. Apparently not to Britain, for they sailed right past it, landing somewhere in Brittany.[9] Although the Bretons were fellow Celts, Columban did not find them open to his preaching (VC 1.10). Accordingly, the Irish monks went to Gaul, where they found a better audience, especially with the King of Austrasia.[10]

Before we proceed further, we should take up the question of Columban's missionary preaching. Although he considered the Gauls basically uncatechized, in fact, as Jonas points out, he was not the first one to preach the Gospel in Gaul:

> At that time, either because of the numerous enemies from without, or on account of the carelessness of the bishops, the Christian faith had almost departed from the country. The creed alone remained. But the saving grace of penance and the longing to root out the lusts

[9] Perhaps at Nantes, the main port of Brittany, from which the Merovingian king later tried, but failed, to deport the Irishmen (see VC 1.47). Local legends claim that Columban and his troop landed at St. Malo, which is equally plausible.

[10] Jonas says this was King Sigebert (VC 1.12), but that cannot be right, since Sigebert died in 575, long before Columban arrived in Gaul. The king must have been Childebert II, who reigned until 595.

of the flesh were to be found only in a few. Everywhere that he went, the noble man preached the Gospel. And it pleased the people, because his teaching
was adorned by eloquence and enforced by examples
of virtue.[11]

At first glance, it might appear that what was at work here
was just Irish chauvinism. Yet while it was true that the Irish
did consider their brand of Christianity superior to any other,
the author of this passage is Jonas, not Columban. And Jonas
was not an Irishman; he was a Gaul.[12] So this statement was
not merely a matter of ethnic disdain.

King Childeric was so impressed with Columban's preach-
ing[13] that he urged him to settle in his territory.[14] Jonas says that
Columban "followed the king's advice and chose for himself
a hermitage" (VC 1.12). It is interesting that Columban chose
for himself a *monastic* site; from the very beginning, Columban
makes it clear that his preaching will take place in a monastic
context. Yet he puts the matter to the king in a subtle way. He
says he has to follow Jesus' words: "Whosoever will come after
me, let him deny himself and take up his cross and follow me"

---

[11] VC 1.11; *Translation from Original Sources*, 6.

[12] Bullough calls Jonas a Burgundian Frank but goes on to point out
that at that time Burgundy extended into what is now Italy. He quotes
book 2 of the VC on Jonas's origins: "the town of Susa, a noble city, once
the colony of the Turians, distant about 140 miles from Bobbio" ("The
Career of Columbanus," 1).

[13] Literally, "the greatness of his learning caused him to stand high in
favor of the king and court" (VC 1.12). This was probably at Chalons-sur-
Saône, the capitol of Burgundy. It could have been at Metz, the capitol
of Austrasia, but that is much farther from Anegray, his first foundation.

[14] Exactly why Childeric was so intent that Columban "not go to other
peoples and leave him" is not clear. Probably he was feuding with his
brother, the King of Neustria, to the west. At any rate, there would come
a time when the king's son, Theuderich, would try to expel Columban
and his Irish confreres.

(VC 1.12; Matt 16:24). Childebert immediately picked up the implication: "If you wish to take the cross of Christ and follow him, seek the quiet of a hermitage." Apparently the king knew that monks need solitude.

At any rate, Columban and his compatriots immediately took up residence at Anegray, a ruined fort in the forests of the Vosges Mountains.[15] This ruined fort no doubt belonged to the king, but that fact did not mean that the monks were wards of the crown. Within a few days they were virtually starving, but a neighboring abbot saved them by sending his procurator with a cartload of provisions to sustain them.[16] This beautiful act of generosity was also heroic, since the horses had to walk through the night across woods unknown to them. Yet a miracle brought them and their load to the monks.

Although the Irish monks settled in a remote area, it did not take long for crowds to flock to Columban for healing (VC 1.14). Perhaps from the social pressure, and no doubt because of his general taste for solitary contemplation, Columban soon took to roaming the woods of the Vosges. At one point, wolves sniffed his clothes but did him no harm (VC 1.15). He found a cave suitable for a retreat, but unfortunately it also contained a bear. No problem: he persuaded the bear to vacate, and the cave

---

[15] Anegray, and nearby Luxeuil, are about fifty miles north of Besançon. Luxeuil is still a town of about eight thousand persons. Both places are situated on the headwaters of the River Moselle, though on opposite sides of it. For an extensive report on the archeological remains of these places, see Henri Leclercq, "Luxeuil," *Dictionnaire d'archéologie chrétienne et de liturgie* (Paris: Letouzy et Ané, 1907).

[16] Jonas (VC 1.14) says this was Caramtoc, Salicis's abbot. A Google search for this man and his monastery turns up nothing. What is worth noting is that there *were* monks in the region before the Irish arrived. In addition, to the south of Besançon were the Jura monasteries of St. Claude and La Balme, founded about a century before Anegray and Luxeuil. So Columban was not the first.

became his favorite retreat (VC 1.16).[17] The cave was remote from water, but Columban commanded his young servant to dig in the nearby rock—and up sprang fresh, pure water!

Finding water in the wilderness is, of course, a hagiographical commonplace. In fact, almost all the episodes in this part of Jonas's account are marked by a miraculous solution. In this sense, the *Vita Columbani* is much like the more famous *Dialogues* of Saint Gregory, written about fifty years previously.[18] Actually, all medieval lives of the saints are replete with the miraculous, a fact that reduces their historicity. Yet that does not mean that a saint like Columban was just an ordinary fellow. Nor does it completely invalidate the basic truth of Jonas's account. In fact, both Walker and Vogüé give Jonas fairly high marks as a historian.[19]

People came to Columban not only for succor but also to join his new monastery. Soon the size of the group prompted Columban to move to another abandoned fort. This was Luxeuil, some eight miles southwest of Anegray and across the River Moselle. But the new monastery was still not adequate for the numbers, so Columban founded another house at Fontaines. This third house was close enough to Luxeuil that Columban could serve as superior in three places. But since he could not be everywhere at once, he also began compiling a written Rule of life for his monks (VC 1.17).[20]

---

[17] By the time of Columban, there was a long tradition of monks dealing fearlessly and peaceably with wild animals. In fact, the prototypical desert hermit, Saint Antony, is reported by his hagiographer, Saint Athanasius, to have lived in harmony with the wild animals around his cave in the remote wilderness near the Red Sea (*Life of Antony*, 50). In Italy, Antony (whose feast day is January 17) is celebrated especially as the patron of wild animals.

[18] Hagiographers are usually happy to recycle episodes from the lives of other saints.

[19] Vogüé, *Vie de Saint Columban*, 48–50; Walker, *Sancti Columbani Opera*, ix.

[20] This was the origin of the famous Rule of Columban, which is the subject of this book. The scenario of the founder's serving as a living

What was life like for the monks at Luxeuil-Fontaines-Anegray? Jonas does not say much about the structure of the community, but one can safely assume that it was similar to that of all the early cenobitic communities. These monks lived a common life of work and prayer, much like what we know from the contemporary Rule of Saint Benedict. But a closer study of their lifestyle in the Rule of Columban shows that they spent a lot of time at the Divine Office, and there was a great emphasis on penance and the confession of sins.

Despite the reticence of Jonas's account, we get an occasional glimpse of daily life in those communities. VC 1.19–20 describes the monks harvesting,[21] and the abbot is laboring among them.[22] Columban is not only working but also driving his monks hard: at Luxeuil he punishes those who claim to be too weak and sick to harvest (VC 1.19); at Fontaines he insists that they go out to harvest in the pouring rain (VC 1.20). As soon as they obediently slog out to the field, the sun comes out!

Although he was abbot of a growing community, Columban was still drawn to the wilderness for solitude. When he was

---

Rule, then to be followed by a written Rule, is outlined in the comprehensive article of Claude Peifer, "The Rule of St. Benedict," in *RB 1980*, ed. Timothy Fry (Collegeville, MN: Liturgical Press, 1981), 65–112.

[21] These accounts show that the Vosges was not entirely dense woods. Still, if the monks had to clear mature timber, that was backbreaking work in those days before power equipment. Actually, harvesting by hand is hard enough. Nor were Columban's monks the only ones to avoid it. Saint Benedict also chides his monks for complaining when they must go out to harvest (RB 48.7-9). See my *Benedict's Rule: A Translation and Commentary* (Collegeville, MN: Liturgical Press, 1996), 388–89.

[22] This may not seem too remarkable until we remember that Columban was already an old man by the time he got to Luxeuil. If he was born about 540, this would make him about sixty years old, a great age in the sixth century. Moreover, Jonas shows him hauling great timbers to repair the Bobbio church shortly before his death at the age of seventy-five (VC 1.60). Clearly he had a strong constitution!

away from the monastery, he tried to live from the land. For an Irishman, that meant fish. Apparently his compatriot Gall was an expert angler. Yet when Columban sent him to fish in the River Brusch, he came home with an empty creel. But Gall had actually fished in the River Oignon, which bit of disobedience Columban knew by clairvoyance (VC 1.19). When he then fished in the right river, he caught his limit. Another act of disobedience by Gall occurred later in Switzerland when he refused to follow Columban to Italy. At that point the irascible abbot forbade Gall ever to say Mass again! For some reason, Jonas entirely omits this whole episode.[23] Did he find Gall's disobedience scandalous? Or was it Columban's harsh reaction he preferred to pass over in silence? Hagiographers do not like to expose the warts of their heroes.[24]

The theme of Columban's exercising a gentle control over the wild animals continued as long as he lived at Luxeuil. The monk Chamnoald once saw him playing with the wild creatures that flocked to him (VC 1.30). Predators stayed away from a dead stag that Columban wanted for the hide (VC 1.27). One time a raven stole his work glove during lunch break, but under Columban's potent threat the bird returned the glove (VC 1.25). But Columban's thaumaturgic power extended to persons as well. He healed the severed finger of Theudegisil (VC 1.23) and the head wound of Winnoc (VC 1.24). He also

---

[23] We have two Lives of Saint Gall, by Wettinus and by Walafrid Strabo, monks of the Abbey of Saint Gall, who wrote in the ninth century. See MGH. Script. Rer. Merov. 4.

[24] Gall went on to become the great missionary of the Alemanni. One of the reasons Gall was so successful with the Alemanni was that he could preach in their language. This fact may have led the author of the entry "Gall" in the *Oxford Dictionary of the Christian Church* to assume that he was of "Frankish or Alemannian origin." But the Gall who appears in VC 1.20 is clearly an Irishman. Saint Gall is commemorated on October 16 in the Roman calendar. He was the founder of the famous Abbey of St. Gall, one of the greatest cultural and spiritual centers of the Middle Ages.

persuaded God to fill an empty granary, and he multiplied loaves and beer for the monks at Fontaines who were engaged in the heavy labor of breaking up clods in the field (VC 1.28).

Columban soon became famous in the Vosges region. When Waldalen, count of Besançon, and his wife were unable to conceive a child, they came to the saint for his blessing. He agreed to give it, but only if the child was consecrated to the service of God. The parents agreed, and the boy, Donatus, eventually became a monk of Luxeuil. Beyond that, he became bishop of Besançon, one of the many bishops produced by Columbanian monasticism. As bishop, Donatus wrote a monastic rule for the nuns of his city. Not surprisingly, it is heavily influenced by the Rule of Columban.[25]

Yet the early history of Luxeuil was not all miracles and growth in numbers. There were also serious conflicts with the local culture, at least for Abbot Columban. The first conflict was religious. The fact that the Irish celebrated Easter according to a different system of dating than the Franks was a source of constant irritation to the local bishops. They must have pressed the monks to conform to local custom, but Columban was intransigent. He not only refused to abandon the Irish custom but also wrote an indignant letter to Pope Gregory in AD 600.[26]

[25] The distinctive thing about the Rule of Donatus, however, is that it is a "mixed rule," composed of sections of the Rules of Columban, Caesarius, and Benedict. The critical Latin text was done by Adalbert de Vogüé, "La Règle de Donat pour l'abbesse Gauthstrude. Texte critique et synopse des sources," *Benedictina* 25 (1978): 219–313; *The Ordeal of Community: The Rule of Donatus of Besançon*, translated by Jo Ann McNamara and John E. Halborg, Peregrina Series 5 (Toronto, Canada: Peregrina Publishing Co., 1990).

[26] Columban's Letters are found in Walker, *Sancti Columbani Opera*, 2–59; Letter 1, pp. 2–12. In this letter, Columban indicates that the confusion has arisen from the mistaken Roman idea that the spring equinox falls on March 21—everybody knows it falls on March 25! In addition, the sheer difficulty of detecting precisely *when* the equinox occurs has

The main purpose of that letter (Letter 1) was to persuade the pope to conform to the Irish date. Needless to say, the pope was not about to do that; in fact, he did not answer the bold monk at all. Columban added an attack on the Frankish bishops, calling them simoniacal. The pope was well aware that many of Gallic bishops had purchased their offices, and he had heard enough about their lax standard of chastity. The bishops, for their part, knew that the pope was unhappy with them, and this fact weakened their case against the stubborn Irishman.[27] But in 603, the new archbishop of Lyons, Arigius, summoned Columban to a council to be held at Chalons-sur-Saône. Columban declined to attend on the grounds that monks are exempt from the jurisdiction of bishops. He also wrote to the council (Letter 2), defying them to exile him and for good measure accusing them of lust and simony.[28]

The French bishops did not succeed in forcing Columban into conformity, because he and his monks were protected by King Theuderich of Burgundy. But this refuge was also coming to an end. Jonas reports that the king liked to spend time at Luxeuil (VC 1.31), but Columban was not impressed with the king, insisting that he get rid of his concubines. Then Brunhilde, the queen mother, tried to force Columban into blessing the bastard sons of Theuderich.[29] Not the type to be

---

bedeviled the church throughout its history. To this day the Eastern Orthodox churches calculate Easter differently than does the Roman church.

[27] Actually, the Frankish date for Easter was also at variance with the Roman date. See Walker, *Sancti Columbani Opera*, xxv.

[28] Letter 2 is printed in Walker, *Sancti Columbani Opera*, 13–23. In both Letters 1 and 2, Columban cites Saint Jerome as his authority for the date of Easter. Curiously, Jonas says nothing at all about Columban's battle with the bishops. Perhaps it would have tainted his hagiographical portrait of the saint.

[29] Brunhilde's reason for favoring her sons' habit of living with concubines rather than with a wife is not hard to fathom. That way, there would be no legitimate queen to challenge her position as the power

pushed into anything by anybody, Columban absolutely refused to bless them (VC 1.32). In addition, he banned the royal
entourage from entering the cloister of Luxeuil, provoking the
king into exiling Columban and his fellow Irishmen on the
grounds that they were violating Frankish hospitality.[30]

Theuderich's soldiers then took Columban to Besançon,
where he made a nuisance of himself by freeing the inmates
on death row. Soon enough, he found himself unguarded and
walked back to his abbey. Soldiers were sent to apprehend
him, but they were terrified to find themselves between a rock
and a hard place: Theuderich and Columban (VC 1.36). As for
the saint, he could see that his resistance was endangering
the whole community, so he decided to go back to Ireland as
a voluntary exile (VC 1.37). He headed west with his compatriots under armed guard. But Theuderich had not won yet;
Columban was not so easily gotten rid of.

Columban's long journey toward Ireland in 610 began with
a boat trip down the River Loire. This voyage, to which Jonas
devotes ten chapters (37–47), is a pastiche of wonders and signs.
Right away a soldier tried to murder Columban but wound
up crippled (VC 1.38). At Nevers, a guard struck one of
Columban's companions; when Columban cursed him, he
drowned in the river (VC 1.40). At Orleans, the locals refused to
feed the Irish monks out of fear of King Theuderich. Yet a Syrian
woman gave them food anyway, so Columban cured her blind
spouse (VC 1.41). Further downstream at Tours, Columban
wished to visit the tomb of Saint Martin; the soldiers tried to
prevent it but were unable to do so. By this time, Columban was

---

behind the throne. One of the best modern experts on Columban, Bruno
Krusch, says that the conflict between Brunhilde and Columban has
been exaggerated, but Vogüé thinks he is wrong in this (see Vogüé, *Vie
de Saint Columban*, 85).

[30] VC 1.33. Not all the monks were exiled from Luxeuil, just the Irish,
showing that the conflict here was more ethnic than religious.

thoroughly disgusted and exclaimed, "That dog Theuderich has driven me away from the brethren!" (VC 1.42). He then foretold the extermination of Theuderich and his family, which soon came about (613).

When the party arrived at the ocean port of Nantes, it seemed as though the efforts of Theuderich II to rid himself of his nemesis had come to a climax. The local count (Theudebert) and bishop (Sufronius), anxious to please the king, hustled Columban on a skiff out to the ocean. But at that point things came to an abrupt halt: the waves and wind drove the boat back to shore (VC 1.47). After three days, the captain saw how things were, so he unloaded the Irish monks and their baggage. Immediately the wind changed and the ship departed for Ireland—minus Columban.[31]

Once it became clear that Columban could not be expelled, he felt free to visit King Chlotar of Neustria. This son of Chilperic, unlike his brother Theuderich II, begged Columban to stay in his kingdom. Columban declined but predicted that Chlotar would control all three Merovingian kingdoms within a short time.[32] In fact, the internecine warfare between the sons of Chilperic in 613 resulted in the deaths of both Theudebert and Theuderich II, leaving Chlotar as the sole ruler. By that time, Columban was in Lombardy, and although Chlotar invited him to return, he politely declined. No doubt he had had enough of the bloodthirsty Franks.

---

[31] It is hard in this regard not to think of the prophet Jonah. Both he and Columban were the cause of trouble for the boats they were in. But there was an important difference: Jonah was fleeing the will of God, so he was a curse; Columban was being exiled against the will of God, as God would not allow.

[32] At this time, Chlotar was king of Neustria, Theudebert was king of Austrasia, and Theuderich II was king of Burgundy. There is a convenient map of the boundaries of these kingdoms titled "Merovingian Kingdoms," on *Wikipedia*, s.v. "Merovingian Dynasty." See also Ian Wood, *The Merovingian Kingdoms 450–751* (New York: Longman Press, 1994), 367–71.

Chlotar then provided safe conduct for Columban to King Theudebert at Metz. This first brought Columban to Paris, where he exorcized a demon (VC 1.49). At Meaux, Columban stayed with a nobleman named Hagneric, who presented his daughter Burgundofare for a blessing. She eventually founded the Abbey of Faremoutier in Brie, which had a strongly Columbanian formation.[33] Columban also visited a certain Antharius, whose sons he also blessed: Ado, who went on to found the Abbey of Jouarre, and Dado, who founded "a monastery near Brieg, on the little river Rebais" (VC 1.50).[34]

When Columban arrived at the court of Theudebert, the latter tried to persuade him to remain in his realm. The Irish party agreed to proceed only to Bregenz on the Lake of Constance far to the south.[35] This journey was accomplished by boat on the Rhine and under the power of oarsmen provided by Theudebert.

---

[33] In fact, the abbot of Luxeuil, Eustace, sent a monk named Waldebert or Walbert to Faremoutiers with the injunction, "Teach them the Rule!" Vogüé says he found this story in Jonas, VC 1.Prol 1. This page is missing from my copy. See Vogué, *Histoire Littéraire XI* (Paris: Les Éditions du Cerf, 2006), 306. Walbert not only did that but also compiled a special amalgam of ancient rules especially designed for women, including the Rules of Columban, Benedict, Cassian, and Basil. The official title of this work is *Regula cuiusdam Patris ad Virgines*, not to be confused with *Regula cuiusdam Patris* for monks. The work, sometimes known as the Rule of Walbert, has never been previously translated into English; it appears in this volume on pages 149–224. The Latin original is found in the collection of Benedict of Aniane called *Codex Regularum* (PL 88:1053–70). Vogüé gives a synopsis of this Rule in *Histoire Littéraire* 11.309–30.

[34] I can find nothing to corroborate this latter reference, but Jouarre became a famous Benedictine abbey of women and remains so today.

[35] Jonas says, "Many brethren had already come to him from Luxeuil, whom he received as if they had been snatched from the enemy" (VC 1.51). Whether these were all Irishmen is not clear, but the general pattern was that King Theuderich allowed the native Gallic monks to stay at Luxeuil, but not the Irish. As for Bregenz, it must have been in Theudebert's jurisdiction, although it was not in Austrasia.

Bregenz was inhabited by the Suevi, a Germanic tribe that was still half pagan. Columban boldly confronted them over one of their rituals, splitting a cask of beer with his prayers. The people were impressed, but Columban was not too impressed with them. He therefore decided to travel further east to evangelize the Slavs, but an angel of the Lord prevented him from doing so. He was supposed to cross the Alps into Italy.[36]

Meanwhile, signs and wonders continued to accompany the charismatic Columban. One of the problems at Bregenz was the scarcity of food: the party was starving. But God sent a flock of birds, much as he had for the Israelites during the exodus (Exod 16:13), and also a gift of grain from a local priest.[37] In another episode involving the monks' hunger, a bear was ravaging the orchard whose fruit the monks needed to stay alive. Columban sent Chagnoald to settle things with the bear by giving him some apples while reserving the rest for the monks (VC 1.55).[38] Not everything went so smoothly at Bregenz. When Columban decided to cross the Alps, he wanted all his monks to come with him. All of them did, except Gall. He had been

---

[36] The episode with the angel is far from obvious to me. The angel said, "You perceive how much remains set apart of the whole world. Go to the right or the left where you will, that you may enjoy the fruits of your labors." As a result of this cryptic message, "Columban remained where he was until the way to Italy opened before him" (VC 1.56).

[37] This was reported by Eustace, who was an eyewitness (VC 1.54). This same Eustace later became abbot of Luxeuil (VC 1.61). He became one of the most important Columbanian monks, so much so that his reign at Luxeuil is recounted in Jonas's second book, which is not included in the English version (see n. 2 above), but Vogüé gives a French version in *Vie de Saint Columban*, 188–203.

[38] Chagnoald was another prominent Columbanian monk. He was with Columban as his "assistant" at both Luxeuil (VC 1.30) and Bregenz (VC 1.55). Later on, he too was sent by Eustace to teach the Rule to the nuns of Faremoutiers (VC 2.7). Finally, he became "pastor" (bishop?) of Laon (VC 2.8.5).

at Bregenz for some time and was having success preaching to the Suevi, so he refused to leave.[39] This is the occasion when Columban forbade him to say Mass ever again—but Columban relented when he was on his own deathbed a couple of years later.

There were also political reasons for Columban's having to flee Bregenz. His protector, King Theudebert, was now dead, having been defeated by his brother, Theuderich II, in the Battle of Zülpich (also known as Tolbiac).[40] So Columban crossed the Alps to elude his old nemesis, Theuderich. But he needn't have worried too much, since Theuderich soon died in a fire at Metz (VC 1.58).[41] That was the signal for the third Merovingian brother, King Chlotar of Neustria (Soissons), to invade the East. He took care to exterminate all five sons of Theuderich, as well as their infamous great-grandmother, Brunhilde. And so the brutal, internecine warfare of the sons of Clovis came to an end.

---

[39] Gall's refusal is recounted by Wettinus, *Vita Galli*, 9. Gall had a history of conflict with Columban (see nn. 23–24 above). Columban's rage seems out of proportion, but we may not know the whole story, since Jonas does not mention it. Gall was already known to be violent and indeed had been expelled from the region of Zurich for destroying pagan temples. But Columban was not exactly a shrinking violet either.

[40] VC 1.57. Zülpich, also known as Tolbiac, is located between Aachen and Bonn, Germany. In 506, the famous battle of Tolbiac was fought there, with the Franks led by Clovis I defeating the Alamans (Suevi). After the Alamannic leader died in this battle, the remaining Alamans accepted Clovis as their king. This was the beginning of the Frankish/Merovingian kingdom (J. M. Wallace-Hadrill, *The Long-Haired Kings* [Toronto: University of Toronto Press, 1982], 168–69). Jonas also says that Columban had tried to persuade Theudebert to become a monk shortly before his defeat in battle but was laughed at for his trouble. See William M. Daly, "Clovis: How Barbaric, How Pagan?" *Speculum* 69, no. 3 (1994): 619–64, here 620.

[41] Columban was not the only cleric persecuted by Theuderich. Jonas (VC 1.54) reports that Theuderich and Brunhilde also drove Bishop Desiderius of Vienne into exile and finally had him murdered.

Columban's first destination south of the Alps was Milan, where he was received with honor by Agilulf, king of the Lombards (VC 1.613). While he was in Milan, for perhaps a year or more, Columban wrote a letter (Letter 5) to Pope Boniface IV (608–615) on behalf of the king, urging him to call a church synod and clarify his opposition to the controversy of the Three Chapters.[42] There was also another conflict between Rome and the Lombards. As a typical Gothic tribe, they had an Arian view of Jesus, namely, that he was inferior to the Father. That being the case, it is curious that Agilulf welcomed Columban, who was an intransigent promoter of Christian orthodoxy and a fierce opponent of anything he considered heretical. Indeed, Jonas reports, "During his stay in Milan, he resolved to attack the errors of the heretics, that is, the Arian perfidy, which he wanted to cut out and exterminate with the cauterizing knife of the Scriptures. And he composed an excellent and learned work against them" (VC 1.59).

Presumably this "learned work" was the same Letter 5, which urged the pope to be reconciled with the Lombard bishops. Apparently, the king wanted that reconciliation to happen, but it is not clear what price he was willing to pay for it to come about. Was Agilulf ready to give up his Arianism? It is not clear, because the letter itself is an extremely convoluted piece of Latin composition that has defied several attempts at analysis.[43]

---

[42] Letter 5, in Walker, *Sancti Columbani Opera*, 36–57. The Three Chapters was a long controversy, triggered by Emperor Justinian II in 543 by his edict condemning three Antiochian theological tracts. He did so to please the Monophysites, but all the edict did was anger the Latin church, which thought it undercut the Council of Chalcedon. See "Three Chapters," in *Oxford Dictionary of the Christian Church*. Bullough ("The Career of Columbanus," 24) suggests that Columban may have been provoked by Bishop Agrippinus of Como, a proponent of the Chapters.

[43] Walker, *Sancti Columbani Opera*, xxxviii, notes that Jean Laporte thought that Letter 5 was in fact a conflation of two Columbanian letters, thus explaining its incoherence (citing Jean Laporte, "Saint Columban, son

At any rate, Columban was looking for another site for a monastery, and he soon found one. Jonas says that a man named Jocundus came forward to point out Bobbio, a ruined church that the monks might restore for their use (VC 1.60). Bobbio is located about fifty miles south of Milan in a fairly secluded spot on the River Trebbia as it winds its way through the hills and down to the Po Valley.[44] Jonas notes that the monks themselves cut timbers to repair the roof, but it was not easy. Because of the roughness of the country, the logs were hard to transport. Columban urged his men to take courage with the task, and sure enough, God helped them finish the job. Jonas also claims that Columban himself helped with the logging, but that is hard to believe, since he would have been roughly seventy-five years old.

Jonas does not tell us much about Columban's doings at Bobbio, mostly because Columban lived only about a year in the new foundation before his death. Jonas does report that King Chlotar attempted to lure Columban back to Luxeuil. He sent Abbot Eustace with a delegation of noblemen to Bobbio, at least a week's journey on horseback, to beg the old abbot-founder to return. But Columban wasn't having any of it, declaring that he could no longer endure such a journey

---

âme et sa vie," in *Mélanges Columbaniens: Actes du Congrès International de Luxeuil, 20–23 juillet 1950* [Paris: Éditions Alsatia, 1951], 78). In Walker's view, however, this theory is unwarranted since there are enough signs showing that Letter 5 is in fact a literary unity. Walker suggests that part of the problem is Columban's evident agitation in addressing the pope.

[44] Bobbio is also close to Genoa, about forty miles as the crow flies. But to get there by bus, one must cross the coastal range of the Apennines, so the trip takes several hours. See Tomás Ó Fiaich, *Columbanus in His Own Words* (Dublin: Veritas, 1974), 130–32. The easier approach is from the northeast, where Piacenza lies another forty miles away, but here the route is flat, through the valley of the Trebbia. The place is very scenic: Hemingway called it "the most beautiful valley in the world." Bobbio today is still an idyllic little town (pop. 3,700) set in an unspoiled countryside.

(VC 1.61). He was probably telling the truth, but one can also guess that he had had his fill of the bloodthirsty volatile Merovingian kings. After the death of Columban (probably on November 1, 615) Jonas continues his account with book 2, containing the lives of some of Columban's abbot-successors (Attala, Eustace, and Bertulf) and the Miracles of Eboriac (Faremoutiers in Brie).[45]

Attala

The monk Attala became the superior at Luxeuil upon Columban's abrupt departure for exile in 610. He was a Burgundian noble who had first tried the monastic life at Lérins but found it lacking in rigor.[46] Jonas says Columban immediately recognized Attala's gifts: "He took him into his personal service" (VC 2.1), perhaps meaning that Attala became Columban's secretary. We are fortunate to have a letter (Letter 4) from Columban to the monks of Luxeuil from Nantes, as he awaited his ship of exile. In this agitated, rather pathetic letter, the abbot appoints Attala superior but says that if he cannot hold the community together, they should choose another leader.[47]

---

[45] Happily, Vogüé includes book 2 of the *Life* in his volume. It comprises about a hundred pages, which is longer than book 1. My only access to this material was this fine French translation. As Vogüé notes in the introduction (*Vie de Saint Columban*, 10), the Miracles of Eboriac were actually a separate document, published as an appendix to James O'Carroll's article, "Sainte Fare et les origines," in *Sainte Fare et Faremoutiers. Treize siècles de vie monastique*, 2 vols. (Abbaye de Faremoutiers, 1956), 3–35, esp. 25–35. So the volume by Vogüé is actually the first to publish all of Jonas's work in translation under one cover.

[46] VC 2.1. Attala was educated by Bishop Arigius of Lyons as a boy. Presumably he came to Luxeuil about the year 600 and was about thirty years of age when Columban was driven out.

[47] Actually, Letter 4 (Walker, *Vita Sancti Columbani*, 26–37) indicates that Columban himself was having a hard time holding the community

This letter shows that there were rifts in the community at that time that worried Columban. Certainly one of the divisive issues was the date of Easter, as the letter states explicitly. With the community becoming increasingly Gallic and less Irish, we can guess that some of the monks would have been less committed to this liturgical practice, which exposed them to the wrath of the local bishops. As we shall soon see, there were other troubling issues involved, but the Irish date for Easter had to be abandoned if Luxeuil was to have a future.[48]

As it turned out, Attala did indeed have trouble ruling the monasteries in the Vosges. For a while, some of the monks chafed at his harsh rule and threatened to leave. At first he put up with them, but something had to give:

> Skillful as he was, Attala began to administer to them the calming agents suggested by his goodness. So he gave them to drink a salutary antidote to make the abscess burst and the pus disappear. He tried to soften their puffed-up hearts. His long efforts at correcting them did not succeed in drawing them to him. So then in his deep affliction he multiplied his pleas with longing looks full of goodness so that they would not distance themselves from him and leave the path that leads in the right way. "Remember," he said, "that our fathers gained the kingdom of heaven by mortification and by despising the present life."

------

together. He sounds profoundly discouraged over this fact. He advises that if Attala cannot rule, the monk Waldelenus should do so. In fact, Eustace became the very effective abbot of Luxeuil soon after Attala.

[48] Although the Gallic bishops did not accept the Irish date for Easter, it seems that the Gallic date was also at variance with the Roman date. This may be why the Gallic bishops did not complain more loudly to the pope. But Columban was not so reticent: in Letter 1 he boldly chastises Pope Gregory (the Great) for being so obtuse about the question. "Why are you celebrating a dark Easter? We ought not hold Easter with the Jews!"

Seeing finally that he was getting nowhere and that he could not keep these spirits who pulled in another direction under the harness of his community, he let them depart in their obstinacy. Once they had parted from him, some of them sought exile on the seacoast,[49] while others went to the wilderness where they could enjoy their liberty.[50] But they soon experienced the troubles that their boldness and pride deserved. (VC 2.1.2)[51]

Jonas takes a good deal of satisfaction at the sad fate of these fugitives, many of whom slunk back to the monastery when things got tough. But Attala himself must have departed rather soon,[52] since we find him at Bobbio, where he succeeded Columban as abbot in 615.[53]

Jonas's account of Abbot Attala at Bobbio is relatively short, concerning only three miracles: taming a raging mountain stream (VC 2.3), reattaching a severed thumb (2.4), and healing a dying child at Milan (2.5). One feature is common to all

[49] Hermits loved islands: see Jerome, Ep 3.4; Sulpicius Severus, VMart 6.5, etc.

[50] See Columban, Letter 1.7, on cenobites who flee to the wilderness (Walker, 8–9).

[51] My translation of Vogüé's French. All of the subsequent English quotations of VC 2 are of this nature. Although a translation of a translation is not ideal, I trust Vogüé's understanding of late Latin so much that I do not feel this procedure is too risky.

[52] One strong indication that Attala did not last long as superior in Luxeuil is the fact that King Chlotar sent Eustace, not Attala, to Bobbio to try to talk Columban into returning to Luxeuil. This must have been before November 615, when Columban died. Probably Eustace was already superior at Luxeuil by that time; otherwise why did Chlotar not send Attala?

[53] In Letter 1 to Pope Gregory, Columban complains about monks who, "inflamed by the desire for a more perfect life, impugn their vows, leave the places of their first profession, and against their abbots' will, impelled by monastic fervor, either relapse or flee to the deserts."

these cases: Attala imposes strict silence on the witnesses. Such modesty, of course, is not unusual for the saints or for the hagiographers. But two other stories are more unusual and therefore more interesting.

In the first instance, Jonas relates an autobiographical element. He tells us that at one point, Abbot Attala ordered him to go visit his parents. Now Jonas was surprised at the command, for he had been asking for home leave for years[54] but had always been refused. Since it was wintertime and Susa was a long way away,[55] Jonas tried to delay the journey. Attala, however, was adamant and sent two confreres along with Jonas. The visit did not go as he expected. His mother was delighted to see him, but he himself fell desperately ill. But then he was convinced that he had to leave immediately for Bobbio because the abbot was dying!

When the party arrived back home, Attala was indeed at death's door. Some time earlier he had had a vision that told him to prepare for a journey he had to make in fifty days. At first he misinterpreted the instruction to mean that he was to make a land journey. His reaction was to set about (rather frantically) fixing the place up—apparently it had fallen into a state of disrepair.[56] But soon he came to understand that his journey was to be spiritual, namely, to heaven. This final scene

[54] Jonas adds (helpfully to a modern biographer) that he had not been home since he had come to Bobbio—at age nine! As we will see, Attala was about to die (in 626 or 627), so Jonas must have been about nineteen years old at the time of this visit.

[55] The text (VC 2.6) notes that Susa is about 140 miles from Bobbio. Jonas claims that his party made half the return journey in three days, and Vogüé is surprised that they covered thirty-five kilometers (= twenty miles) a day (Vogüé, *Vie de S. Columban*, 188).

[56] VC 2.6: "He reinforced the monastic cloister, had the roofs redone, and shored up all the buildings so as to not leave anything shaky upon his departure. He made all the beasts of burden lie down, and he made sure the books were firmly bound. On his order, people cleaned things

(VC 2.7) is characteristic and even humorous. When Attala senses that he is about to die, he orders all the monks to leave him alone. But Blidemund "stayed on behind the back of the Man of God, holding his breath." His reward for this act of pious disobedience was to witness the abbot's final ecstatic moments and, of course, to report them.

Eustace

Next (VC 2.2) Jonas turns his attention to Eustace, the abbot of Luxeuil (ca. 611–629). Jonas probably never met him, but no doubt he talked to people who knew him well.[57] The bulk of his account of Eustace concerns a long conflict he had with a renegade monk (VC 2.6–16). But before that, Jonas portrays Eustace as an extremely successful propagator of the monastic ideal and of monastic foundations. Most of his missionary work took place at Brie, just east of Paris, but he also worked in Bavaria.

On a visit to the court of King Chlotar at Soissons, Eustace stopped at the home of Chagneric, near Meaux. As was his custom, he blessed the children. But he found the daughter, named Fare, stricken with blindness and sick in bed. She told him that this was because her father was forcing her to marry, although she wished to become a nun.[58] Eustace healed Fare

---

up, resewed what was unraveling, repaired what was broken down, and put all the boots into good shape."

[57] As we have seen, Eustace visited Bobbio before 615 (VC 1.61), but Jonas only came there in 617. Twenty years later, Jonas was commissioned by Abbot Bertulf to write the life of Columban (638). He not only did that but also expanded the project to include the successors of Columban, including Bertulf. And to do research for his work, Jonas went to northern Gaul, where he surely visited Luxeuil—all in all, a rather modern approach to biography (or hagiography).

[58] Probably she was severely depressed: psychosomatic illness can take severe forms.

and then confronted her father. Chagneric capitulated, but as soon as the abbot was out the door, he went back on his word. On his way home from Soissons, Eustace again found the girl distraught. This time he furiously cursed Chagneric, who gave up the fight. Eustace then founded a female monastery on the family property and made Fare abbess.[59] Faremoutiers (also known as Eboriac) became one of the greatest monasteries in Europe. It was a double monastery, with the abbess as the overall superior.[60] In fact, the Brie region later became a hotbed of monasticism, as we will see further on.[61]

Eustace also worked toward the east, where he preached to the pagan tribes called Warasques[62] and Boii (Bavarians). In this he followed his master, Columban, but he also resembled him in failing to accomplish much. Probably language was again a major barrier. On one of his trips to a village near the headwaters of the River Meuse, he found a girl named Salaberg, who,

[59] It seems likely to me that Fare herself was the founder and the author of the *Regula cuiusdam Patris ad Virgines* (the Rule of Walbert); see my article, "Who Wrote the Rule of Walbert?," in *A Not-So-Unexciting Life: Essays on Benedictine History and Spirituality in Honor of Michael Casey, OCSO*, edited by Carmel Posa, CS 269 (Collegeville, MN: Cistercian Publications, 2017), 214–32. Whatever the exact facts of the case, she clearly needed Eustace to overcome her father.

[60] This was a familiar pattern in medieval monasteries. Typically, the daughter of a founder, or a near relative, would serve as abbess. This, of course, was an aristocratic monasticism that persisted throughout the Middle Ages. But since cloistered women had a hard time finding lucrative work, novices had to bring a dowry, something only the rich could manage.

[61] In VC 2.2.5, Jonas says that Eustace also healed Agila, who became abbot of Rebaix. Rebaix is also a small river near Meaux, the site of a monastery founded by Audinus (Ouen) who later became bishop of Rouen. See VC 1.50, n. 7. Jonas does not name the men's superior at Faremoutiers.

[62] In his note on VC 2.3.2, Vogüé locates the Warasques thirty kilometers northeast of Besançon. This place was near Montbeliard, and it had a monastery called Cusance.

like Fare, had gone blind. Eustace healed her as well, in typical dramatic fashion.[63] Salaberg did not want to become a nun, but she later became the lay monastic founder of a convent at Laon.

Then Jonas narrates another story, about a man named Agrestius, who he makes clear was possessed by the devil.[64] Agrestius was a Burgundian with connections who joined Luxeuil as an adult, whereupon he immediately began agitating to do mission work among the Bavarians. Abbot Eustace held him back as long as he could but eventually let him go. Predictably, Agrestius got nowhere with the pagans, so he crossed the Alps to Aquileia, where he found what he was looking for: a schism. Naturally, he sided with the northern Italian bishops against the pope and wrote an insulting letter to Abbot Attala at Bobbio,[65] trying to get him to join the schism.

Because of Agrestius's conduct in Italy, Abbot Eustace banished Agrestius from Luxeuil. The unhappy man then turned his rancor against the monastery itself and its observances. He roamed the countryside drumming up support: "He grunted like a pig rolling in the mud, and he tried to enlist the proud folk of his type to grunt with him. He had the backing of Abelin, bishop of Geneva, who was a close relative of his. This Abelin then bent all his effort toward the neighboring

---

[63] In fact, Eustace asked her if she "aspired to the service of divine love." She said yes but probably understood him in a general sense. But these healings cost Eustace a good deal: "He then set to work, afflicting his body with two days of fasting, arming his soul with faith, and applying blessed oil to her eyes" (VC 2.8.4).

[64] Curiously, Jonas here uses the title Chelydre, which comes from Virgil's *Georgics* 3.415, suggesting that he had a classical education. Since he came to Bobbio at the age of nine, the monks must have taught him well. Jonas was obviously widely read, as was typical of medieval hagiographers.

[65] Jonas ruefully notes that when, as Attala's secretary, he handled this letter, he forgot to file it and so it got lost (VC 2.2.7). As for Attala, he disdained to answer it.

bishops so as to form a league to support Agrestius" (VC 2.2.9). Agrestius and Bishop Abelin then got King Chlotar to call a synod of bishops at Mâcon (626–627), where both the excommunicated monk and his abbot were called to testify. First off, Garnier, the mayor of the palace and an enemy of Eustace, dropped dead at the hand of God (VC 2.2.10). He had taken up Agrestius's cause, which now looked much shakier. Agrestius did not help his own case with his testimony: "Babbling away, but holding to his worthless and badly conceived attack, he said that their customs included practices that were opposed to canon law. They pressed him to explain himself. He ended by making a single accusation: the Rule wants the spoon they use to be blessed many times with the sign of the cross. He also said that the Rule demands a blessing every time someone enters every building in the monastery, whether one is entering or leaving."[66]

In contrast to Agrestius, Eustace made a much better impression on the bishops:

> It is for you who are the glory of the priesthood to discern who are those who fill the churches with the seeds of truth and justice and who are the ones whose teaching is opposed to the truth and true religion. For all that departs from the true rule of conduct ought to be cast out of the body of the church. It is up to you to discern whether the practices of which we are accused are opposed to the teachings of Scripture. (VC 2.2.11)

Apart from this *captatio benevolentiae*, it is interesting that Eustace does not back off an inch from the Columbanian

---

[66] I think it must be significant that Agrestius does not mention the date of Easter in his complaints against the Columbanian observance. If that Irish custom had still been in force at Luxeuil, surely the bishops would have been unhappy about it. It is therefore quite clear that the problem departed from Luxeuil with the founder.

customs that Agrestius had held up to ridicule, namely, the multiple blessings of spoons and the requirement to get a blessing on entering and leaving a building. He calmly and sweetly provided a spiritual rationale for these Irish customs, and the bishops found for him and against Agrestius. But since Agrestius persisted in vilifying the Rule of Columban, Eustace finally finished him off with this tremendous curse: "Before the bishops here present, I, a disciple and successor of him whose Rule and teachings you condemn, summon you to the divine Judgment to be confronted with him before the end of this year. You will thus undergo the examination of the Just Judge, whose servant you are trying to dirty by speaking evil of him" (VC 2.2.12).

After this awful pronouncement, the assembly forced Agrestius to ask for the pax, which Eustace then bestowed. But it was a feigned peace for Agrestius, and he was soon up to his old routine of touring the country and stirring up trouble. The next place he struck was at Remiremont, a new foundation located about fifteen miles to the northeast of Luxeuil. Its founder was Romaric, a Burgundian noble who had joined Luxeuil shortly before.[67] Remiremont was a convent for nuns located on the property of Romaric. The founder lived there with Amatus, whom Eustace had appointed to teach the nuns the Rule (VC 2.2.13).[68] When Agrestius arrived at Remiremont, he found the ground prepared for his nasty activity, for it seems

---

[67] This man was famous enough to merit a *vita*, namely the *Vita Romarici*. According to this hagiographic text, he had been converted by the Columbanian monk Amatus when he was at the court of Chlotar in 613.

[68] In his note on this passage, Vogüé comments, "The following shows that it was a double monastery." Apparently this was the same pattern that obtained at Eboriac and other convents: Luxeuil sent monks to teach the women the Rule of Columban. Some of these monks stayed with the nuns, but the abbess was in charge. The monks served as auxiliary personnel, discharging liturgical functions and doing heavy labor.

that Eustace had visited the place shortly before and did not like what he found:

> At this time, in fact, Amatus and Romaric had both been chastised by Eustace for certain relaxations of monastic discipline. Seeing them thus stung, Agrestius took the opportunity to draw to his views their irritated spirits. Little by little he injected into their still healthy spirits his poisoned ideas, and he spread his own crazy disdain for the Rule of Columban. Alas! These terrible counsels and damaging advice corrupted the healthy teaching with Agrestius's own insanity. Rejecting the former Rule, the masters tried to give these worthless teachings to their sheep. But then, according to the word of Job, the hand of God, like a wise woman, made the serpent come out of its den, not fearing to turn up with its jealous envy. (VC 2.10.13)

Agrestius, who was apparently free to go where he liked, next journeyed to Faremoutier to try to corrupt Abbess Fare. But here he met his match. She rebuked him with the words, "I know these men whom you slander. I have had direct experience of their miracles. I have embraced their salutary doctrine, and I know that their teachings have led many to the Kingdom of heaven." Undeterred, Agrestius returned to Remiremont, where the nuns were more receptive. But God is not mocked, and Jonas devotes VC 2.15 to explaining the terrible punishments this community was subject to: a suicide and a terrific lightning strike that killed fifty of them! Yet Amatus and Romaric "demanded pardon from Blessed Eustace, and they obtained it when they banished all negligence" (VC 2.16).[69]

---

[69] It seems that Remiremont did not remain in the Columbanian system. Yet it became one of the most famous Benedictine abbeys of the Middle Ages.

Apart from conflict, Eustace's reign was marked by considerable institutional growth, at least in the sense of an increasing number of monasteries that took on the Rule of Columban. In VC 2.2.17, Jonas lists three important founders in other locales: Eloi, Bertoare, and Theodulf. Between them they founded seven monasteries, mostly of women.[70] Eustace himself retired sometime around 629, when Walbert took over as the third abbot of Luxeuil. Eustace's final days were unusual, although much like those of many other Merovingian deaths described by Jonas:

> As he was awaiting his departure from this life, Eustace gave over all his energy to pondering the mysteries contained in revelation. His soul tended toward God alone, and he poured out prayer that he might rise up to him. He had been involved in this exercise for many years when the time arrived for his call. A sentence of the just Judge decided that some days of corporal suffering would heal that which had not yet been purified in the years past when he had suffered various trials. While this fever was consuming him, he was asked in the course of a nighttime vision whether he preferred forty days of light suffering or entering heaven to enjoy the blessed life after thirty days of hotter flames. He answered that it would be better to undergo fiercer torments for a shorter time than to be consumed by gentler flames for a longer time. So then he suffered the corporal pain that he had foreseen and chosen. (VC 2.10.18)[71]

Overall, it can probably be said that Eustace was one of the greatest Columbanian saints and also a cornerstone of

---

[70] The seven were Solignac, Paris St. Martial, Bertoare's female house, Isle at Charenton, Jouy at Sancoins, Carenton (River Marmande), and Nevers.

[71] Jonas, *Life of Eustace*, 18–19; *Vie de Saint Columban*, 203.

Merovingian monasticism. As we will see, his successor, Walbert, was in the same class.

The Miracles of Eboriac

Next comes a section of Jonas's account that breaks into the series of the abbatial successors of Columban. The scene shifts abruptly from Luxeuil under Eustace to Faremoutiers/Eboriac under Fare.[72] Jonas does not write a general history of this great female Columbanian monastery or even tell of its founding.[73] He also does not deal in this section with the role of the Luxeuil monks, especially Walbert, in teaching the Rule to the nuns. His only concern in this rather long unit[74] is to tell of the miracles of Eboriac. Indeed this unit is one long string of miracle stories.

How did Jonas come to know about this material? Faremoutiers is hundreds of miles north of Bobbio, perhaps a week's journey in those days. But apparently Jonas had at some point made that trip, because in describing the death of Gibitrude (VC 2.5), Jonas casually mentions "those of us present." How he got there and why he was there is not clear, but in a note on the passage, Vogüé says the year was 634 or 635.[75] Apparently the nuns had witnessed many remarkable

---

[72] Of course, Fare was a successor of Columban since he had blessed her as a child (VC 1.50), and she accepted the Rule of Columban for her new monastery. Fare was one of the great monastic founders of the early Middle Ages. See n. 60 above.

[73] See nn. 60–62 above for the sketchy role of Abbot Eustace in the founding of Faremoutiers.

[74] Comparatively speaking, this is the second-longest unit in the VC. Of course, VC 1, on Columban, is by far the longest, at sixty-seven pages in Vogüé's version. But at twenty-four pages, the section on the Miracles of Eboriac is longer than the material on Attala (ten pages), Eustace (sixteen pages), or Bertulf (fourteen pages).

[75] In another place (introduction, p. 20), Vogüé gives the year as 633/634, citing J. Guérout, "Fare (sainte)/Faremoutiers," DHGE 16 (1967):

deathbed scenes by this time, and they shared them with their Italian visitor.[76] Jonas came back north again at the end of the decade (ca. 638) and in fact finished his book at St. Amand near Lille in 641.[77] So he may well have stopped in again at Eboriac. He probably knew the place well.

Jonas's long unit on the miracles of Eboriac has a unique character. Not only is it almost entirely miraculous, but it is also resolutely eschatological. All of these stories have to do with deathbed occurrences and also with their implications for the afterlife. In fact, some of the dying nuns are transported to heaven by angels as a sort of preview and then returned to earth for a final adieu.[78] One of the deathbed scenes, that of Sisitrude (VC 2.1–2), is representative of all of them.

Sisitrude was not a young novice when she came to die but probably an older nun, for she held the responsible post of cellarer of the monastery. Like many of the nuns of Faremoutiers, at least the ones described in the miracles, she was granted a vision warning her to put her life in order, for she would die

505–31, 534–45. Guérout says Jonas spent a month at Faremoutiers, so he had plenty of time to collect stories.

[76] Since the community of Faremoutiers was only about ten years old in 633, one wonders why so many nuns were dying. Yet two of the stories, of Ercantrude (VC 2.6) and Deurechilde (VC 2.10), explicitly say that the dying nun was young. Of course, many people, in particular young nuns, did die young before the advent of modern medicine, especially from tuberculosis.

[77] Vogüé thinks it took Jonas three years to write it (*Vie de Saint Columban*, 20). Jonas came to Lille as an assistant to Bishop Amand in 641.

[78] Thus Sisitrude (VC 2.1) and Gibitrude (VC 2.5). But although the other nuns do not depart for heaven only to return, some of them behave in such an ecstatic way that they seem to be in heaven before death: Ercantrude (VC 2.7), Deurechilde (VC 2.10), Ansitrude (VC 2.11), Wilsinde (VC 2.12), Leudebert (VC 2.13), and Landeberg (VC 2.18).

in forty days' time.[79] After thirty-seven days, she was granted a three-day journey to heaven,[80] which may not have included the Beatific Vision, but the next thing to it. When she returned to her body, the other nuns refused to believe she was really dying. But she would not take no for an answer and called for Mother Fare.[81] Soon she saw two angels from heaven return again to fetch her, and she cried out joyously, "I am dying, my lords, I am dying! I do not wish to remain any longer in this life full of misery. I want to return to that light from which I have come!"[82] But the assisting community members did not see the angels, so they were puzzled: "Mother Burgundofare asked her who she was talking to. 'Don't you see,' she said, 'these young men dressed in white robes who led me into heaven day before

---

[79] Forty days here is not just biblical shorthand for a long time but a precise prediction. In Gregory's Dialogues 4.18.1, Musa is also given thirty days' notice by the Blessed Virgin Mary. We will list below the frequent similarities and citations from Dial 4 in the Sisitrude story as an indication of how much Jonas was influenced by Gregory's stories. (A good modern edition of *Dialogue* 4 is in Gregoire le Grand, *Dialogues*, vol. 3, ed. Adalbert De Vogüé, SCh 265 [Paris: Les Éditions du Cerf, 1980]).

[80] In Dial 4.16 (not 4.6, as Vogüé has it in *Vie de Saint Columban*, 204, n. 5), Romula is given three days to prepare for death. In Dial 4.27, Armentarius also has a three-day vision anticipating his death. He also performs language miracles, learning to speak Greek in heaven. Sisitrude is escorted to heaven by two men in white robes, a reminiscence of Sulpicius Severus, VMart 7.6. This was also a favorite hagiographic source for Jonas and other medieval authors.

[81] In virtually every story in this cycle, the dying nun calls for Mother Abbess Fare. In itself, this is not surprising, since monks and nuns expect to be attended on their deathbed by the superior. But the constant mention of Fare in this account suggests to me that she herself may have written it.

[82] Similar deathbed exclamations are recorded by Gregory for a priest of Nursia (Dial 4.12.4) and the young girl Musa (Dial 4.18.2). Of course, pious exclamations are remembered by deathbed observers, but it is significant that these exclamations are addressed to angels, not to mere observers.

yesterday, and now are ready to lead me there again?"[83] She said a final goodbye to her astounded mother and to all those surrounding her, and then she died."[84]

After the departure of Sisitrude for heaven, the onlookers "heard angel voices chanting for longer than a human ear could hear them."[85] Of course, these liturgical niceties are not the essence of a holy death, but they make it more attractive and also more compelling for the onlookers and the readers. And that, after all, was and is the basic purpose of hagiography. As Jonas says in concluding the story of Sisitrude, "This was the first of the encouragements that the Lord was pleased to give to his servants in this monastery, so that although they were still held here below, they could aspire with all their souls to the perfection of the religious life" (VC 2.22.21).

The story of Sisitrude, like most of the deathbed visions in this section, ends happily: after a peaceful death, she goes to heaven. But not all the episodes are of that kind, since some of the nuns are not in good spiritual health when they come to die. Consequently, they must undergo a virtual conversion before they can be admitted to eternal glory, and this may be a harrowing experience:

> Likewise, another young girl by the name of Beractrude had lived in the above-mentioned monastery for a long time without even trying to observe the precepts of regular discipline. Then the devil put into her soul soiled by disobedience the thought of

[83] This sequence is almost verbatim from Dial 4.12, where the priest of Norcia is quoted. In addition, he angrily drove his wife away from his deathbed, an act that obviously has no parallel in Sisitrude. Probably Pope Gregory could not resist inserting a plug for clerical celibacy.

[84] Jonas, *Miracles of Eboriac* 11; *Vie de Saint Columban*, 205.

[85] Gregory says the same thing about Romula (Dial 4.16.7), even more artfully than Jonas. Another sign of a happy death in early hagiography is a pervasive sweet odor. See regarding Gibitrude, VC 2.3.5.

eating in secret all that she could get her hands on. This
disobedience had besmirched her soul for a long time
when the just Judge drew from her a just penalty: she
was possessed by a fever, so that burning like fire she
cried, "Woe is me!" After having blurted out this cry,
she fell into such torpor that everybody believed her
to be dead. After many hours, when she was breath-
ing with difficulty, she cried, "Bring the Abbess! Bring
the Abbess!" Then those who heard hastened to call
Mother Burgundofare. When she saw her arrive, the
dying woman, in a supreme effort, divulged to her in
confession all the faults that she had accumulated. On
their side, the sisters awaited the end of her life, but her
condition improved and she pulled herself together.
She stayed alive for some time, wasted by fever, and
then she finally died. (VC 2.22.21)

Even though Beractrude managed to overcome her final
sorrows, she apparently had to pass through them for purifica-
tion. But she arrived at reconciliation only after she confessed
her sin of gluttony to the abbess. In fact, confession of sin was
a key element in the spirituality of the Columbanian monasteries. Thus Ercantrude can only have a happy death after she
has confessed to the superior during the morning ritual in the
dormitory (VC 2.37).[86] Yet not everyone found it possible to
divulge her sins. In one long saga (VC 2.3.15–17), two young
nuns are persuaded by Satan to leave the monastery. But no
sooner are they out than they feel the need to return. Yet there
was no real conversion, since they found it impossible to make
a clean breast of their sins:

[86] This is the first of three confession periods, which is called *secunda*,
probably because it takes place about the second hour of the day (7:00
a.m.). See Walbert, Reg 16 [= Wal 2.16], and Donatus, Reg [RDon] 19.2–3.
Of course it was not sacramental confession, but it could very well have
been one of the roots of the church's later practice of private confession.

For a long time, they received the reproaches of the whole community without drawing any profit from the reprimands, but both of them, struck by the divine justice, learned how to submit to these well-merited punishments. In seeking the cause, the mother superior, whom we have already mentioned many times, could not drag the truth out of them. She exhorted them again to reveal their crime, at least at their last hour. But their hard hearts refused this remedy; in their tortures they cried out, "Back off a bit, back off! Don't press us like this. Wait!" The sisters then asked them whom they were begging to wait. They answered, "Don't you see this mob of Ethiopians who are coming, who wish to grab us and carry us off?" (VC 2.19.16)

This terrible case is one of the saddest episodes in this collection. The author makes two things clear: these nuns are possessed by the devil, and they cannot escape his clutches (do not want to!) and so are damned. This outcome is proven by the fact that their corpses are later found incinerated in their graves. At this point, we might ask why Jonas, or any other hagiographer for that matter, would recount such a gruesome tale. Apparently he was reproached for precisely this, and his answer is as follows: "If the deeds that we report promote the progress and the advancement of the just, or even the amendment of sinners, we should not see them as a collection of useless details. There is no doubt, in fact, that the punishments serve as a warning to many and render them more vigilant to acquire the heavenly goods" (VC 2.3).

So edification need not be entirely consoling. It can also be admonitory, since it can build people up (*edificatio*) by forcing them to examine their own consciences. But there is yet another aspect of these grim stories that might be noted, namely, realism. They may be full of grotesque details, and they may also be laden with otherworldly implications, which we might deem rather unrealistic. But they do frankly admit that some of the nuns at Faremoutiers were no angels. Some pretty rough characters joined the ranks of the holy virgins, and some of them remained unconverted sinners. After all, they were fresh from the rather brutal Merovingian society, so we should not expect them to lack some rough edges.

Moreover, we should remember that this collection of stories about the nuns of Faremoutiers is narrow in its purview since it is made up exclusively of deathbed happenings. Such stories alone can hardly give us an idea of life what was like in a seventh-century convent. Everything in these accounts is a matter of life and death, but ordinary existence cannot be that way.

Sources

We should not pass on before we have reflected a bit on the literary sources of these stories. As we have seen in the one story we presented in some detail, namely, that of Sisitrude, there is a heavy reliance here on the *Dialogues* of Saint Gregory, especially *Dialogue* 4. What are we to make of this? First, how does it affect the historicity of Jonas's account of the nuns of Faremoutiers?[87] Clearly it cannot but undermine it to some degree. Even though Jonas rarely quotes Gregory verbatim, enough of the details are parallel that we must conclude that the Columbanian monk knew Gregory's stories so well that they color his accounts. How much they do so is always a question. It is certainly not enough that we can accuse Jonas of flat-out plagiarism. The old writers had no idea of what that was. But on the other hand, we just cannot accept these stories as factual reportage. They all have a spiritual purpose.

---

[87] It is also quite possible that the nuns themselves knew the stories in Dial 4 and that these colored their accounts of what they had seen and heard. For our discussion here, it does not matter who was the author or who had read Gregory. Someone had!

There is also a scholarly controversy on this material. Some years ago the British scholar Francis Clark published a massive study of Gregory's *Dialogues*, in which he claimed that they were not written by Gregory at all. Rather, said Clark, they were the work of an eighth-century forger working in the Papal Scrinium (archives) at the Lateran.[88] As Clark points out, the early medieval period saw a good deal of this kind of fraudulent activity; the infamous Donation of Constantine is the most famous example. At any rate, one of Clark's ostensible proofs lies in the fact that he could find no literary source that actually quotes Gregory before about 750, leaving a gap of 150 years between the putative date and the evidence. But if Jonas of Bobbio wrote in 640, that date cuts Clark's gap down by at least a hundred years. Gregory's *Dialogues* are a problem for scholars, but it does not seem that we can claim he did not even write them.[89]

Bertulf

To close the pious account of Saint Columban and his followers, Jonas tells us of Bertulf, the third abbot of Bobbio. Like the other abbatial successors of Columban, Bertulf was not an Irishman but a Burgundian Frank.[90] Jonas says he was a

---

[88] Clark's first study of this question was published as *The Pseudo-Gregorian Dialogues* (Leiden, Netherlands: Brill, 1987). He published many other versions of the same thesis until his recent death.

[89] I myself perhaps contributed to the confusion by my article "Who Wrote the *Dialogues* of Saint Gregory? A Report on a Controversy," in which I more or less agreed with Clark (*CSQ* 39, no. 1 [2004]: 31–39). I was happy to hear that other scholars better than I (e.g., Claude Peifer, Henry Wansborough) were also impressed with Clark's thesis. But some years later Paul Meyvaert assured me that the evidence is heavily against Clark. On the basis of my own experience with Jonas's use of Gregory, Dial 4, I have to conclude Meyvaert is right.

[90] Although it appears that mostly the Irish monks were expelled from Luxeuil and presumably went to Bobbio, there is no evidence for

nobleman, related to Bishop Arnoul of Metz,[91] who became a monk under Eustace at Luxeuil. Bertulf met Abbot Attala when the latter visited Luxeuil and was given permission to accompany him back to Italy.[92] The monks must have been impressed by him, for they soon elected him to the abbacy.[93] He ruled that community until his death in 640. One of the most significant things that Bertulf did was to assign Jonas to write the life of Columban. Since he wrote it in 641, after Bertulf's death, Jonas made sure to include him in his lineup of saintly Columbanians.

Although Bertulf is a worker of wonders (VC 2.4.10–11), as are all of Jonas's heroes, his main significance is more theological, and even political. As soon as he began to govern Bobbio, "the Ancient Serpent decided to aim some hostile blows at his peaceable soul" (VC 2.4.4). Probus, the bishop of Tortona,[94] decided to assert his purported right of control over

---

their presence at Bobbio in the seventh century, and very little for the eighth century either, but that does not prove that they were not there (see Pius Engelbert, "Zur Frühgeschichte des Bobbieser Skriptoriums," *Revue Bénédictine* 78 [1968]: 220–60).

[91] Arnoul long harbored a desire for monastic solitude, and on his retirement (ca. 628) he went to live at the Columbanian monastery of Remiremont. It had been founded by his friend Romaric. Arnoul died in 640.

[92] We don't know exactly when Bertulf went to Bobbio. Jonas says he lived at Luxeuil "a long time," which could mean a lot of things. Since Attala died in 626, Bertulf must have come to Bobbio a few years before that.

[93] Jonas does not say much about Bertulf's character, except that he was "loved by all" at Luxeuil (VC 2.4.2). This statement may seem merely gratuitous, but it is not a typical remark among cenobitic monks. The Columbanian Rule does not arrange for abbatial elections, but in Columban's Letter 4.9, the founder tells the monks of Luxeuil to "unanimously choose" a leader if Attala prefers to go to Bobbio (Walker, *Sancti Columbani Opera*, 36–37). They chose Eustace.

[94] Tortona was an ancient Roman town located about thirty miles west of Bobbio. Vogüé says it is sixty-eight kilometers distant, but that

the monks. To bolster his claims, Probus appealed to the Lombard King Ariowald at Milan, but the king refused to interfere in church affairs: "It is not for me to decide between priests."[95]

When Bertulf got wind of the affair, he appealed to the pope.[96] Not only that, but he asked the king to transport him and his entourage to Rome. When we consider that Ariowald was an Arian, and also that Rome was at least a week away on horseback, this was no small request. Yet Ariowald "sent him to Rome in a royal carriage" (VC 2.4.6), so apparently Abbot Bertulf was in good favor with the Lombard court. Moreover, Pope Honorius[97] was also impressed by Bertulf: "The abbot was eager to describe it to the pope in all its details; and blessed Honorius was well impressed by the regular observance, the practices of religious life and the marks of humility. He retained Bertulf for some time, striving to build him up by daily conversations in his resolution not to abandon his laborious

---

measurement must allow for winding mountain roads. The place has 27,000 inhabitants today, but to judge from the rest of Jonas's account, it was not a place where the monks did business.

[95] VC 2.4.5. The term used here for priests is *sacerdotum*, which could also apply to bishops. See Albert Blaise, *Dictionnaire latin-français des auteurs chrétiens* (Strasbourg, France: Le Latin Chrétien, 1954), s.v. *sacerdos*. According to Vogüé, *Vie de Saint Columban*, 231, n. 16, Bertulf was a *presbyter* "by privilege of (Pope) Honorius." Exactly what that means escapes me, but it is not germane here.

[96] This was probably a shrewd move, for a synod of north Italian bishops would have been unlikely to favor the monks, who were feuding with the pope over the Three Chapters. It also seems that King Ariowald wanted this schism healed.

[97] Pope Honorius I (625–638) was one of the most effective popes of the early Middle Ages. Unfortunately, he came down on the wrong side of the Monothelite controversy, writing of "one will" in Christ in a letter to the Byzantine emperor. Hence he was used as an argument against papal infallibility at Vatican Council I (1870). See *Oxford Dictionary of the Christian Church*, s.v. "Honorius I."

enterprise and not to give up in defeating with the sword of the Gospel the abominable heresy of Arianism" (VC 2.23.6).

As Jonas points out, the pope was glad to have found another ally against Arianism. But of course Bertulf came to Rome on a different mission, which was also successful: "[Honorius] granted the favor asked and conceded the privilege of the Holy See according to which no bishop could pretend to exercise authority over a monastery under any title" (VC 2.23.7). This decision, based on a dispute between an obscure but ambitious bishop and a remote, rural monastery, is usually pointed to as the earliest instance of the exemption of religious men and women in church history.[98] For this alone Abbot Bertulf deserves the eternal gratitude of monks.

After his signal success with the pope, Bertulf fled the notorious Roman summer, but apparently he did not quite escape the danger. According to Jonas's eyewitness account,[99] when the party had reached Bismantum,[100] Bertulf was laid low with fever, almost to the point of death. But at that point he was graced with a vision of Saint Peter, who assured him that he was not going to die but would return safely to Bobbio.[101]

---

[98] The term "religious exemption" has a different meaning in the United States, where it applies to juridical decisions granting various groups exemption from various laws on the basis of religious privilege. For papal exemption, see *Oxford Dictionary of the Christian Church*, s.v. "exemption." Since monasteries must be under some higher authority, they exist either directly under the Vatican or in a religious congregation.

[99] VC 2.23: "I myself was in the party." Presumably the royal carriage was also available for the return trip of about four hundred miles.

[100] Vogüé, *Vie de Saint Columban*, 232, n. 20, locates Bismantum fifty kilometers southwest of Reggio Emilia, so the party was almost home but still in the mountains and probably in the wilderness.

[101] A nice touch to this vision is that Peter grants it on his feast day (Saints Peter and Paul). This fact enables pinpointing the event to June 29, 628. We also know that the exemption decree was issued on June 11, so

Although the abbot modestly endeavored to conceal this vision from Jonas, he finally disclosed the whole event.[102]

Yet not all Bobbio's dealings with the Arian Lombards were as irenic as this. For example, when Duke Ariowald, before becoming king, sent one of his men to Abbot Attala for healing, the latter granted the favor but haughtily refused the presents offered by the duke: "As for the presents, he would never, never accept anything from an impious heretic" (VC 2.24 [15]).[103] Yet a back story places this refusal in its proper context. This possessed, and healed, Lombard was not just anyone. He was in fact a henchman of Ariowald, who had mugged Blidulf, one of the Bobbio monks, near Pavia—on a contract from Ariowald! Blidulf revived, but the thug did not get off so easily:

> However, the man who had been sent to do the foul deed, when the monk had departed from Pavia, was invaded by a demon. He was tortured by various chastisements that burned him, and he confessed the terrible deed that he had committed. To the ears of all, he proclaimed that whoever would do to the monks of Bobbio what he himself had done would undergo the same punishment. And he added that whoever let himself be persuaded by the Arians would suffer a like punishment from the Just Judge. (VC 2.24 [14])

What had provoked Ariowald to this vicious deed? When he met Blidulf on the street, the following nasty exchange had ensued:

---

the laborious return trip in the Italian summer heat took about twenty days. Even today a slow train ride up the Italian peninsula takes forever.

[102] Embarrassment by the recipient of a miracle is a recurring theme: see VC 2:6, 21, 25.

[103] Bracketed numbers indicate subtitles in the text.

Seeing Blidulf, Ariowald said, "There is one of the monks of Columban; he refuses to greet me." When he drew near, he saluted him in a derisory manner. Blidulf responded, "I would greet you, if you did not aid and abet those who deceive you and their erroneous doctrines. You call them priests, but that is a deceptive title. It would be better to confess the ineffable Trinity and the One God, not three powers but three persons, not one person under three names but three true persons, Father, Son, and Holy Spirit,[104] who have but a single power, a single will and a single essence." (VC 2.24 [12])

From this encounter, it is clear that the ecumenical movement had not yet begun in Lombardy. It is clear that the Arians had no use for the monks of Bobbio, and vice versa. The miracle is that the monks from Luxeuil were ever admitted into the territory.

Jonas of Bobbio

After describing Jonas's account of Columban and his disciples and successors, we might focus briefly on Jonas himself.[105] As we have noted, he came to Bobbio as a child of nine,[106]

---

[104] See Columban, Sermon 1.2: *Deum . . . unum potentia, trinum persona; unum natura, trinum nomine,* and, further on: *De veritate autem personarum Patri, Filii et Spiritus Sancti* (Walker, *Sancti Columbani Opera*, 60, 62).

[105] After I finished my commentary on these Rules, I came across a new article on the work of Jonas of Bobbio: Jamie Kreiner, "Autopsies and Philosophies of a Merovingian Life: Death, Responsibility, Salvation," *Journal of Early Christian Studies* 22, no. 1 (2014): 113–52. Kreiner claims that Jonas revolutionized seventh-century hagiographical deathbed scenes. I plan to explore her ideas in the future.

[106] See Vogüé, *Vie de Saint Columban*, 55. It could have been that by the time of Jonas the Columbanians had taken on the continental custom of admitting child oblates.

even though the Irish practice was not to admit child oblates but only adults. Probably Jonas was somewhat educated when he came to the monastery and then received a good grounding in letters. At any rate, by age eighteen, in 626, he was serving as secretary to Abbot Attala. By 633, he was sent by Abbot Bertulf to Faremoutiers, probably to collect material for the life of Columban that Bertulf wanted him to write. No doubt he also on that trip visited Luxeuil and other important sites for the Columbanian "Order."

In 638, shortly before Abbot Bertulf died, he again sent Jonas north. This time he accompanied a traveling missionary bishop named Amand, who worked in the area of modern Lille. There Jonas seems to have written the bulk of his book on the Columbanians. Although he had been ordered to write only the Life of Columban, he now expanded his project to include the lives of several other disciples of the great saint. This additional material became book 2 of the present *Life of Columban*. Jonas was soon named abbot of Marchiennes, near Tournai. He must have pursued his craft as hagiographer for a good long time, since we know that in 659 he traveled to Reomé in southern France to write the *Vita Iohannis*.[107] From the little we know about Jonas, we can still say that he was a serious scholar and writer. Bertulf would not have commissioned him to undertake this great task unless he had a high respect for his ability. Nor would he have been allowed to travel so extensively except in pursuit of an important work. For a medieval monk, to be roaming hundreds of miles doing this kind of research was remarkable in itself.

But beyond these bare facts, what kind of writer was Jonas? First of all, he was obviously not a modern biographer. Plenty

---

[107] Jonas, "Vita Sancti Iohannis Monachi et Abbatis," in *Ionae Vitae Sanctorum Columbani, Vedastis, Iohannis*, ed. Bruno Krusch, Scriptores Rerum Germanicarum (Hannover and Leipzig: Hannoverae Impensis Bibliopolii Hahniani, 1905), 321–44, here 321, 326.

of evidence shows that his basic interest was hagiographic: to edify. Like all writers of this type, his stock in trade was miracles, by means of which he wanted to show God's power at work in his saints, and in sinners. Like almost all ancient hagiographers, Jonas was not primarily interested in character development. Nor did he spend much time presenting the specific characteristics that modern readers relish in biographies.[108] Rarely do the special quirks and idiosyncrasies of his subjects peep through his account. Still, he can tell a good story, and he knows how to keep the account moving. Only in the section on Faremoutiers does the reader long for relief.

What kind of education did Jonas have for this task? We don't know exactly, but at least we can say that he was well read. All of the Irish monks and their descendants prized learning, but Jonas was *learned*. We know this because he quotes and alludes to a wide variety of sources, and he does so without obvious effort. He rarely depends slavishly on his sources, but to a scholar like Vogüé, who knew the ancient literature so well, the references are clear. Jonas was especially influenced by the *Dialogues* of Gregory the Great.

What kind of historian is Jonas? According to Vogüé, he is a rather good one. He is not a good writer: his Latin is poor, and he is very repetitious. But he is very original and informative, and his material is coherent. Actually, he is not all that well informed on the life of Columban before the Irishman traveled to Bobbio, but he is generally reliable in all the other parts, as Vogüé says:

> But although Jonas is a mediocre writer in the details,
> he has realized a remarkable literary work. In the literary
> ary desert of the seventh century, when only dwarfish

---

[108] For a discussion of this point, see Thomas J. Heffernan, *Sacred Biography: Saints and Their Biographers in the Middle Ages* (Oxford: Oxford University Press, 1992).

trees are found, he is indeed a giant. Not only does the *Life of Columban* tower over its competition in regard to size, but it also evidences a real capacity for composition. Adapting his material to the canons of traditional hagiography, Jonas has produced an original work whose structure and design do not depend on any known model. His rich prosopography, his precise topography, his rather numerous historical facts, even if they sometimes lack cohesion and exactitude, provide an important source for our knowledge of this era.[109]

Thus we come to end of our rather long introduction on the *Life of Columban*. We are now in a position to examine the details of three Rules.

---

[109] Vogüé, *Vie de Saint Columban*, 34. My translation.

The Rule of Columban

The Rule of Monks
(*Regula Monachorum*)¹

Thus begins the Rule for Monks of Saint Columban Abbot. First of all we are taught to love God with our whole heart and with our whole mind and with all our strength, and our neighbor as ourselves; then {come} works:

I. Obedience²

1. At the first command of the senior, all who hear him must stand up to obey, because obedience is shown to God,
2. as our Lord Jesus Christ said, "Whoever listens to you, listens to me" [Luke 10:16].
3. So if anyone hears the command but does not immediately rise up, he is to be considered disobedient.³

¹ This translation is based on the critical edition with facing-page English translation of G. S. M. Walker, *Sancti Columbani Opera* (Dublin: Dublin Institute for Advanced Studies, 1970), cited in footnotes below as Walker. Walker's emendations from the Long Text appear in the text below in brackets; my own insertions are in curly brackets. A French translation appears in *Règles et pénitentiels monastiques*, trans. Adalbert de Vogüé with Pierre Sangiani and Jean-Baptiste Juglar, Aux sources du monachisme colombanien vol. 2, Vie monastique 20 (Bégrolles-en-Mauges, France: Abbaye de Bellefontaine, 1988), cited below as Vogüé, Règles.

² The title (T) "Obedience" and verses 1 and 2 are based on RB 5.4, 6, and RB 5.15, though not verbally. Benedict quotes Luke 10:16 in both places.

³ "if anyone hears the command . . . to be considered." Basil, *Regula* 70.1 has the same wording, except that he has *non obtemperans* for *non statim surrexerit* (hereafter RBasil).

4. But if someone contradicts {the superior}, he is guilty of insubordination,

5. ⁴and therefore he is not only guilty of disobedience but is to be reckoned the destroyer of many because he opened the door of contradiction to others.

6. If anyone murmurs, but obeys grudgingly, he is to be held disobedient.⁵

7. Thus his work is to be rejected until he manifests good will.

8. On the other hand, what is the limit of obedience?⁶

9. It is certainly commanded to the point of death, for Christ obeyed the Father for us unto death.

10. He himself recommended this to us when he said through the apostle, "Have this mind in you that was also in Christ Jesus.

---

⁴ These verses quote RBasil 69.1–2: "Q. Is it permissible for anyone to excuse himself from the work he is charged to do and to seek something else? R. Since it is defined that the measure of obedience is even *unto death* [Phil 2:8], anyone who avoids what he is charged to do and seeks something else is first of all guilty of disobedience and manifestly shows that he has not yet *denied* himself [Matt 16:24; Mark 8:34; Luke 9:23]. Second, he becomes the cause of many more ills both for himself and for others. For he opens the door of contradiction to the many and accustoms himself to contradicting" (*The Rule of St. Basil in Latin and English: A Revised Critical Edition*, trans. Anna M. Silvas [Collegeville, MN: Liturgical Press, 2013], 165).

⁵ Here is Silvas's rendition of RBasil 71.T–2: "Q. What of someone obeying who murmurs? R. Since the apostle says: *Do all things without murmurings or hesitations* [Phil 2:14], a murmurer is estranged from the unity of the brothers, and his work is rejected. For such a one is manifestly sick with want of faith and does not have the sure confidence of hope for the future."

⁶ The source here is RBasil 65.T–1: "Q. What ought to be the measure of obedience of one who desires to fulfill the rule of being well pleasing to God? R. The apostle shows when he sets before us the obedience of the Lord, *who was made obedient*, he says, *unto death, even death on a cross* [Phil 2:8], and he prefaced it with, *have this mind in you which was also in Christ Jesus*" [Phil 2:5].

11. Although he was in divine form, he did not think he should cling jealously to his equality with God.

12. No, he abased himself by accepting the role of a slave.

13. Not only did he behave like an ordinary person, but he humbled himself, becoming obedient to the Father unto death, death on a cross" [Phil 2:5-8].

14. Therefore truly obedient disciples of Christ ought not refuse anything, no matter how hard and strenuous it is. It should rather be welcomed with the warmest joy,

15. [7]for unless obedience is of that sort, it will not be acceptable to the Lord. For he said, "Whoever does not take up his cross and follow me is not worthy of me" [Matt 16:24].

16. Therefore he says of a worthy disciple, "Wherever I am, there my servant will be with me" [John 12:26].

II. Silence

1. It is decreed that the rule of silence is to be carefully observed, for it is written, "But the fruit[8] of righteousness is silence and peace" [Isa 32:17].

---

[7]Now Columban returns to RB 5.14-18: "But this same obedience will only be acceptable to God and humanly attractive if the command is not executed fearfully, slowly, or listlessly, or with murmuring or refusal. For obedience given to superiors is given to God, who said, 'Whoever listens to you listens to me.' And it should be given gladly by disciples, for 'God loves a cheerful giver.' If a disciple grudgingly obeys and murmurs not only out loud but internally, even if he carries out the order, it will not be acceptable to God. For he sees the heart of the murmurer" (*Benedict's Rule*, trans. Terrence Kardong [Collegeville, MN: Liturgical Press, 1996], 104). Overall, Columban makes more use of Basil than of Benedict in this first chapter, but he has effected a workable combination. RB 5 is one of the most rigorous chapters in the whole Rule, and Basil is also very stern on obedience. So Columban has put together a tough chapter.

[8]"Fruit." The *Oxford Latin Dictionary* doesn't give this meaning for *cultus* but Vogüé does. As the perfect passive participle of *colo*, it makes sense. The NAB for Isa 32:17 has "Right will produce calm and security."

2. Therefore, so as not to be accused of verbosity,[9] one must maintain silence except for useful and necessary matters. For according to Scripture, "In much talking there will be sin" [Prov 10:19].[10]

3. Therefore the Savior says, "You will be justified on the basis of your words, and you will also be condemned on the basis of your words" [Matt 12:37].

4. They will be rightly condemned who, when they could have spoken justly if they wished,

5. instead preferred to speak evil, unjust, impious, silly, injurious, dubious, false, hostile, disparaging, wicked, outlandish, blasphemous, harsh, and devious words, and with extreme verbosity.

6. Therefore, we should avoid these and like words, and speak cautiously and reasonably. Otherwise, detractions or loud arguments may erupt in a vicious flood of words.

III. Food and Drink

1. Let the food of the monks be plain, and taken in the evening. Their food should [help them] avoid gluttony and their drink inebriation; it should sustain and not harm them. They should eat vegetables, beans, and flour cooked in water accompanied by a small loaf of bread. Thus the stomach will not be overloaded nor the spirit stifled.

2. Those who desire an eternal reward should only consider how such things are useful and compatible with their lifestyle.[11]

---

[9] The literal sense here is more verbose: "Therefore, lest one be convicted of being guilty of verbosity."

[10] Gregory, *Moralia in Iob* (hereafter Mor) 7.XXXVII.58 has the same quotations (Isa 32 and Prov 10) but in reverse order. In Mor 10.II.2, the same two quotations are given but in the usual order.

[11] "Useful and compatible with their lifestyle." The Latin *utilitati et usui* is much more compact but also cryptic. Walker does not advance our understanding much with "usefulness and use" (*Sancti Columbani Opera,*

3. Therefore, their lifestyle ought to be moderate, and so should their manner of working. True moderation consists in maintaining the possibility of spiritual progress[12] along with an abstinence that mortifies the body,

4. for if abstinence goes too far, it is a vice and not a virtue. Virtue sustains and contains many good things.[13]

5. So we should fast every day, just as we should eat every day.[14]

6. Since we must eat daily, we should feed the body with simple food, and not much of it. We need to eat every day because we need to make daily progress by praying, working, and reading.

IV. Poverty or Conquering Greed

1. Monks ought to avoid avarice, "for the world is crucified to them and they to the world" for Christ. It is damnable for them not only to possess, but even to wish to do so.[15]

127; all footnoted references to Walker refer to the editions in this book). Vogüé, Règles, has "Util et avantageux à usage," which I tried to render even more explicitly. I settled on "lifestyle" for *usus,* although "monastic observance" would probably also fill the bill. Vogüé, Règles, refers to Cassian, Inst 5.5, for "Usage modéré de la vie," but I don't get the point.

[12] "Possibility of spiritual progress." The idea here is probably that excessive fasting can destroy basic health and therefore impede spiritual growth. This is one of the emphases of Cassian, Conf 2.18–22.

[13] "Virtue sustains and contains many good things." This gnomic aphorism seems to continue the thought of the previous verse. As such, it insists that abstinence from food, or any other commendable act of ascesis, not become an obsession that vitiates the rest of the moral life. What follows expands this idea.

[14] We will not be able to lead a *balanced* monastic life of prayer, work, and *lectio* unless we maintain our strength by eating enough to have some energy.

[15] Cassian, Inst 7.21–22, also insists that true poverty lies in the will. The same point is made by Basil in RBasil 4.8.

2. It is their will that counts, not their bank account.[16] They have left everything and followed Christ the Lord daily with the cross of fear,[17] so they will have treasure in heaven [Matt 19:21].

3. For this reason, since they will possess much in heaven, they ought to be content on earth with just enough to stay alive.[18]

4. They know that cupidity is leprosy for monks who are imitators of the sons of the prophets. For a disciple of Christ it is treason and ruin, and it is death for the doubting followers of the apostles.[19]

5. Therefore, nakedness and disdain for riches are the first perfection of monks.[20] The second is the cleansing away of vice. Third is the most perfect, continuous love for God,

---

[16] "Bank account" (*census*). Jerome has the same idea in Ep 68.1, with *res* instead of *census*. Strictly speaking, it does not matter whether a monk handles money; in fact, some monks *must* handle large sums. What counts is whether one is attached to or detached from it.

[17] "Cross of fear." In Inst 4.34, Cassian begs God to pierce his "flesh with the fear of the Lord," a reference to Ps 118:120.

[18] "Just enough to stay alive," my free translation of *parvo extremae necessitatis censu*. I translated *census* rather differently in the previous line; like *res* it is very adaptable.

[19] The references here are all biblical and also lifted directly from Cassian, Inst 7.14: "sons of the prophets" refers to Gehazi in 2 Kgs 5:27; "disciple of Christ" refers to Judas in Matt 27:5; "doubting followers of the apostles" refers to Ananias and Sapphira of Acts 5:5 and 5:10.

[20] These three "perfections" correspond to Cassian's three "renouncements" of Conf 3.7 and 8. As Vogüé remarks (Règles, 57 n. 5), only the third member of the series is usually considered a spiritual perfection. The first perfection is also quoted verbatim by Columban from Cassian, Inst 4.43. Perfection number two is a direct transcription of Inst 4.39. For the third number, however, Columban makes an important change: where Cassian (Conf 3.6.1) has "to contemplate the future and to desire the invisible," Columban simply substitutes the love of God.

and also of the divine law.[21] This comes after the forgetful-
ness of earthly things.

6. This being the case, according to the saying of the Lord,
   we need few things.[22] Indeed, we need only one.

7. There are very few true necessities without which we cannot live, or even one thing, like food, literally speaking.

8. But we require purity of understanding by the grace of
   God, so as to understand spiritually the few things of love
   suggested to Martha by the Lord.

V. Conquering Vanity

1. The peril of vanity may be shown from a few words of our
   Savior. When his disciples were crowing with vanity, he
   said to them, "I have observed Satan fall from lightning
   from the sky" [Luke 10:18].[23]

---

[21] "Divine law" (*divinorum iugus*) could also refer to the religious life
(Albert Blaise, *Dictionnaire latin-français des auteurs chrétiens* [Strasbourg:
Le Latin Chrétien, 1954], s.v. *jugum*).

[22] "Few things, or even one." This is the formulation of Cassian in
Conf 1.8 and Conf 23.3. Although Cassian has slightly altered Luke 10:42
("only one thing"), he follows the gospel faithfully in making the one
thing contemplation. Columban interprets it (temporarily) as food. Vogüé,
Règles, 58 n. 8: "In Conf 1.8, the *pauca* (few things) are "the acts and ad-
mirable services of the holy ones," the objects of a contemplation inferior
to that of God ("the only one").

[23] "The peril of. . ." Vogüé, Règles, 58 n. 1 points to a similar formulation in Cassian, Inst 11.10 (*quam perniciosus*), which also pertains to vanity.
Although Columban interprets Jesus' words—"I have observed Satan fall
like lightning from the sky" (NAB)—as a reproach, as does Gregory the
Great in Mor 20.V.13 and 23.VI.13, that is not the only possible meaning of
this passage. For example, the note in NAB (1986) at Luke 10:18 says, "As
the kingdom of God is gradually being established, evil in all its forms
is being defeated; the dominion of Satan over humanity is at an end."

2. And when some Jews justified themselves, he told them, "What men esteem as high is abominable in God's eyes" [Luke 16:15].[24]

3. From these examples, and from the most famous one of the Pharisee who justified himself, we gather that vanity and self-importance destroy all good deeds. For the good deeds the Pharisee bragged about perished, but the sins confessed by the tax collector vanished.[25]

4. So let's have no big talk from monks lest their big efforts be in vain.

VI. Regarding Chastity

1. The chastity of a monk is judged by his thoughts, and he was doubtless the target of the Lord's words to the disciples when they gathered to listen to him: "Whoever ogles a woman is guilty of defiling her in his heart" [Matt 5:28].[26]

---

[24] "Justified." In Luke 16:8-13, Jesus unleashes a diatribe against avarice. The Pharisees, overhearing, take it as aimed at them. They must have been right, because Jesus then rounds directly on them, accusing them of hypocrisy in addition to greed. The result is that the aphorism is restricted to the Pharisees: "What men esteem as high is abominable in God's eyes." According to Vogüé (Règles, 58 n. 2), Gregory also cites Luke 16:15 in Dial 1.4.18 but "in another manner." He must refer to the different wording in the two texts: Gregory's version reads *quia quod hominibus altum est, abominabile est ante Deum*. Columban has *quod autem altum est in hominibus abominatio est in conspectu domini*. In fact, Gregory is quoting the Vulgate exactly, but Columban is not. Perhaps he is quoting from memory.

[25] The allusion here is to Luke 18:9-14, about the Pharisee and the tax collector. Note that Columban explicitly affirms that the Pharisee *did* do a great deal of good—but vitiated it with his vanity. This is also the theme of Cassian in Inst 11.19. The Pharisee and publican are referred to by Gregory, Mor 23.VI.13, just before Luke 10:18. All in all, Gregory is the main influence on this little chapter of Columban's Rule.

[26] Matt 5:28 is similarly quoted by Cassian in Inst 6.12, which is devoted to the "the spirit of fornication." Like Cassian, Columban knows

2. When the One to whom {the monk} is consecrated scrutinizes his vow, he should be afraid that the One might find something abominable.

3. {Then he would fall under} the judgment of Saint Peter: "They have eyes full of sensuality and adultery" [2 Pet 2:14].

4. What good is it to be a physical virgin if one is not a spiritual one?[27]

5. For "God is spirit" [John 4:24], who dwells in the spirit and mind that he sees is pure, in which there is no adulterous thought, no stain of an impure spirit, no blemish of sin.[28]

VII. The Divine Office

1. Regarding the *synaxis*,[29] that is, the Office of psalms and prayers in the canonical form, certain distinctions must

---

well enough that the spiritual problem here lies deeper than the eyes: it is the thoughts that count in this regard. Inst 6.13 stresses the scrutiny of the thoughts, as does the remainder of this chapter of the Rule of Columban.

[27] In Inst 6.4.1, Cassian develops this idea by means of special vocabulary. He claims that abstinence (*enkrateia*) indicates mere bodily virginity. But one may be a physical virgin through mere lack of opportunity. Chastity (*agnon*), according to Cassian, is a very different thing, for it is embraced with full intentionality.

[28] The idea that the spiritual God, or Holy Spirit, will only come to dwell in a human heart/spirit that is pure of defilement is a commonplace with the Fathers, including Cassian, Inst 6.15. But Columban is original in citing John 4:24. Vogüé, Règles, 59 n. 5, lists the following "possible echoes" for the last items of this list: Song 7:22, 25; 1 Cor 7:1; 2 Pet 2:13.

[29] *Synaxis* is a term from Greek monasticism that means "gathering." It can refer to the community itself, as it usually does in Cassian's writing. In Inst 2.12T and Conf 7.34, however, it means the Divine Office. Columban uses it three times for the Office, here and in Coen II.6 and IV.4. Since he always uses it with a gloss, he must think his audience may not understand it. Cassian complains in Inst 2.2 that he has found a bewildering variety of methods of apportioning the psalms. He probably is referring to Gallic authors, for whom he proposes to solve these problems by laying

be made because the thing has been handed on to us in various ways by different authors.

2. Therefore, I must also arrange things variously to suit our way of life[30] and the succession of seasons.

3. Because of the changing of seasons, it should not be a uniform program.

4. When the nights are long, the Office should be long; when the nights are short, the Office should be likewise.

5. So, with the custom of our elders, from June 24, when the nights grow appreciably longer, the Office begins to grow from twelve *chora*, the smallest number allowed for Saturday night and Sunday, until the beginning of winter, that is, November 1.[31]

---

down the Egyptian norm (Inst 2.3). "Psalms and prayers in the canonical form" is traditional language, found already in Cassian, Inst 2.9: *orationum canonicarum modum.*

[30] "Our way of life." Walker has "the nature of man's life," but Vogüé has "notre manière de vivre," which makes better sense.

[31] Vogüé's explanation of the Columbanian Night Office is instructive: "Let us enter then at Luxeuil or Bobbio some morning, at daybreak, when the monks come to end the longest of their daily Offices, that is, *matins*, where they sometimes recite half the psalter. They rise for the first time at midnight to recite twelve psalms; then they go back to bed. They rise again for the great *vigil* of the last hours of the night. This varies according to the seasons from twenty-four to thirty-six psalms on ordinary days, and from thirty-six to sixty-five on Saturday and Sunday. The enormous number of psalms is lightened by abridgements and incessant alteration. After each psalm, they stop for a brief prayer. They kneel for this during ordinary time and bow for it on Sundays and during Paschal Time. The monks silently recite the verse *Deus in adjutorium* three times and rise up. To these interruptions of the chant are added changes in the mode of execution: after two psalms recited by soloists, the third is chanted antiphonally by all. Each one of these groups of three psalms, which give rhythm to the psalmody, is called a *chora*" (from the General Introduction of Columban, *Règles et Pénitentiels Monastiques,* II [not vol. III, as p. 60 n. 5 of the work reads]).

6. Of these, they sing twenty-five antiphonal psalms, which always follow two psalms, that is, twice the same number,[32] in the third place. Thus they sing the whole psalter on the aforementioned two nights. But for the other nights in winter, they limit themselves to twelve *chora* (thirty-six psalms).

7. At the end of winter, throughout spring, they drop three psalms each week, so that twelve antiphonal psalms remain on only the holy nights[33] (Saturday and Sunday). This applies to the thirty-six psalms of the daily Office in winter.

8. But there are twenty-four psalms for the whole of spring and summer up to the autumn equinox, that is, September 24.[34]

9. So the manner of the *synaxis* is like the spring equinox, that is, March 24, seeing that the Office gradually increases and decreases by mutual changes.[35]

---

[32] "Twice the same number" (*eiusdem numeri duplicis*). This phrase has puzzled commentators from Germain Morin ("Mélanges d'érudition chrétienne," *Revue Bénédictine* 12 [1895]: 193–203, here 200–201) to Walker, who considers it an interpolation to be left in brackets after "twenty-five antiphonal psalms." Vogüé, however, takes it in stride, though he moves it, as I have. The huge number of psalms sung at Luxeuil had an Irish origin but was also characteristic of Gaul. In Inst 2, Cassian struggles to convince the Gauls to limit the psalms of Vigils to twelve, but to judge from texts like Caesarius's *Rule for Nuns* (Reg Virg), he did not succeed. "Other nights of winter" begin on September 24 and end March 24. Modern calendars place the equinoxes on the twenty-first or twenty-second day of the month.

[33] "Only on the holy nights." Although Walker understands the Irish Office well enough, he contributes to the confusion by writing "only twelve antiphons remain on the holy nights, that is, the thirty-six psalms of the daily winter office." The Latin is rather obscure, but the sense requires that this sentence refer to the dropping of three psalms a week in daily Vigils. I do not believe either Walker or Vogüé makes this clear enough in his translation.

[34] As far as I can understand, the "whole of spring and summer" here means May 1 to September 24. The period of decrease is March 24 to May 1.

[35] "Increases" must refer to a spring transition from twenty-four (winter) to thirty-six (summer) psalms, which parallels the decrease that

10. Thus we must proportion our vigils to our strength, especially since we are commanded by the author of our salvation to watch and "pray at all times" [Luke 21:36]. And Paul orders us to "pray ceaselessly" [1 Thess 5:17].[36]

11. But we need to know the measure[37] of the canonical prayers, at which all come together at set hours to pray together, after which each one should pray in his room [Matt 6:6].

12. Therefore, our ancestors have decided that three psalms[38] should be said at the Day Hours,[39] taking into account the work to be done in the intervals.

13. {We should add} versicles that intercede first for our sins,[40] then for the whole Christian people, then for priests and

---

occurs in September. It seems to me that this opaque sentence could well mean that the psalmody should match the hours of daylight. That is, the longer the night, the longer the Office of Vigils.

[36] While Columban's arrangement of the psalms may strike us as excessive, and even grotesque, he presents it here as a *restriction*, the purpose of which is to enable us to "pray ceaselessly" (1 Thess 5:17).

[37] "Measure." *Modus* can mean either "manner" or "measure," the first referring to quality and the second quantity. Walker has the first, but Vogüé the second, I believe correctly. The issue here is the *quantity* of vigils. Cassian spends much of Inst 2 discussing this very question. For him, 1 Thess 5:17, "pray ceaselessly," is a capital text. In Conf 9–10, he insists that this is the true monastic ideal, which prevailed in Egypt. In Syria (including Palestine), they set down great numbers of psalms to be sung at fixed hours, but in Cassian's view that does not implement "pray always" but undermines it. As for Columban, he often cites Cassian, but he seems to follow the Syrian model.

[38] These three psalms were presumably short ones if Columban was serious about work. As it is, formal prayer every three hours can preclude certain kinds of sustained work—especially agriculture. In Inst 3.3, Cassian says that only three psalms are said, precisely to allow for work.

[39] "Day Hours." *Diurnae horae* is technical language referring to Prime, Terce, Sext, and None, the Little Hours of the Office. In occurs in the earlier RB at 16.3; 18.20; and 43.10.

[40] "For our sins." In the Rule of the Master, chap. 50, the monks are told to give thanks every three hours for having survived the previous

the other orders of the holy people that are consecrated to God. Next [we should pray] for those who give alms and for peace among kings.

14. Last {let us pray} for our enemies,[41] lest God hold it as sin [Acts 7:60] when they persecute and slander us, "for they do not know what they are doing" [Luke 23:34].

15. At the beginning of the night twelve psalms are chanted, and the same thing is done at midnight.[42]

16. At Morning Office, twice ten plus twice two {= twenty-four psalms} are set down.[43] This is when the nights are short, as I have said. But more are always set down for Sunday and Saturday nights, at which seventy-five psalms are sung one after the other[44] at a single Office.

17. These things have been said regarding the common Office.

---

three-hour interval free of sin. Indeed, this seems to be the very purpose of the Day Hours for the Master. Columban does not seem to have been influenced by the Rule of the Master, although he was very concerned with the forgiveness of sins.

[41] "Our enemies." Columban did not have to use his imagination on this score, since he had frequent troubles with the Merovingian kings. In fact, one of them, Theuderich (see Jonas, VC 1.35), tried to deport him back to Ireland but gave up when the winds would not let the ship depart from the port of Nantes (see p. 13 of the introduction above).

[42] Adamnan mentions three night Offices in his *Life of Columba* 3.28. The one at the beginning of the night, which would be equivalent to Vespers or Compline, is called *duodecima* (twelve) in Columban's Coen III.2. Cassian, Inst 2.4, insists on twelve psalms (only) for the Night Office.

[43] "Set down" (*dispositi*). When or where these were "set down" is not clear to me. Since this Rule was written soon after they arrived in Gaul, presumably the model for Columban was what he had learned at Bangor, Ulster, where he was trained.

[44] "One after another" (*sub uno cursu*). How this relates to the system of *chora* (VII.5–6) is not obvious. The *chora* was a block of three psalms, with the third always done antiphonally. It is unclear whether there was a pause between *chorae*, but at least the variation of performance would introduce some variety in this interminable lineup of seventy-five psalms.

18. However, as I have said, the true tradition of prayer varies so that the capacity of the person devoted to it should be able to perdure without undermining his vow. It also depends on whether one can actually do it and whether one's mental capacity allows for it, considering the necessities of one's life.

19. It should also be varied as the fervor of each one requires, according to whether he is free or alone, to how much learning he has, to how much leisure he has, to how much zeal he has, or at what age he arrived at the monastery.

20. And so the realization[45] of this one ideal[46] should be variously valued, for the demands of work and place must be taken into account.

21. So although the length of standing or singing may be varied,[47] a person will achieve equal perfection in prayer of the heart and continual attention to God.[48]

22. There are, however, some Catholics[49] for whom the same number of psalms is canonical, whether the nights are short or long.

Surely it would have taken at least two or three hours to sing half the Psalter?

[45] "Realization" is Vogüé's inspired rendition of *perfectio*; Vogüé notes that the word has the same connotation in v. 18. Although *perfectio* will have its more usual sense of faultlessness and total excellence in v. 21, the point being made here is that "perfect" prayer is precisely what suits the individual. "Pray as you can, not as you can't" (John Chapman).

[46] "This one ideal" must refer to the ideal of constant prayer, which the author admits must be tailored to the actual condition and circumstances of the monk.

[47] Walker's rendition of this verse is as follows: "And thus, although the length of standing or singing may be various, yet the identity of prayer in the heart and mental concentration that is unceasing with God's help will be of singular excellence." Compared to Vogüé's French translation, which I have used as a model, this is far from clear.

[48] "Attention to God," literally "attention with God's help" (*cum Deo jugis attentio*).

[49] "Catholics" (*Catholici*) is a typical Irish expression; "Christians" was the usual term in the days before the Reformation. But Walker's

23. But they celebrate this canon[50] four times a night:[51] at the beginning of night, at midnight, at cockcrow, and at morning.

24. This Office seems rather little to some people in winter, but in summer they find it a heavy burden, for the frequent celebrations[52] in the short night cause not just weariness but downright exhaustion.[53]

---

note is important here: "The phrase quoted from Cassian immediately afterwards suggests that these are the Egyptians; they made the same distinction as Columban between 'holy' and other nights, but maintained an invariable number of appointed psalms throughout the year."

[50] "Canon" is not a reference to canon law, which did not exist at that time, and which also has never laid down liturgical minutiae. Yet in Inst 2.5, Cassian presents the "Rule of the Angel," a traditional story about the early Christians of Alexandria. When they were unsure how many psalms to sing at night, an angel appeared, sang twelve psalms, and departed. In *Lausiac History* 32.6–7, Palladius claims that an angel came in a vision to Pachomius and gave him detailed regulations for his community. Regarding the Office, he "commanded that they pray twelve prayers each day and twelve at lamp-lighting time, and that at all-night devotions they say twelve prayers, and three at the ninth hour." When Pachomius objects that the "prayers are too few," the angel replies that this was laid down for the weak, not the strong. The Pachomian expert Armand Veilleux says that Palladius actually knew little or nothing about Pachomian monasticism. Veilleux states that the Pachomians said far fewer psalms than Palladius claims.

[51] "Four times a night." To sing 4 x 12 psalms was still a considerable labor. Since Cassian's purpose in Inst 2.12 is to counter Gallic excess in this matter, his emphasis on just twelve psalms was restrictive. But to turn around and multiply that by four was subversive. Yet it was consistent with the Gallic tendency, which Columban happily follows.

[52] "Celebrations." The Latin term is *expeditionibus*, but none of the meanings given in the classical Latin dictionary of Lewis and Short seem appropriate. Albert Blaise, *Dictionnaire*, however, gives several possible meanings found in Christian Latin: *travail, execution, accomplissement*. Vogüé provides the liturgical term *celebration*. Walker has *risings*, which has little connection to the Latin but does fit the case: these long Offices were ill suited for the short summer nights of northern Europe.

[53] "Not just weariness but downright exhaustion." Vogüé's French is much more evocative: *lassitude/fatigue écrasant*.

25. But on the holiest nights, namely, Sunday and Saturday, the same number is repeated in the morning three times, that is, thirty-six psalms.[54]

26. The great number and holy lifestyle of these people[55] have led many others to experience the sweetness of this canonical number. And that also applies to the rest of their observance, for no one has found their Rule wearisome.[56]

27. Yet though they are such a great throng that a thousand monks are said to live under one archimandrite, no quarrel between monks is reported to have taken place since the founding of the cenobium.[57]

28. It is clear that this would not be possible if God did not dwell there, for he says, "I will dwell among them, and I will walk among them. I will be their God and they will be my people" [2 Cor 6:16].[58]

[54] "Thirty-six." The huge number is not a misprint or a mistranslation of *ter denis et VI* (three times ten and six).

[55] "Of these people" is rightly added by both Walker and Vogüé, though the Latin *quorum* could refer to the nearest antecedent, namely, the thirty-six psalms. Yet "holy lifestyle" cannot apply to the psalms.

[56] "Wearisome." Here Vogüé forgets that he just translated *lassitude* as "weariness," and now he uses *ecrasé.* V. 26 twice makes the point that the number of psalms is not a burden for the monks of Egypt, but v. 24 tells a different story. Since many Gallic Rules prescribe great quantities of psalms, we must presume that it was a national predilection. But commentators from Cassian to Vogüé have complained about the resulting imbalance in early Gallic monasticism.

[57] The situation reported here could be taken from the *Dialogues* of Sulpicius Severus. Columban's use of *abbates* for monks and *archimandrite* for superior shows some familiarity with eastern monasticism. Exactly why one superior for a thousand monks should make it unlikely for peace to reign is not clear to me.

[58] This is a composite quotation woven from many OT texts: Exod 25:8; 29:45; Lev 26:12; Ezek 37:27; Jer 31:1.

29. Thus they have deservedly grown and continue to grow, thanks be to God, since God dwells in their midst. And may we merit salvation from our Lord through their merits.[59]

VIII. Discretion

1. How necessary discretion[60] is for monks is shown by the error of many and the ruin of some. Because they started out without discretion and did not acquire moderating knowledge, they have not been able to come to a praiseworthy end.

2. For just as those who proceed without a map fall into error, those who live indiscreetly soon end up in excess. Excess is contrary to those virtues located in the middle between both extremes.[61]

3. It is very dangerous to do things in excess, for our adversaries place stumbling blocks of wickedness and pitfalls of various errors along the straight path of discretion.[62]

---

[59] If Columban is still talking about the Egyptian cenobites, and especially the Pachomians, we might wonder if they were still "growing" by the time this was written (ca. 600). Although we do not know much about Coptic monasticism at this time, I suspect that Columban knew even less.

[60] Discretion is a major theme of Cassian, who devotes Conf 2 entirely to the subject. Although the Latin vocabulary is different, the last sentence of Conf 2.8 is similar to this verse of Columban's Rule: "Thus the falls and experiences of many show how dangerous it is not to have the grace of discretion" (John Cassian, *The Conferences*, trans. Boniface Ramsey, Ancient Christian Writers 57 [New York: Paulist Press, 1997], 90). It is interesting that Columban thinks people can "acquire" discretion, or at least "moderating knowledge." Experience seems to indicate that discretion (in the sense of common sense) is very hard to replace if it is not part of one's makeup.

[61] Cassian makes this same point in Conf 2.16.2, where he says that there can be an "excess" of virtue, hard as that might be to imagine. Thus excessive fasting is as damaging as overeating. See Vogüé, *Règles*, 64 n. 2.

[62] Vogüé, *Règles*, 64 n. 3, suggests that the source of this verse is probably Basil's *Latin Rule* (RBasil), Question 140. Not only does Basil also use

4. Therefore we pray continually to God that he will bestow on us the light of true discretion to illuminate this earthly path surrounded on both sides by inky darkness. Then his true adorers can avoid these shadows without error on the way to him.[63]

5. Discretion gets its name from *discernere*, because by means of it we distinguish between good and evil, and also between means and ends.[64]

6. For both good and evil have been divided from the beginning like light and darkness after evil was begun by the devil by the deprivation of good, but God first accomplished the separation by creating light.[65]

---

the same term, *periculum est* (to deviate from the path of discretion), but he also uses the word *semitam* for "path," quoting Ps 139:6. Walker translates the rare word *impactio* as "onset," but Vogüé simply connects it with discretion from the previous sentence (*passer la mesure*). Since it better fits the context, I have gone with that reading.

[63] "On the way to him" (*ad se*). The need for Christian discretion is not just to avoid error, or even serious inconvenience. Rather, it is to maintain a straight path on the journey to God.

[64] Columban seems to think his reader will need some help connecting *discretio* with its root verb *discernere*. "Means and ends" is Vogüé's inspired rendition of *media . . . perfecta* (*La Vie de saint Columban*). The dictionaries do not indicate the instrumental usage of *media*, but it makes good sense. Although Cassian does not use this terminology in his treatise on spiritual means and ends (Conf 1), the sense is the same.

[65] This long sentence is so overloaded as to be nearly unintelligible. Vogüé makes it clearer, but it takes him forty-seven French words to explicate thirty-one Latin words! The problem seems to come from the mixing of two creation accounts. On the one hand, there is good and evil, which were caused, according to Columban, by the Devil's "depriving" creation of the good. Good and evil are compared to light and darkness, but of course the creator of this contrasting pair is not the Devil but God. Another translation of *per deum illuminantem prius ac postea dividentem* is offered by Walker, 135 ("through God's agency Who first illumines and then divides"). This rendition leads better into the next verse on Abel and Cain.

7. So holy Abel chose the good, but wicked Cain fell into evil.
8. God made all he created to be good, but the devil sowed[66] bad things over them by sly craftiness and crafty persuasion to dangerous ambition [Matt 13:24-30].[67]
9. What then are these good things? They are those that are whole and incorrupt and that have remained as they were created. "God alone created and prepared them," according to the apostle, "that we might walk in them. These are the good works in which we were created in Christ Jesus."[68]
10. Good, integrity, piety, justice, truth, mercy, charity, healthy peace, spiritual joy with fruit of the Spirit—all these, with their fruits, are the good things.[69]

[66] "sowed over" (*superseminavit*). Here Columban makes it clear that he understands that God created all things good before the Devil was able to cause some of them to fall into evil. This clarification prevents us from taking "from the beginning" in v. 6 too literally.

[67] "To dangerous ambition," that is, in Eve and Adam. Vogüé (*Vie de Saint Columban*, 65) has "of dangerous persuasion," pertaining to Satan. *Ambitio* can mean either "ambition" or "persuasion." Blaise, *Dictionnaire*, s.v. *ambitio*, has as the first meaning the spreading around of rumors.

[68] V. 9b is a virtual translation of Eph 2:10, which reads in the NAB version, "For we are his handiwork, created in Christ Jesus for the good works that God has prepared in advance, that we should live in them." Lionel Swain makes this comment on Eph 2:9-10: "The ultimate extent of God's power at work in Christians is that they should be 'created in Christ Jesus,' not only in their being but in their activity. It is this new creation in Christ that is the basis and principle of all Christian morality. Christian activity consists less in man's activity than in God's action in man through Christ. Man's role is to respond to that action" ("The Inspiration of Scripture," in *A New Catholic Commentary on Holy Scripture*, ed. Reginald C. Fuller [London: Thomas Nelson and Sons, 1964 (1969)], 1181–91, here 1186).

[69] Goodness, charity, peace, and joy also appear in Paul's list of fruits of the spirit in Gal 5:22. Each list, Reg VIII.10 and Gal 5:22, has nine members, with four overlapping. "Healthy peace" renders *pax salutaris*, which Vogüé translates as "peace that procures salvation." My version is less spiritual, but it is meant to avoid a merely complacent peace.

11. But here are the evils that are contrary to them: wickedness, perversion, impiety, crookedness, lying, avarice, hatred, discord, and bitterness, with the many effects that arise from them.[70]

12. The offspring[71] of these two contraries, that is, good and evil, are innumerable.

13. The first evil that departs from the goodness and integrity of creation is pride, the primeval wickedness.[72]

14. Contrary to this is the humble attitude of a pious and good person who acknowledges and glorifies his Creator, which is the primary good of the rational creature.[73]

15. So it is that the rest of the vices and virtues have gradually developed into a vast forest of names in two parts.[74]

---

[70] A list of vices (fifteen) appear in Gal 5:19-20, but they are labeled "works of the flesh" (5:19) and include several sexual aberrations, of which Reg has none.

[71] "Offspring" is a literal, colorful rendition of the verb *procreantur*.

[72] "The goodness and integrity of creation" is a rearrangement of *bonitate condita et integritate*. Vogüé (Règles, 65 nn. 12–13) points to Gregory the Great, Mor 31.XLV.88–90, for similar teaching on pride as the first vice. This moral lesson is told in mythological form in Isa 14:12-20, where Lucifer, a powerful angel, is cast out of heaven for pride, to become the prince of devils. See *Catechism of the Catholic Church*, 391–92; 1 John 3:8.

[73] "Humble attitude of a pious and good person," my version of *piae bonitatis humilis existimatio*. The "primary good of the rational creature" must refer to the deference the creature owes to the Creator, if one has any sense. But "primary good" also sounds like it could refer to the Creator himself.

[74] "Developed into a vast forest of names" retains the concreteness of *in immanem nominum silvam creverunt*. Columban seems to be referring to the long lists of vices and virtues, which he has no hesitation in repeating in this chapter on discretion. Perhaps he means that it is fine to study the distinctions between the vices, as in, say, Cassian's Inst 5–12, but the basic distinction for spiritual discretion is between pride and humility.

16. This being the case, we must hold firmly to the good we receive by God's help,[75] which we should pray for in good times and bad. Otherwise, we may be puffed up with vanity in our prosperity or driven to despair by adversity.[76]

17. Therefore we must avoid both dangers, that is, from all excess by illustrious temperance and true discretion, which holds to Christian humility and opens the way of perfection to soldiers of Christ.[77]

18. This is accomplished by always discerning rightly in doubtful cases[78] and by everywhere dividing justly among the good and the evil. This means judging external matters, either between flesh and spirit in the inner life, or between

[75] I am not sure of the precise point of the first part of this verse. "We receive" (*habentibus*) is a dative agent of the perfect passive periphrastic *tenenda*. Perhaps an alternative translation could be "We must hold fast [to the fact that] the good we receive is by God's help."

[76] A good biblical reference here is Prov 30:8-9: "Put falsehood and lying far from me, give me neither poverty nor riches; [provide me with only the food I need], lest, being full, I deny you, saying, 'Who is the Lord?'" In Conf 10.10, Cassian makes a great point of the efficacy of this prayer for divine help: *Deus in adjutorium meum intende, Domine, ad adjuvandum me festina.*

[77] "True discretion" is described by Cassian (Conf 2.10.1), as by Columban later in this verse, as that "obtained by humility" (translation of Boniface Ramsey). Then Cassian, but not Columban, goes on to specify this humility as demanding consultation with the elders about one's ascetic plans. Perhaps Columban could take this more for granted with his cenobitic audience, but Benedict spells it out plainly in his eighth step of humility (RB 7.55).

[78] "Doubtful cases," strictly speaking, are the real object of discretion, since clear-cut, black-and-white matters need no particular virtue or skill to decide. The examples given of "good and evil" are the various distinctions that are useful in sorting out complex matters. Cassian makes this point forcefully in Conf 1, where he insists on the necessity of distinguishing spiritual means and ends.

acts and habits, or between action and contemplation,[79] or finally between the public and the private.

19. So then evils should also be avoided: pride, envy, lying, seduction, heresy, evil transgression of morals, gluttony, fornication, avarice, wrath, sadness, flightiness, vanity, bragging, slander.[80]

20. The goods of the virtues[81] are also to be sought after: humility, kindness, purity, obedience, abstinence, chastity, generosity, patience, joy, stability, fervor, energy in work, watchfulness, silence.

21. These virtues[82] are to be carried out with suffering courage and moderating temperance, as if placed on some scale of discretion.[83] This we do in order to weigh our habitual

---

[79] "Action and contemplation" is Walker's (137) interesting rendition of *curam et quietem*. "Administration" is one of the meanings given for *cura* in the *Oxford Latin Dictionary*; another option is "care" as worry, but it is hard to see why one would need discretion to discern about that.

[80] This list of vices is the second one in this long chapter, the first one occurring in v. 10; here it is the mirror image of nine virtues given in v. 9. The second list of evils is longer (fifteen items); it precedes the virtues and does not correspond to them.

[81] "The goods of the virtues" (*bona . . . virtutum*) seems awkward, but it picks up the basic contrast between good and evil in v. 18, which will be carried forward in the next two verses.

[82] V. 21 is notable because of its lack of verbs and its plethora of nouns. I have broken it into two more manageable sentences, which then requires me to supply a verb (*weigh*) for the second one. These two sentences seem to divide into two separate ideas: 21a: When performing the virtues, we need to keep them in balance. 21b: This kind of moderate activity will help us evaluate our daily activity as to whether we are trying hard enough to achieve moderation in all things.

[83] "Scale of discretion" (*ponderatrice discretionis statera*). The image is of a balance-bar scale with two matching pans on which our performance of the virtues is to be balanced.

acts according the possibilities of our efforts, for we try to measure up in all things.[84]

22. There is no doubt that the person for whom sufficiency is not enough has exceeded the measure. And it is obvious as well that whatever exceeds the measure is a vice.[85]

23. Therefore, the rational mean between too little[86] and too much lies in the middle. It always calls us back[87] from excess[88] on one side or the other. When the rational mean is applied in all cases, it obtains what is really necessary[89] but shies away from the unreasonable demands of rampant desire.[90]

[84] "For we try to measure up in all things" (*sufficientia ubique quaerentibus*). This rather free rendition is complicated by the obscure status of the participle *quaerentibus*. Probably it is a dative plural somehow connected to *statuenda in actu*. The plural pronoun is again inferred from *nostri*.

[85] Now Columban shows that he is using *sufficiency* in the strict sense of "enough and no more." The idea that a virtuous person should be satisfied with a decent minimum may be influenced by Sulpicius Severus, DialSul 1.18: "Much will not profit the person who is not satisfied with a little." Columban quotes this passage three times in his other works: Ep 6.1, and Instr 1.3 and 3.4. Unfortunately, it seems that capitalism has a way of undermining this sense of moderation in people, to the point where they cannot distinguish between their wants and their needs.

[86] "Too little" (*parvum*), literally "little." But the obvious sense here is a happy medium between extremes. Vogüé, Règles, 67, has *trop peu*.

[87] "It always calls us back." The personification of "rational mean" here is no accident; it continues throughout this long verse and also the next one (24).

[88] "Excess." We don't usually think of excess in regard to paucity, but all ascetics learn about it sooner or later. An extreme case is anorexia.

[89] "Really necessary" (*certum ubique necessitatis*). Walker has the plausible, if wordy, alternative: "what is universally fixed by human need." Vogüé's laconic *le necessaire* seems a bit too terse to express the issue here: what do I *really* need?

[90] "Rampant desire" may be an overinterpretation of *superfluae voluntatis*, but the sense seems to require an expression of the real culprit in this matter of ethical imbalance, namely, unchecked hunger. Part of the

24. And this mean of true discretion, by weighing in the scales of justice[91] all our acts, never allows us to deviate from the just norm. Nor does it let us fall into error if we always follow it closely as our leader.

25. For we must always keep away from both extremes, according to that saying, "Keep away from both the right and the left" [Deut 5:32]. Discretion means we must always hold to the straight course, that is, by the light of God.[92]

26. We should often repeat and chant the verse of the victorious psalmist: "My God, light my darkness, for in you I will be snatched from temptation" [Ps 17:29-30].

27. "For life on earth is temptation" [Job 7:1].[93]

IX. Mortification

1. The main element[94] of the rule of monks is mortification, since they are told by Scripture, "Do nothing without counsel" [Sir 32:24].

---

human dilemma is the way that people's wants imperceptibly become their needs.

[91] "Weighing . . . in the scales of justice" (*pondere trutinans iusto*). As in v. 21, Columban employs specific, concrete vocabulary to illustrate the workings of discretion. In v. 21, he spoke of the balance-bar of the scale (*statera*), and here he uses the curious word *trutinare* to describe the fussy action of adjusting the weight indicator. Clearly Columban spent some time in the market.

[92] "To the straight course" (*in directum*). Cassian speaks of the "royal road" (*via regis*) in Conf 2.2.9 and 4.12.5. The road for the king supposedly went straight as a ruler, deviating for no obstacle. The image is not perfectly apt, however, for kings go straight because they are powerful, but the discreet person goes straight to preserve virtue.

[93] "Temptation" (*Temptatio*). Apparently Columban got *temptatio* from Gregory the Great, Mor 8.VI.8, but I do not know where Gregory got it. The Vulgate has *militia*, and the Hebrew, at least as rendered by RSV, has "hard service."

[94] "The main element" renders *Maxima pars*, which here refers not to quantity but to quality. Columban has a generally severe reputation for

2. Thus if nothing should be done without counsel, counsel is to be sought in all matters.

3. And Moses also commands us, "Ask your father and he will tell you; your elders and they will instruct you" [Deut 32:7].[95]

4. This discipline may seem hard to the hard-headed,[96] namely, that a person should always be subject to the word of another.[97] Yet those who fear God will find it a source of enjoyment and security, if they keep it fully and not just in part.

---

asceticism and penitence. In fact, he has left a treatise titled *de penitentia*, so the title *de mortificatione* might point in that direction. But the real topic of this chapter is discretion gained by following counsel or advice. Suffering is discussed because people sometimes get advice that goes against their inclinations. The same biblical warrant given here (Sir 32:24) is also used by Benedict in RB 3.13, but the focus there is different. Here the monk is urged to heed the counsel of the seniors; in RB 3.13 the focus is on the abbot (*senior*), who must pay attention to the opinions stated by the monks in the chapter meeting. Vogüé (Règles, 68 n. 1) points out that Cassian's Conf 24 is also labeled *de mortificatione* but that the true source of Columban's chapter IX is Cassian's Conf 2.10, on discretion.

[95] "Your elders" in the original sense of Deut 32:7 refers to the Jewish elders of the exodus, but for Columban's monastic audience *maiores* meant officials or seniors: "The eighth step of humility [RB 7.55] is when a monk does nothing except what is encouraged by the common rule of the monastery and example of the veteran members of the community" (Kardong, *Benedict's Rule*, 134). My "veteran members" translates *maiores*.

[96] "Hard-headed" (*duris*) could also be construed as "hard-hearted," which is what both Walker and Vogüé have. But I don't think the issue here is malice so much as a certain inability to learn from others. Pachomius in SBo 105 claims that openness to the lessons of others is the key virtue of cenobites. Although, again, Cassian's Conf 24 is not the main source for this chapter of Reg, nonetheless Conf 24.25 does teach that some monastic practices that at first seem very hard eventually produce great satisfaction.

[97] "Always be subject to the word of another" (*semper de ore pendeat alterius*). This remark suggests that the real topic here is obedience more than counsel. The cenobite is always subject to a superior. Unlike the anchorite, who chooses whom to listen to, the cenobite is not free in that

5. For nothing is sweeter than a more certain conscience,[98] and nothing more certain than a soul without fear of punishment.[99] No one can bestow this on himself because it belongs strictly to the judgment of others.

6. What defends us from the fear of Judgment[100] is that we have already been subjected to the scrutiny of a judge. For the latter bears the weight of his client's burden, and he bears the whole responsibility he has undertaken.[101]

7. As it is written, "The responsibility of the one judging is greater than that of the one who is judged."[102]

---

way. Therefore, Columban, as a cenobite, cannot be completely dependent on Cassian, whose Conf 1–10 are aimed at anchorites.

[98] "Sweeter" and "more certain" (*dulcius/securius*) are repeated from the previous verse. Indeed, *securius* is repeated twice in this verse. This makes it clear that Columban urges his monks to seek counsel as a means of peace of mind. The idea is "no one is a judge in his own case." This idea, of course, assumes that the counselor or superior possesses some spiritual wisdom.

[99] "A soul without fear of punishment" (*animae impunitate*). If this is carried to its logical conclusion, it could lead to the teaching found in RM 7.55: if the monk carries out the orders of the abbot, good or bad, he has nothing to fear at the Last Judgment. Yet this was precisely the plea of the Nazi henchmen at the Nuremberg trials: "I only did what I was told." The plea was rejected by the judges.

[100] "Judgment." I have capitalized the word here because I think it refers to the Last Judgment. The stress here on the responsibility of the superior or advisor could be crushing unless it is remembered that the subject or directee is a free agent who may accept or reject counsel. RB 2 also makes heavy demands on the abbot but consoles him as well: "Still, if he has faithfully shepherded a restive and disobedience flock . . . he will be acquitted at the Lord's judgment" (2.8-9).

[101] "Responsibility" is Vogüé's rendering of *periculum* (= danger!). Columban's use of this loaded word shows he has not thought this matter through so well as Benedict.

[102] The quotation seems to be from Sextus, *Sententiae* 184. But in fact only two words are identical: "judging" (*iudicantis*) and "judged" (*iudicatur*). Columban, like Saint Benedict, must have known this word from

8. Therefore, whoever seeks counsel[103] will never go astray if he carries it out. For if the response of another person sometimes goes astray, the faith of the believer and the effort of the one who obeys never will.[104] Those who seek counsel will not lack a reward.

9. Now if someone decides for himself what he should have consulted about, he is guilty of having erred. He presumed to judge when he ought to have submitted to judgment. Even if his resulting act is correct, it will be held against him, for he has gone astray in this matter.[105]

10. The person whose role is only to obey will not dare to judge anything for himself.[106]

Rufinus's translation of it from Greek to Latin. Again, Walker has the literal meaning "peril" for *periculum*, while Vogüé has the accommodated "responsibility."

[103] "Seeks counsel" renders *interrogaverit* in the sense of what precedes. "Will never go astray" confirms my feeling that this discussion is really not about discretion but about obedience. Discretion must remain free to decline advice given. And a good counselor/councilor must not take it amiss when his suggestions are declined by the one seeking advice.

[104] "Faith" and "obeys" show that this is really a discussion of religious obedience. "Another person" (*alterius*) must mean someone seeking counsel in a secular context.

[105] Now we are presented with the mirror opposite of the obedient monk of v. 8. This person decides for himself what he should have submitted to an elder for a decision. "He is guilty of having erred," not because things did not turn out well, but because he presumed to make a decision that was not his to make. To judge from Saint Benedict, who uses it dozens of times and always pejoratively, "presuming" is about the worst thing a cenobite can do.

[106] This verse, which Vogüé (Règles, 69 n. 10) lists as an allusion to Jerome's Letter 125.15, points toward either an extreme form of cenobitic obedience or the mentality of a slave. RB 5.12 has a similar statement: "They no longer live by their own judgment . . . rather according to another's decision." But the whole context of RB shows it was not meant literally: Benedict wants his monks to use their heads. For the willful, arrogant Jerome to teach this kind of slavish mentality is curious, to say

11. Since this is the case, monks must everywhere avoid a proud independence. The obedient must learn true humility "without grumbling and hesitation."[107]

12. That way they will experience the truth of the Lord's saying that the "yoke of Christ is sweet and his burden light" [Matt 11:30].[108]

13. Otherwise, until they learn the humility of Christ, they will not experience the sweetness of his yoke and the lightness of his burden.[109]

14. For humility of heart is the rest of a soul weighed down with vices and troubles and its only refuge from so many evils.[110]

---

the least. The role of an adult is to make responsible decisions. Where people are not allowed to do this, we have a school for infantilism.

[107] "Without grumbling and hesitation" quotes Phil 2:14, where it follows closely on the great christological hymn. Because Christ humbly assumed the human condition and the humiliation of the cross, the Christian must accept the will of God. For the monk, this includes obedience to the abbot.

[108] "The yoke of Christ is sweet and his burden light." This is the conclusion of Matt 11:29-30: "Take my yoke upon you, and learn from me; for I am gentle and lowly in heart, and you will find rest for your souls. For my yoke is easy and my burden is light." Christ's yoke is easy for those who have learned—but that is not an easy lesson to learn! In his magisterial commentary on RB, Vogüé claims that this text is the New Testament undergirding for Benedict's "school for the Lord's service" (RB Prol.45). Strange, then, that Benedict never quotes it, nor does he invoke it in RB 7 on humility. Undoubtedly it is a capital text for humility.

[109] Vv. 12–13 summarize six pages of discourse in Cassian's Conf 24.22–25 (Ramsey version).

[110] Again following Conf 24.25, Columban makes the important spiritual point that a life of dissipation itself becomes a burden. This is an ascetical-spiritual interpretation of Matt 11:28: "Come to me all who labor and are burdened." It is not so clear that Matthew meant it that way. Perhaps he meant it as relief for oppressed Palestinian peasants.

15. The more the soul is drawn to this consideration from so many external vain and erroneous interests, the more it rests within itself and is refreshed.[111]

16. The result is that what was bitter to it becomes sweet, and what it previously considered harsh it now finds level and easy.[112]

17. Moreover, mortification,[113] which is intolerable to the proud and hard-hearted, is actually a consolation to the person who is only pleased with what is lowly and mild. The monk should know, however, that he will not be able perfectly to accomplish this happy martyrdom,[114] nor

---

[111] In this verse, Columban goes even further than Cassian in spiritualizing Matt 11:29-30. He indicates that the yoke and burden come from involvement with "externals" (*foris*); the answer is to turn "inward" (*intus*).

[112] "Level" translates *plana*. The reference is to Isa 40:4: "The rugged land shall be made plain" in regard to the coming of the Messiah. Cassian discusses the same text in Conf 24.25.4. Notice that the question here is not about objective reality but subjective perception. As Benedict assures us in RB Prol.46-49, what first seems very hard to the monastic novice should eventually become easy and even attractive. Hence, Vogüé's translation of *plana* as "natural" is perfectly plausible.

[113] Finally Columban discusses the purported subject of this chapter, namely, mortification. Actually, though, he admits that mortification becomes consolation for someone who is truly humble. In his sixth step of humility (RB 7.49), Benedict speaks of being "content with low and dishonorable treatment" (*omni vilitate vel extremitate contentus sit monachus*). Columban may go him one better by asking the monk to be "pleased only" with what is lowly and mild. "Lowly and mild" is a reference to Jesus in Matt 11:30, although Reg has *mansuetum* instead of *mite* (Vulgate Latin) for "mild."

[114] "Happy martyrdom" (*martyrii felicitatem*) is a highly charged expression. Although it is a rather brilliant oxymoron, and expresses very well the message of vv. 17–18, it is still troubling. The idea of the monk as martyr goes all the way back to the *Life of Antony*. Antony, the proto-monk, was alive during the persecution of Diocletian (ca. 310), and, according to Athanasius, he went to Alexandria purposely in order to be martyred. When he was denied this privilege, he went home disappointed

cope[115] with unforeseen situations, if he has not devoted himself single-mindedly to this quest. Otherwise, he may be found unprepared.

18. For if, in addition to this quest,[116] a person wishes to pursue and foster his desires, he will immediately be absorbed and troubled by these preoccupations. He will not be able to follow wholeheartedly[117] where the commandment leads. Nor will he be able to fulfill it as he ought, precisely because he is upset and ungrateful.

---

but a "martyr to his conscience" (*Greek Life* 47). Later monastic literature sometimes pursues this theme. For example, the Rule of the Master, in its fourth step of humility (10.53), uses the loaded term *constantia* (courage) for the monk's behavior under perceived persecution. This is martyr language, based on NT *hypomone*. But Saint Benedict carefully replaces *constantia* with *conscientia*. I think he wants to avoid anything that might feed into monastic self-pity.

[115] "Cope with unforeseen situations." This is my admittedly free rendering of *aliud quid utile superveniens*. Another possibility, which is offered by Walker, is "nor any other benefit that follows." I opt for "unforeseen" (Vogüé) because it will be repeated in the final member as "unprepared."

[116] "In addition to this quest" (*iuxta hoc studium*). This is a key element in this long and overloaded sentence. The reference is to the same *studium* Columban urged on the monk in the previous verses to seek the worst and the meanest in every situation. To pursue a parallel (*iuxta*) program of self-indulgence is not going to work. This kind of double game will come a cropper because desires (*intentiones*) have a way of becoming needs.

[117] "Wholeheartedly" (*gratus*) appears to correspond to "single-mindedly" (*singulare*) in the preceding verse. Of course, it adds the element of good will to the theme of focus and purpose. But Columban's point is well-taken: it is unrealistic to pursue a life of mortification with anything less than full motivation. That is the tragedy of the "tepid religious": he usually becomes a "lax religious."

19. Thus there are three levels [118] of mortification: not to disagree [119] mentally, not to blab freely,[120] not to wander about.[121]

20. Although the superior [122] commands vexing things,[123] the mortified monk says to him, "Not as I will, but as you wish" [Matt 26:39],

21. according to the example of our Lord and Savior, who said, "I came from heaven, not to do as I please, but to follow the will of him who sent me, that is, the Father" [John 6:38].[124]

---

[118] "Levels," literally, "The structure [*ratio*] of mortification is." The three levels are then listed, ranging from thought to word to action. In positive terms, the three virtues associated with mortification are equanimity, silence, stability.

[119] "Disagree" (*discordare*) refers to a state of resentment in which one holds the tongue but argues internally with everything that is being done by other people.

[120] "Blab freely" renders *lingua libita loqui*: to speak with a loose tongue.

[121] "Wander about" is my somewhat terse version of *ire quoquam absolute*. The hard word is the adverb *absolute*, which can be taken generally or specifically. Thus Vogüé has "without permission," but Walker has "with complete freedom."

[122] "Superior" is in fact "senior" (*seni*), which can mean a monk who is senior in rank (see RB 63) or any monastic official. In either case, the obedient and mortified monk must defer to him.

[123] "Vexing" renders *contraria*. Strictly speaking, *contraria* could mean orders that are incoherent. But of course they would still be vexing.

[124] The biblical citations that appear in vv. 20–21, namely, Matt 26:39 and John 6:38, are also found, in reverse order, in Cassian's Conf 24.26.14. Columban is clearly basing his rules on Cassian here, for he also puts these biblical citations in the mouth of "our Lord and Savior." Cassian also makes the context a "hard" order given by a "senior." See Vogüé, Règles, 70 nn. 20–21).

X. The Perfection of the Monk[125]

1. The monk should live in a monastery under the discipline of a single Father[126] and the communion[127] of many.[128]
2. The purpose is to learn humility from the one and patience from the other.[129] The first should teach him silence[130]

[125] Chapter X is copied almost verbatim from Letter 125.15 of Jerome. It is not found in the manuscripts of Reg in the Paris Bibliothèque Nationale, but it is included in those kept at Turin (from Bobbio).

[126] "Father" as the title of the cenobitic superior is also consonant with RB 2.1-3. Historically, the term *abbot* as head of a monastic community did not emerge before the writings of Sulpicius Severus and John Cassian (ca. 400). Jerome does not use it in his writings. For a good historical summary, see Claude Peifer, "Appendix 2: The Abbot," in *RB 1980*, ed. Timothy Fry (Collegeville, MN: Liturgical Press, 1981), 322–78, here 322–24.

[127] "Communion" translates *consortio* and is one of the meanings given by Blaise, *Dictionnaire*, s.v. *consortium*.

[128] One is reminded of RB 1.2: "The first are cenobites, who live in monasteries and serve under a Rule and an abbot." While it is true that Benedict has three elements (community, Rule, and abbot) while Columban has only two (Father and community), this sentence implies that he is writing a monastic rule.

[129] "To learn humility . . . patience." The idea of the monastic community as a place where one can learn virtues from others is brought out well by Pachomius in SBo 105. From the Latin word order, it seems that one learns humility through obedience to the "Father" and patience through daily interaction with the community. Cassian notes that patience is a crucial virtue in living with flawed others in community (Conf 19.9). While his take on shared life is probably too pessimistic, it cannot be denied that patience is a key communal value.

[130] "Silence." Although RB 6.6 teaches that "the master's role is to speak and teach; the disciple is to keep silent and listen," this is not a principle Benedict presses very far in the rest of his Rule (see RB 68). The idea seems to come out of the desert tradition that Jerome knew from experience. That does not mean that Jerome himself sat silent at anybody's feet for very long! Moreover, the master-disciple dialogues presented by Cassian are by no means one-sided.

and the second mildness.[131]

3. The monk should not do whatever he wants.[132] Rather, let him eat what he is told [133] and have only what he receives.[134]

4. He should do the work [135] assigned him and submit to what he does not wish.[136]

---

[131] "Mildness" is my version of *mansuetudinem*, a word that Benedict rarely uses (RB 66.4; 68.1). The idea seems to be that community life should rub the rough edges off a person.

[132] "Whatever" is literally "what" (*quod*). The point is not, however, that whatever we want as monks is therefore wrong and forbidden, as is actually stated in RM ThP40. Rather, the perilous situation for the cenobitic monk is to be entirely his own boss. I assume this is what Columban means.

[133] "Eat what he is told" is a prescription that is rarely found in ancient monastic Rules. The more humane Saint Benedict admits in RB 39.2 that some people cannot eat certain dishes. Therefore, he arranges for at least two cooked dishes at every meal. Of course, Columban may merely mean that the monk should eat what is put before him.

[134] "Only what he receives" may seem like a cliché, but is in fact a bedrock idea of cenobitic poverty. The alternative is to take care of oneself, which is one of the great commandments of capitalism. Although pure receptivity can engender laziness and infantilism, "abuse does not take away use." Receptivity is indispensable in a follower of Jesus: "Ask, and it will be given you" (Matt 7:7).

[135] "Work" is *pensum*, which refers to a certain amount of wool weighed out (*pensare*) for each slave to spin that day. Benedict uses the term in RB 50.4 to indicate the amount of psalmody to be prayed by the monk whether in choir or alone: *servitutis pensum*. He also uses the phrase to mean the monastic life as such (RB 49.5).

[136] "Submit to what he does not wish," could also be construed as "to *whom* he does not wish." That is the way both Walker and Vogüé read *cui*, and it may be required by *subiciatur*. This could imply "mutual obedience," which can be difficult. But it does not make much sense to tell a cenobite to submit to his superior even if he does not wish to do so.

5. Let him come to bed exhausted [137] and fall asleep on his feet.[138] He must be forced to rise before sleep has been completed.[139]

6. When he has suffered some wrong,[140] he should say nothing. Let him fear the superior of the monastery as a master but also love him as a father.[141]

---

[137] "Exhausted." *Lassus* is a strong word and probably needs a more extreme translation than Walker's "weary" or Vogüé's *fatigué*.

[138] "Asleep on his feet" renders *ambulansque dormitet* (walking asleep). Jerome may present his kind of regular sleep deprivation as ideal for a monk, and Columban may share this sentiment, but the present writer does not. I see nothing spiritually advantageous with being perpetually worn out. Moreover, a successful monastic Rule like RB makes sure the monks get enough sleep. RB 8.1-2, which leads off the liturgical section, reads, "In wintertime, that is, from November first until Easter, right reason dictates they should arise at the eighth hour of the night. That way they can rest a little more than half the night and rise with their food digested."

[139] "Forced." Jerome/Columban seem to assume a communal waking system such as is found in RB 22. Still, if the monk has internalized monastic discipline, if he is motivated by love, and if he has gotten enough sleep, he should be able to get himself out of bed. Of course, "before sleep has been completed" again indicates that sufficient sleep is undesirable for a monk.

[140] "Suffered some wrong." Since the rest of this verse is about obedience to the superior, it seems reasonable to assume that the monk here thinks he has been wronged by a superior. If so, says Jerome, he should not protest. RB 7.35 says the same, but RB 68 allows some discussion. Of course, Christian discipleship demands "turning the other cheek" (Matt 5:39), but it can also promote tyranny.

[141] "Master . . . father." These words actually exist in separate sentences, but it is hard to separate them conceptually. The idea of fearing the abbot as a master does not sit well with most modern monks, but then neither does the notion of parental love ("father" here is *parentem*). In fact, a religious superior cannot be exactly equated with any other social role.

7. He should believe[142] that whatever the superior commands is in his best interests. He must not second guess[143] the decision[144] of the elder. His job is to obey and carry out[145] what he has been ordered to do.

8. As Moses says, "Hear, O Israel," etc. The Rule ends here.

[142] "He should believe." No one can force another person to believe anything, but the subject can operate under the general presuppositions that (1) authority is usually right and (2) the subject almost always benefits by obeying. In rare cases, however, the plain facts force one to believe otherwise.

[143] "Second guess" translates *iudicet*.

[144] "Decision" renders *sententia*, which Walker misconstrues as "opinion." No one can be obliged to conform to the opinions of another.

[145] "Obey and carry out." This laconic definition of the monk's job (*officium*) sounds a lot like RB 6.6: "Speaking and teaching are the master's task; the disciple is to be silent and listen." Such a definition comes close to military obedience. Whether the Irish actually lived this way is not clear to me. Certainly Jerome did not!

Cenobitic Rule of Columban
(*Regula Coenobialis*)

Here begins the Cenobitic Rule of the Brothers.[1]
[The various kinds of faults ought to be healed by various penitential remedies. Therefore, beloved brothers,][2]
    I. It has been decreed, dearest brothers, by the Holy Fathers[3] that we make confession before dinner or before going

---

[1] Although the following material is labeled Cenobitic Rule of the Brothers (Coen), it is in fact a system of penances for typical monastic faults. Since there is another Columbanian text labeled *Paenitentiale* (Paen), this could be a source of confusion. What is very clear, however, is that these monks had a highly developed system of penances.

[2] This translation is based on the critical edition with facing-page English translation of G. S. M. Walker, *Sancti Columbani Opera* (Dublin: Dublin Institute for Advanced Studies, 1970), cited in footnotes below as Walker. Walker's emendations from the Long Text appear below in brackets; my own clarifications appear in curly brackets. Four manuscripts of the work list its contents, included by Walker on pp. 142–45; I have not translated them here. A French translation appears in *Règles et pénitentiels monastiques*, trans. Adalbert de Vogüé with Pierre Sangiani and Jean-Baptiste Juglar, Aux sources du monachisme colombanien vol. 2, Vie monastique 20 (Bégrolles-en-Mauges, France: Abbaye de Bellefontaine, 1988), cited below as Vogüé, Règles.

[3] The Holy Fathers are also mentioned in Paen 1 (A1). See Reg VII.12. Probably this refers to the monks in Ireland, who were well-known experts on the subject of confession of sins and faults.

to bed or whenever it is convenient,[4] because confession and penance free us from death. Thus not even small sins are to be neglected in confession, because as it is written, "The one who neglects small things gradually declines" [so confession should be made before dinner or before going to bed or whenever it is convenient].[5] So if someone does not come on time for the table blessing[6] or does not respond "Amen," he should receive six blows.[7] Six blows are given to one who speaks during the meal unless to serve the needs of another brother.[8] [He who calls anything his own should receive six blows.] [Six blows]

[4] This regulation refers to minor faults as well as serious sins. Vogüe, Règles, 120 n. 1.1–3, points out that other Columbanian texts such as Wal 6 and Jonas, *Vita Columbani* (VC 2.19), say confession was done three times a day. But Columban himself, in this passage, calls for only one confession a day—which is still a lot!

[5] Walker records that The Long Text of Coen (found in two manuscripts) has omitted this clause where it appears early in the paragraph in the Short Text (found in eight manuscripts) (Walker 144–47).

[6] "Does not come on time" (*custodierit*). The Latin is general ("keep"), so this sentence could simply refer to eating alone. But the matter of responding "Amen" clearly comes from common meal prayers.

[7] "Six blows" (*sex percussionibus*). Walker (147 n. 1) says, "Those were inflicted with a leather strap on the hand" (see E. J. Gwynn and W. J. Purton, eds., *The Monastery of Tallaght* §37, Proceedings of the Royal Irish Academy 29.C.5 [Dublin: Hodges, Figgis, & Co., 1911], 142). The stipulation of *six* blows is the beginning of "tariff penance," namely, precise penalties assigned to the specific faults. The Irish monks were famous for this system, which is often regarded as the root of private confession in the Catholic Church.

[8] Silence at meals was normative in all ancient monasteries, and most modern ones. But the exception allowed here by Columban is also interesting. One of Saint Benedict's maxims for meals is "The brothers should serve one another" (RB 35.1). Here Columban allows a diner to speak to serve the needs of another, not himself.

for one who does not bless the spoon he eats with,[9] and for someone who shouts, that is, speaks with a loud voice.[10]

II. Six blows are levied on the monk[11] who does not bless the lamp, that is, when it has been lit by a junior brother and not presented for the blessing of a senior.[12] If he calls anything his own, six blows. [If he does some frivolous work, six blows.] He who gouges the table with his knife should be corrected with blows. If a brother is charged with cooking and serving but spills something, he must be corrected by prayer in church after the Office, so the brothers will pray for him.[13] The person who forgets to prostrate in the *synaxis* [Office], that is, the prostration in church at the end of each psalm, should be similarly punished.[14] Likewise, one who has wasted crumbs should be

---

[9] This may seem to be an inconsequential rule, but in fact it got the Columbanian monks in some trouble. In 626/627, a Columbanian monk named Agrestius denounced this rule, probably as a strange Irish custom, to an episcopal synod at Mâcon in France (see the introduction, 26). Columban had at that time been dead for about ten years.

[10] "Shouts" (*qui locutus fuerit in plausu*), literally "speaks while clapping." But the next phrase explains that it just means loud speech.

[11] I have inserted the word *monk* here, although Columban has simply the verb *signaverit* (*Si non signaverit . . . VI percussionibus*). According to Vogüé (Règles, 134 n. 4; see n. 134 on p. 111 below), Columban only uses the term *monachus* once in the entire *Regula Coenobialis* (Coen). He often uses *frater*, brother, when speaking of his monks.

[12] Although the Latin is clear enough (*et non exhibeatur ad seniorem ad signandum*), one wonders if the phrase is really meant to be negative. I suspect that this warning is addressed to a senior who neglects to bless the lamp presented to him.

[13] This provision seems to be redundant if the brothers are told twice to pray for the delinquent. Perhaps it is the erring brother who must stay after Office to pray. Or maybe he just "knelt out" during the *oration*.

[14] "Prostrate" (*humiliare*). This was standard practice in early monasticism. One rarely, if ever, hears of this practice today, even among "primitive observance" communities. Most modern monks could not get

corrected by prayer in church. But this small penance should be assigned him if he has spilled only a little.[15]

III. But if through negligence or absentmindedness or failure of precaution the monk loses an unusual amount of liquid or solid, he must make a long penance in church.[16] He should lie prostrate at the Office of the twelfth hour,[17] not moving a muscle while the monks sing twelve psalms. Now if he has spilled a great deal, he should calculate[18] the amount of beer or whatever he lost by negligence {by going without}[19] what would have rightly and normally been his portion for an equal number of days. Let him know what he has lost by drinking water instead of beer.[20] When someone spills on the table and it runs off, we think it sufficient to seek pardon while staying in his place at table.

---

up if they had prostrated. And what modern choir is spacious enough to allow it?

[15] That this seemingly trifling arrangement was taken very seriously by monks at this time is also seen in RM 23.34–37 and RM 25.1–12. In that detailed presentation, the table servers gather the breadcrumbs after every meal. On Saturday a bread pudding is confected, to be ceremoniously dished out by the abbot to each monk. This custom was actually carried out at Cluny (John of Salerno, *Vita Sancti Odonis* 1.35).

[16] "Penance" (*venia . . . paeniteat*). *Venia* usually means forgiveness, but here it must go with *paeniteat* to mean penance.

[17] "Twelfth hour" (*dum duodecim*) is Vespers or Compline, called the "beginning of the night" in Reg VII.15 and VII.23. This Office ended with the pax or general absolution, according to the *Bangor Antiphonale* 34.

[18] "Calculate." Walker has "supply" for *supputans*, perhaps thinking of *supponans*. But the monk can only "supply" what he has wasted by going without.

[19] My addition.

[20] "Let him know by drinking." The grammar here is not crystal clear to me. If the *ut* clause is one of purpose, as Walker has it, I fail to grasp the idea. I think it is a result clause: by abstaining from beer, one learns existentially, physically, what one has wasted.

Twelve blows should be applied to the monk who leaves home without bowing to ask for prayer.[21] Upon receiving the blessing he must make the sign of the cross before the cross.[22] Likewise, the person who forgets to pray before and after work should receive twelve blows.[23] Twelve blows for the person who eats without first praying. But the brother who confesses all these faults and others, up to those that merit a day of deprivation, will receive a semi-penance, that is, a half-penance.[24] From such faults, one should henceforth abstain.[25]

IV. The person who coughs[26] at the beginning of a psalm, and thus does not sing well, should be beaten with six blows. Who bites the Chalice of Salvation, six blows.[27] He who does not maintain the proper order at Mass [for offering] receives

---

[21] "Bowing" (*see humiliaverit*). Walker (147) has "prostrated," but Vogüé has "s'incliner." Strictly speaking, this Christian word could mean either, but it seems to me that prostration is a rather extreme sign of abasement. It is almost impossible for old folks, and it is also hard on the clothes.

[22] "Before the cross." Walker (149) comments, "The Irish were accustomed to place standing crosses at doorways and other frequented spots."

[23] "Pray before and after work." Presumably this prayer was to be said aloud; otherwise who else would know whether it had been said or not? Most, if not all, of the faults listed in this Rule were public ones. RM 50.20 and 50.47–50 demand similar prayer.

[24] This is Vogüé's rendition and my translation of his French. I fail to fathom the point here: what is a half-penance? Walker's version is unhelpful.

[25] Vogüé calls this ending "grammatically uncertain and obscure." He also says the previous sentence sounds like a conclusion, implying that this verse is a later addition.

[26] "Who coughs." The Latin form *tusse* appears to be incorrect, and Walker gives *tussem* C, *tussiens* Och, as alternatives. Vogüé construes it as a present participle without further comment.

[27] "Chalice of Salvation," no doubt so called to make sure the reader knows it is a sacred vessel. Ancient chalices were sometimes made of glass, but Columban preferred bronze (Walafrid, *Life of St. Gall*).

six blows.[28] Six blows for the priest who says Mass with un-
trimmed fingernails, for the deacon who neglects to shave, for
a monk who comes directly from plowing to take the chalice
at Mass.[29] The monk who smiles[30] in the *synaxis*, that is, the
Office of Prayers, deserves six blows. But one who laughs out
loud shall receive a more severe penance,[31] unless it happens
accidentally.[32] [The priest celebrating Mass, and the deacon
carrying the Host,[33] must be careful not to let their eyes rove
about. If they gaze around, they should be corrected with six
blows. If someone forgets his chrismal[34] when going out to

[28] "The proper order." Vogüé thinks this sentence refers to the order
of the monks receiving Communion. That the cenobites kept strictly to
their rank for the ritual is clear from RB 63.4. Walker, however, seems to
think *ordinem ad sacrificium* pertains to the proper rubrics for the priest
offering Mass. This latter interpretation probably lies behind the Long
Text's addition [for offering].

[29] "From plowing." *De rustro*, probably error for *de rastro* ("hoe"). At
least Walker thinks so. Vogüé omits the word entirely, thus making the
unshaven deacon approach the chalice.

[30] "Smiles." While we might consider a smile anything but reprehensible, Columban thought otherwise. *Subridens* definitely means *smile*, not
laughter, which is treated in the next sentence.

[31] "A more severe penance." *Superpositio* is called by Walker 149
n. 2, "an intensified or prolonged form of the penance involved." Vogüé,
Règles, 123, translates it as "a day of privation." In RM 53, *superpositio*
means a day of complete fast.

[32] "Accidentally" (*veniabiliter*). The literal meaning is "without fault."
Here it may refer to situations where something so ridiculous is said or
happens that someone bursts out laughing.

[33] "Carrying the Host" (*sacrificium custodientes*). Since *custodientes* is
plural, it could refer to both priest and the deacon, as Walker and Vogüé
both translate it. But I prefer to take *sacrificium* not as Mass but as the
Host. Either way, the grammar is confusing.

[34] "Chrismal" (not *chrism*) was a small container holding either the
Host or blessed oil (Blaise, *Dictionnaire*, s.v.). Walker quotes *Vitae Sanctorum Hiberniae* 2, p. 11, to the effect that Comgall sometimes wore a
chrismal around his neck as a pyx-pendant while working in the fields.

work at a distance, he should receive five times five blows. If he drops it on the ground but immediately finds it, he then gets ten times five blows. If he hangs it on a tree, thirty blows; if it remains there overnight, a day of complete fast.[35] The monk who receives the blessed bread in a state of impurity receives twelve blows.[36]] If someone forgets to prepare the offerings before going to Mass, one hundred blows.[37]

One who tells idle tales to another should be pardoned if he immediately accuses himself, yet if he does not accuse himself [but denounces the way these things should be excused][38] he should receive a whole day's silence and fifty blows as a penance.[39] When something is being discussed, if a brother instinctively excuses himself rather than immediately saying,

---

[35] "Hangs it on a tree . . . overnight." Although the casual treatment of the Host may seem strange to us, it was almost inevitable if people carried it on their person everywhere, as they were expected to do—at least to judge from the previous verse.

[36] "Blessed bread" (*eulogias*) was the excess bread that was offered at Mass but not consecrated. It was often sent as a gift to those who could not be at Mass. Walker has "unclean hands," but Vogüé thinks it is a moral issue (*Vie de Saint Columban*, 123 n. 6).

[37] "Going to Mass" (*ad offerendam*). Vogüé, Règles, 123 n. 7, on the basis of the Long Text (Mss. B and C), has the person going to Office. He also thinks that this regulation is addressed to the deacon. But I suspect that the severe penalty indicates that someone has forgotten to set up for Mass.

[38] "The way these things should be excused." Vogüé has "and tries to excuse himself," which makes better sense. Yet I do not see how it accounts for the Latin: *sed detractaverit qualiter eas excusare debeat*. I think Walker's rendition ("but has declined the way in which he ought to excuse them") is more accurate.

[39] "Whole day's silence" (*superpositione silentii*). This expression shows that *superpositio* itself does not specify the content of the penance, but merely the length. Blaise, *Dictionnaire*, s.v. *superpositio*, defines it as "the act announcing that the fast extends to the next day (and not to such and such an hour)."

"forgive me, for I am guilty!" he gets fifty blows.[40] Fifty blows are coming to the monk who instinctively sets counsel against counsel.[41] Someone who strikes the altar gets fifty blows.

V. If a monk abandons all restraint in bellowing with a loud voice, unless there is some necessity, he is subject to a day of complete silence plus fifty blows. Someone who makes excuses instead of satisfaction[42] should be similarly punished. When a confrere tries to tell him something, the monk who immediately counters with "It is not as you say!" should be punished with a full day of silence and fifty blows. That response is only permissible for seniors reacting to juniors. Or a monk is entitled to respond to a confrere of equal rank who has said something he remembers as less than the full truth: "If you remember well, brother. . . ."[43] And when the other person hears this, he should not insist on his statement, but humbly say, "I

---

[40] "Instinctively" (*cum simplicitate*). Walker has "honestly," but Vogüé has "without reflection." It appears to me that the setting here is the community *culpa*, and the culprit is trying to wriggle free of punishment. If Walker's rendition is accurate, it is hard to see why the monk should be punished at all.

[41] "Instinctively." This sentence proves conclusively that *cum simplicitate* must have a negative meaning here. "Setting counsel against counsel" means that one seeks advice not in the service of truth, but to further one's agenda. Thus King Ahab of Israel, in 1 Kgs 22, surrounded himself with prophets who could be counted on to tell him what he wanted to hear instead of what God wanted to tell him.

[42] "Satisfaction" (*veniam*). This is Vogüé's suggestion. Walker has *pardon*, which is the usual meaning. But here the idea would have to be excuses to obtain pardon.

[43] "If you remember well." In other words, "If you had a better memory, you would speak differently." This response, by avoiding flat-out contradiction, preserves an exquisite atmosphere of harmony. Vogüé (*Vie de Saint Columban*, 124 nn. 3–5) cites Jonas, VC 1.5 (11), to the effect that the first companions of Columban avoided contradicting each other. I once had a professor, in a class in Greek Composition, who never contradicted us. He always said, "What you *meant* to say. . . ."

believe you remember better than I do. My lapse of memory has caused my tongue to slip. Please forgive me, for I have said something wrong."[44] Here is the way the sons of God should talk: *Do nothing from selfishness or conceit, but in humility count others as better than yourselves* [Phil 2:3].[45] Otherwise, someone who excuses himself should not be considered a son of God but a carnal son of Adam.

VI. Whoever does not flee to the restful harbor of Christ's humility[46] but opens the door of contradiction by others through persistence in proud talk, that one should be segregated from the liberty of Holy Church to do penance in a cell. This should continue until his good will is obvious and he is reinserted through humility into the holy congregation.

If someone loudly upbraids the gatekeeper because the gatekeeper has not kept his hours,[47] he is to receive a day of

[44] This contrived scenario should probably not be taken literally but be seen as an example of a community where harmony is highly prized and discord and contention avoided. It definitely should not be taken to suggest that *all* conflict must be suppressed. What is needed, and not easy to learn, is calm and thoughtful discussion, even of touchy issues.

[45] The subject in Paul's letter is not just speech but the whole of Christian life and conduct. Since this passage leads into the famous *Carmen Christi* ("Christ became obedient"), it is quintessential Christian doctrine.

[46] The overall message of this long and complex sentence is not difficult: the monk who insists on upsetting the community with inflammatory language should be excommunicated until he learns some humility. The best model of monastic humility is Christ himself, who once described himself as *meek and humble of heart* (Matt 11:29-30). In that same passage, Jesus assures the disciples who take on his humility, *You will find rest for your souls*. This crucial connection between peace and humility is made by Columban in Reg IX.13–14. See Vogüé, *Vie de Saint Columban*, 124 n. VI.1–3.

[47] "Has not kept his hours" (*horas non bene custodierit*). There are at least two possible explanations of this regulation: (1) the porter has missed some of the Hours of the Divine Office; (2) the porter is not on duty to open the gate when he should be. Since the culprit here is not the

silence and fifty blows. Whoever hides some fault he sees a brother committing but then accuses the brother (when that man is corrected for that vice or another one) is subject to three days of penance. The punishment for one who badmouths or slanders the works of other brothers is three days of penance. If a monk immediately corrects one who corrects him, that is, chastises his chastiser, he also rates three days' penance.[48]

VII. Whoever runs down another brother or listens to someone else doing so is subject to three days of penance unless he corrects him {the badmouther}.[49] If a monk expresses bitter contempt at someone, he also does three days' penance.[50] When a brother notices something out of line but does not wish to report it to his temporary superior[51] and waits to tell the senior father, he shall merit three days of penance (unless he

---

porter but the monk who has blown his top at the gatekeeper, I suspect this sentence is based on real-life experience. Probably the monk returned home only to find the gate barred—and the porter unresponsive.

[48] "Chastises his chastiser." The problem here is not one of truth: the chastiser may well be as guilty as the culprit. What is at stake is the principle of corrigibility: am I open to correction or not? Obviously, no one likes it, and the first instinct is retaliation. Also, if I accept criticism only from perfect brothers, this practice greatly reduces the pool of eligible correctors.

[49] Vogüé (Règles, 125 n. 1) indicates Basil, RBasil 43T, as a possible source of this prohibition (see *The Rule of St. Basil in Latin and English*, trans. Anna M. Silvas [Collegeville, MN: Liturgical Press, 2017], 147). It is similar to Paen 11 (A10).

[50] "Bitter" (*cum tristitia*). *Tristitia* often means sad, but that would not make too much sense here. *Contempt* implies anger, but sadness is melancholic.

[51] "His temporary superior" (*praeposito suo*). *Praepositus* in itself can mean any superior, but here it must mean a subordinate because it is contrasted with *pater senior*. This explanation, however, still leaves some ambiguity. In Letter 4.2, Columban speaks of leaving a *praepositus* in charge of the brothers during his absence. Vogüé, but not Walker, thinks that is what Jonas means in VC 1.10 (Règles, 125 n. 3). Perhaps a reluctance

does this more calmly [52]). If some brother is upset [53] [if possible, he should be calmed], he should postpone his report until his rancor has subsided and he can speak more calmly; [54] [let the brothers pray for him]. If anyone says to his relative who lives as a hermit, [55] "It would be better for you to live with us, or with some other community," three days' penance. Someone who vilifies another monk who obeys a brother deserves a similar judgment.

VIII. A monk who tells his relative who is learning some trade [56] or anything else imposed by the superiors, "You would

---

to report to the *praepositus* was interpreted as a rejection of the substitute superior.

[52] "More calmly" (*verecundiae*). This word normally means "modesty," which is what Walker makes of it. Vogüé has *retenu* ("caution"), which is quite different. We will see in the next sentence that it is a question not of modesty but of prudence. All of this hangs on the correct construal of *tristitia* as anger, not sadness.

[53] "Upset" (*tristis*). Now it becomes clearer what was going on in the previous verse, which seems closely bound to this one in terms of vocabulary. As I noted above, *tristis* can mean "sad," which is the way Walker (mis)construes it. The Long Text does the same, for it speaks of possible consolation. Vogüé has *chagriné*, which is heading in the right direction but does not quite get there. I think the monk is simply too agitated to make a balanced and judicious report.

[54] "Calmly" (*verecundius*). By now we can see that "modesty" has little to do with this case. The monk needs to cool off and regain his equilibrium. This is an example of the considerable psychological acumen that Columban shows in his Rule. Note also the way he deftly shifts gears in this paragraph. He begins by demanding quick reporting of faults but soon remembers that prudence sometimes requires a waiting period to let the sediment settle and the waters clarify.

[55] "Lives as a hermit" (*in loco optimo*), literally, "in the best place." Both Walker and Vogüé think this means a hermitage. Walker notes that the Irish prized eremitical life. The alternative ("live with us") means to live in community.

[56] "Trade" renders *artem*. At issue here may be the distinction between manual arts and intellectual skills such as reading. Of course, monks

be better off learning to read," three days' penance. If a monk should dare to say to his immediate superior,[57] "You shall not judge my case, but our abbot or the other brothers will" or "We will all go to the father of the monastery," that one must be punished for forty days [on bread and water]. This is so unless [he prostrates himself before all the brothers] and says, "Please forgive me for what I said." If some brother is kept at some work although he is worn out, he may speak to the overseer[58] on his own behalf: "If it's all right with you, I will speak to the abbot; if not, I won't." He may speak on behalf of another monk:[59] "If you persist, I hope you don't take it amiss if I speak to the abbot." This is to preserve obedience.

[When someone does not return what he has borrowed[60] until the next day, he gets six stripes if he remembers and

---

needed to read in the liturgy, so legislators like Pachomius required that candidates learn how to read (Pr 139–40). Yet in RBasil 81, Basil condemns an inordinate desire for reading in a monk. Note too that obedience is involved here: the monk has been *ordered* to learn a craft. Moreover, this paragraph, like the last one, involves a relative (*consanguineum*), and no superior wants relatives undermining his authority.

[57] "Immediate superior" (*praepositus*). This paragraph is similar to the previous one, where the same vocabulary for officials is used: *praepositus*, *senior*, *pater*. I have taken the liberty to call the major superior *abbot*, but the habitual title for Columban and his successors was *pater*. See Jonas, VC 1.11, quoted by Vogüé, Règles, 126 n. VIII.2–3.

[58] "Overseer" (*oeconomum*). The term ordinarily refers to the monk who manages the temporal goods of the monastery. Here it may refer to someone who is supervising a monastic work crew. Note that the monk is told to address this subordinate official with special deference—in contrast to the cheeky monk in the previous verse.

[59] "On behalf of another monk" (*in alterius causa*). I understand the quotation that follows as still addressed to the overseer. Now the over-taxed monk is speaking on behalf of another monk who is also hard-pressed. Vogüé has, "If you only repeat your order."

[60] "Borrowed" (*commodat*). Walker has the more general "furnished," but Vogüé's *emprunté* makes more sense.

brings it back. But he gets twelve if he has to be reminded. If he forgets to ask what his penance is until the next day, six stripes.[61] If someone murmurs and says "I won't do it unless the abbot or his assistant tells me to," three full days' penance.[62] No one is permitted to hold hands with another.]

[The cellarer should provide food and lodging[63] for pilgrims or visiting brothers, and all the brothers should be ready to minister to guests with every kind of service[64] for God's sake. If the cellarer is not aware {of the arrival of guests}[65] or even present, others should carefully do what is necessary for them.

[61] I take this sentence to be a continuation of the previous one. But the two may be only juxtaposed because both contain the same word *crastinum* (next day).

[62] This is an intriguing prohibition, concerned with mutual experience. According to this crucial principle of cenobitic life (see RB 71–72), a monk should be open to good counsel from any confrere. Yet there are some matters that can be decided only by the superior, and the wise monk knows how to distinguish one from the other.

[63] "Food and lodging" (*de humanitate . . . adhibenda*). Since Columban charges the cellarer (business manager) with providing *humanitas* (*hospitalité*, Vogüé, Règles), this points to physical support. Some legislators, like Benedict, arrange for a special guestmaster for accommodating travelers (see RB 53). Columban here may limit the service of the cellarer to providing provisions, while "all the brothers" do the serving. Still, large monasteries always have specially designated staff to care for guests.

[64] "With every kind of service" (*cum omni famulatu*). The unusual word *famulatus* literally means slavery. Of course, the old monks were slaves of nobody, even the nobility who sometimes came as visitors or pilgrims. But this term could refer to the servanthood of Christ, who washed the feet of his disciples. The theological dimension is secured by the final words *propter Deum*, which keeps monastic hospitality from degenerating into public relations.

[65] Here it becomes apparent that Columban (or his successors, for this is from the Long Text) did not have a guestmaster. Given that lack of organization, it was all the more necessary for *someone* to take charge of guests on arrival. It creates a bad impression when a guest is made to wait a long time before receiving a welcome.

And they should guard their luggage until they can assign it to a watchman. But if they neglect this, the priest[66] should sentence them to an appropriate penance.]

When a monk is corrected, he must undergo a day of penance if he does not beg pardon. If he visits confreres in their cells without permission,[67] a day of penance. A like penalty applies to someone who enters the kitchen after Nones[68] [without an order or permission]. For someone to leave the compound, that is, the precinct,[69] of the monastery without permission, a day of punishment. When the boys[70] violate the period when

[66] "The priest." This is the first appearance of such a figure in this Rule. It would appear that this is an especially grievous offense that demands a serious penalty. The phenomenon appears in the Rule of Saint Augustine (Praec 4.29), where, after a long discussion of punishment for offenses that normally involve the *praepositus*, the priest is called in for the extreme case of expulsion.

[67] "Permission," literally "asking" (*interrogatione*), but that must imply asking the superior for permission. This is interesting, because it also shows that Columban's monks had private rooms (*cellae*) but that people were not free to enter the room of someone else *ad libitum*. Since Saint Benedict's cenobites did *not* have private cells, one wonders if this was not, like private confession, an Irish custom.

[68] "Nones" (*nonam*) Since the single meal of the day was taken about 3:00 p.m., this prohibition was connected to the general culinary discipline of the early cenobites. In RB 43.18-19, Saint Benedict strictly prohibits eating before or after meals. That would rule out unauthorized monks hanging around the kitchen, as a source of temptation. Cooks, of course, had to be in the kitchen before meals, but, again, not after meals.

[69] "Compound, that is, precinct" (*vallum, id est extra sepem [saepta]*). These are somewhat vague terms, but I suspect they refer to a sort of stockade with several small buildings contained therein. But whatever the physical arrangement, Columban maintained a strict monastic enclosure.

[70] "Boys." *Iuvenculi* is a generic term for adolescents, but the question here is whether they were young monks or boys in the monastic school. Vogüé, Règles, 127 n. 8, thinks the former, but Walker, 155 n. 2, thinks the latter. Three days of fasting or silence seems harsh for schoolboys, and Vogüé notes that the proper term for students was *alumni*. One wonders,

they may not speak to each other, they are subject to three days' penance. [Let them say only this: "You know we may not speak with you."] And if someone tells them to do something that is not permitted,[71] they should say, "You know that we may not do that." But if the other person makes further demands, he is subject to three days of privation. They, however, should say this: "We will do what you say, so as to preserve the good of obedience."[72] They should especially avoid communicating through a third party when they may not engage in mutual conversation.[73] But if they deliberately violate this principle, they should be punished as if they engaged in forbidden conversation. When the monk's chrismal falls off, even though it is not broken, he should be corrected with twelve blows.[74]

IX. If someone engages in chitchat, he should be condemned to observe the following three hours[75] in silence, or

---

however, why Columban would have monks so young that he would call them *iuvenculi*.

[71] "Not permitted." Although I am not exactly sure what is going on here, it seems a case of conflicting orders (*praeceperit*) in the community. This can befall young monks who are junior to everybody. This is the reason that novices are sometimes told to obey no one but the novice master.

[72] "The good of obedience" (*bonum oboedientiae*), as in RB 71.1. There too the monk is told to obey everybody—but especially the superior. Here, though, the argument takes a surprising turn. The monk has been told to fend off conflicting orders. Now, though, he is told to comply with them, with a resigned comment about the "good of obedience." Perhaps the point is that it is better to give in for the moment than to risk an unseemly row.

[73] "Mutual conversation." Now Columban returns, somewhat surprisingly, to the previous prohibition regarding forbidden conversation. Was conversation also the topic of the conflicting orders just discussed?

[74] "Is not broken" (*nihil confringens*). Presumably the problem is not about breakage but lack of respect for the Sacred Host that was housed in the *chrismal* (pyx). See n. 34 above.

[75] "Three hours" (*inter duas horas*). Walker takes *horas* as intervals of time, but Vogüé, Règles, 128 n. 1, sees it as a reference to the Hours of

else twelve stripes. When the monks are doing penance, they should only wash their heads on Sunday, that is, the eighth day, even if they are doing heavy or dirty work.[76] But if not, at least every two weeks, or when someone, according to the judgment of the superior, needs to wash his long, flowing locks.[77] Six stripes are the punishment of the monk who turns aside from the path without asking permission or blessing. If the immediate superior becomes aware of minor infractions[78] at table, he should levy a penance then and there, but not more than twenty-five blows.

Penitent brothers and those who need to do a penance of psalms, whether it be thirty or twenty-four psalms in order, or fifteen or twelve, should sing them kneeling—even on Sunday

---

the Divine Office. Since these occur every three hours, at least during the day, he thinks this penalty is commensurate. Moreover, he thinks Columban operates a coherent system of penalties where twelve stripes equals three hours of deprivation.

[76] "Heavy and dirty work" (*opera difficilia et sordida*). The idea of washing only once a week strikes a contemporary American as preposterous, but in my novitiate (1956–1957), we were allowed to shower only once a week. This was "whether you need it or not," and we certainly did, for we were gardening. This was imposed on us not as penance but simply as a rigorous observance of RB 36: "The sick may take baths whenever it is advisable, but the healthy, and especially the young, should receive permission less readily."

[77] "Long, flowing locks" (*fluentium capillorum incrementum*). Apparently "the Celtic tonsure covered the forehead only, permitting a considerable growth of hair on the back part of the head" (Walker, 155 n. 4). If the Irish thought rare bathing was punitive, their general level of cleanliness must have been fairly high. Of course, in poorly heated medieval buildings, *any* washing in wintertime could be punishing.

[78] "Infractions" (*paenitentias*). Strictly speaking, this means "penances," but it is hard to see why penances should be punished. The reference here must be to table behavior, like tardiness, that calls for penance. Twenty-five blows seems exorbitant for minor offenses.

night or during Paschaltide.[79] This applies to those who have psalms to chant to expiate night visions due to diabolic illusions or some {other} kind of dream.[80]

[If the abbot or the second has given someone a command and he repeats[81] it to the brothers, it is to be obeyed as when a junior obeys a senior. But he should take care to transmit the order accurately.[82] If the abbot or head overseer commands something but the assistant overseer repeats something different, the monk ought to obey but quietly[83] point out what

---

[79] "Sunday night or during Paschaltide." According to Cassian, Inst 2.18, the Egyptians did not genuflect or kneel during Paschaltide.

[80] "Night visions" (*visione nocturna*). Praef Gildas 22 and *Liber Davidis* 8–9 speak of "psalms to be chanted to expiate nocturnal pollution" (Vogüé, Règles, 128 nn. 6–7). But such ideas were not peculiar to Ireland. John Cassian also considered nocturnal pollution at least indirectly sinful. He thought that people are subconsciously aroused by what they have seen or thought of during the day. Consequently, he teaches in Inst 6 that anyone who keeps his consciousness pure can completely avoid nocturnal emission. The present writer cannot vouch for the validity of this theory.

"Some other kind of dream" (*aut pro modo visionis*). I would guess that the reference here is a dream that stems from conscious, and therefore culpable, activity. Vogüé, Règles, 128, has "according to the nature of the dream," which seems to beg the question. But my translation supplies "other," which is not in the Latin.

[81] "He repeats it" (*iteraverit*). Vogüé must mistake this verb for *itineraverit*, which he renders "d'aller en voyage." The point here is the need for orders sometimes to be delegated. In section VIII, Columban condemns a monk who refuses to accept an order except directly from the abbot's mouth.

[82] "Accurately." It would be possible to translate this clause as "see whether what he tells them is correct." But surely the point here is faithful transmission and not critical censorship.

[83] "Quietly" (*in silentio*). *Silentium*, of course, usually means no talk. But Vogüé has "à voix basse" (Règles, 129), which better accounts for "point out." The purpose here is not contradiction but truth-telling. Presumably the assistant overseer would want to know the correct order. This is a situation where the original order is public knowledge.

the head overseer said. Within the monastery, however, no one should give a contravening order, unless he be the major superior.[84]

[From daybreak until evening there is one change of clothes,[85] and another at night. Separate prayers should be made on each occasion. The monk who, on Sunday or another solemnity, serves in the bath[86] for the ablutions or some other necessity, should make one prayer on both entry and exit. But let him ask for prayer.[87] If one is not going far, only a sign of the cross is needed. He may sign himself as he walks, and there is no need to turn east. When someone leaves the house in a hurry, he does not have to face east as he signs himself. When he meets someone when he is hurrying by, he should also ask a prayer and bow. In the monastery where genuflection is out of place, a bow is to be made.

[If someone prefers, he may prepare the Sunday oblations on Saturday; when the washing is over, the priests should change clothes if this is convenient. But the deacons should

---

[84] "A contravening order" (*alio imperio praecellente imperet*). Here I follow Walker's "with another overriding commandment" (157). Vogüé, Règles, 129, has "quand un autre n'a le pas sur lui," which would make good sense except for the concluding clause: "unless he be the major superior." I think *alio imperio praecellente* must be an instrumental ablative rather than an ablative absolute.

[85] "Change of clothes" (*commutatio vestimenti*). This probably refers to the change into and out of the night habit mentioned in Cassian's Conf 9.5. But Vogüé does not accept Walker's reading, *intermutentur*. He prefers *interrogentur*, which refers to the prayers to be said at both changes. Walker thinks the issue is modest, private (*separatim*) disrobing.

[86] "Serves in the bath" (*ministrat . . . ad lavacrum*). I suspect this means "uses the bath," but I am not sure. The old monks all bathed on the same day, but no doubt individuals could bathe any time this was deemed necessary. Vogüé has "to serve the bath" (*fait service*).

[87] "Ask for prayer" (*interroget*). Walker takes it as asking permission, but Vogüé reads it as a request for prayer, as he did in the previous entry.

carry out their appropriate service either before or after the conference.[88]

[If a monk has an impure dream or pollutes himself[89] or is doing penance, he must remain standing during the instruction.[90] But on solemn feast days, when they hear the signal during the daily conference, when it is halfway over, they should sit down.[91] Then when they hear the signal inviting them to the *synaxis* of the day's assembly,[92] they should wash before entering the oratory—unless they have already washed.

---

[88] Vogüé, Règles, 142, notes for 8l and 8m, points out that the author continues to "lighten Sunday morning" (*alleger*). He cites a number of sixth- and seventh-century cenobitic rules that call for bathing and a conference between Prime and Mass. He says the bath was because of the Eucharist. Why the priests are mentioned is not clear to me. Did they concelebrate? As for the deacons, their ministry probably involved preparation for the liturgy.

[89] "Pollutes himself" (*coinquinatus fuerit*). For the early monks, nocturnal pollution was a worrisome moral problem. Cassian devotes the whole of Conf 22 to the subject, even suggesting that wet dreams will entirely cease if the individual completely avoids carnal thoughts during waking hours.

[90] "Instruction" (*praeceptum*). The same word (*praecipitur*) is used later in the same line to mean "command." Actually, the sentence could read, "When he is commanded, he is commanded to stand." *Praeceptum* has the same meaning of instruction in the following sentence.

[91] Presumably this refers to the monks who have been standing because they are in a state of pollution or penance. And this may also be why they need to wash before entering the Divine Office.

[92] "*Synaxis* of the day's assembly" (*sinaxim . . . diei conventus*). Vogüé, Règles, 143 n. 8p, thinks *diei conventus* is an explanatory genitive with *synaxis*. Normally, *synaxis* means the Divine Office (Blaise, *Dictionnaire*, s.v.). Taken with *conventus*, that is the most probable meaning here. Yet one wonders why they have to wash before Office. This can hardly mean a full bath; it must be a quick wash in the fountain, found outside every refectory. Walker has *initiantem* instead of *invitantem*, conjecturing that this *synaxis* "begins the day's assemblies." But I have the impression that these events are transpiring in mid-morning.

[It will be arranged that the senior monk intone the first psalm and then the second; they must not genuflect, but only bow.[93] The seniors should stand in the middle of the oratory, but the others arranged to the right and left, except for the celebrant and the one assisting him.[94] Every Sunday, the Sunday hymn should be sung, just as is done on Easter.[95] When a monk approaches the altar for communion, he should prostrate three times.[96] But the newcomers, because they are untutored, and similar persons, should not approach the chalice. And no one should be reading privately during Mass,[97] or communion, except in the case of necessity. Every Sunday or solemnity, anyone

[93] "Senior monk" (*primarius*). Walker thinks this means head cantor, but Vogüé, Règles, 143 n. 8q, thinks it refers to the senior monk (*premier en grade*). The latter bases his opinion on Pachomius, Pr 16–17. In traditional cenobitism, psalms were often intoned in seniority when recited. But sung Offices were intoned by cantors. The next prescription also talks about seniors (*ordines qui priores*).

[94] "Celebrant" (*offerentem*). This was traditional patristic language for the priest offering Mass. "The one assisting" (*adherentem*) was probably the deacon. Probably the community of monks stood facing the celebrant across the freestanding altar, as in many monasteries today.

[95] "The Sunday hymn" (*hymnus diei . . . dominice*). Walker, 159 n. 1, says specimens of this hymn can be found in the *Bangor Antiphonal*. "Just as is done on Easter" (*et in die inchoante pasche*) is anything but clear. A more literal rendition might be "on the day beginning Easter." But that could be confusing, as is shown by the Rule of Walbert (*Regula Cuiusdam Virgines*), which thinks it means the opening hymn on Holy Thursday! But Pascha begins on Sunday, not Thursday.

[96] "Approaches" (*inchoaverit accedere*). As in the previous sentence, *inchoaverit* appears superfluous here. Since genuflections are prohibited a few lines previously, that must have referred to the psalmody before Mass, not Mass itself.

[97] "reading privately" (*legatur*). Walker has the very different "compelled by force" (*cogatur coactus*). Vogüé prefers *legatur* on the basis of Wal. Before Vatican II, many people followed Mass in a book such as the *St. Andrew's Missal*. Others read other devotional books. A "reading Mass" was one in which the monks were supposed to be doing their

who is forced by necessity to be absent when the brothers are pouring forth their prayers to the Lord should pray alone.[98] During Mass there should not be a lot of coming and going. Moreover, when a penitent monk[99] must make a journey and is walking with a group who are lawfully using food, if the third hour arrives and they have a long walk ahead of them, let him receive some food for the moment. He should take the rest of his food at the end of the journey.[100]]

Every day and night,[101] at the end of the psalmody in common, at the time of the closing prayers, the brothers should calmly[102] kneel in prayer (unless prevented by infirmity), saying in silence, "God, come to my aid; Lord, hasten to help

---

lectio divina for the day. Why it would be "necessary" to read during Mass, I am not sure.

[98] "Should pray alone" (*oret ipse*). Why monks should miss Sunday Mass is not obvious, but Paen B29 speaks of cooks and porters sometimes coming late for the exhortation or sermon. On rare occasions, some essential work like calving might take precedence, and of course sickness is an excusing cause. But wherever one finds himself, one can pray.

[99] "Penitent monk" (*Paenitens*). No doubt a penitent would normally eat late in the day, but those engaged in a long journey on foot can hardly have done without food all day. The third hour was 9:00 a.m. or mid-morning. Vogüé, Règles, 145 n. 8x, cites several sixth- and seventh-century texts that say a monk should not eat before the third hour. He also thinks this regulation is somehow connected to Sunday Mass, typically held at 9:00 a.m.

[100] "End of the journey" (*ubi quiescat*, literally, "when he rests"). If "they have a long walk ahead of them" refers to a journey, this could have been late in the day. In other words, when one is traveling, there is no need to observe all the duties of ordinary life.

[101] "Every day and night," that is, at all the Offices.

[102] "Calmly" (*aequo animo*). Walker has the puzzling "uniformly." Vogüé, Règles, 131, seems closer to the mark with *de bon coeur*, but one wonders what the problem was. Saint Benedict, RB 31.17, uses *aequo animo* for the cellarer, who should maintain his equilibrium even though he is sometimes overworked.

me!"[103] When they have silently repeated[104] this verse three
times in prayer, let them rise together from kneeling in prayer.
But on Sundays, and from the first to the fiftieth day of Paschaltide, they should bow slightly during the psalmody,[105]
praying carefully[106] to the Lord without genuflection.

X. If any brother is disobedient, two days on bread and
water (a single loaf).[107] If someone says "I won't do it!" three
days with one loaf and water. Whoever[108] murmurs will go two
days on one loaf with water. If anyone does not ask pardon
but makes an excuse, two days on a single loaf and water. Two
brothers who quarrel about something to the point of anger

---

[103] This psalm verse (69:2), which is recommended by Cassian as the
ideal spiritual nostrum (Conf 10.10), is used by Saint Benedict to *begin*
Offices (RB 17.3, 18.1), not end them.

[104] "Silently repeated" (*tacite decantaverint*). The literal sense would
be "chanted," but that makes little sense. Blaise, s.v., cites Jerome, Ep
106.49, who uses the term *decantare* in parallel with *meditari*. The latter
verb means "to repeat silently."

[105] I don't understand why he should talk about what is done *during*
the psalmody, since it seems the subject in question is the prayer *after*
the psalmody. However, I may be looking for too much chronological
precision here.

[106] "Carefully" (*sedule*). Although the meaning is clear enough (Vogüé,
Règles, 131, has *avec zèle*), one has the feeling that the adverbs in this
section are slightly out of focus. Maybe the point is that one doesn't have
to kneel down to engage in fervent prayer.

[107] "A single loaf" (*una paxmate*). According to Cassian, Inst 4.14, the
Egyptian monks ate two of these a day. Since they weighed half a pound
(160 gr.), that means that the Columbanian penal fast was serious. See
Vogüé, Règles, 56, note. It is interesting that the Irish were still using
Cassian's vocabulary for bread after two hundred years. This whole
paragraph is organized around the penalty of "one loaf," spelled *paxmatio*
in all but this first case.

[108] "Whoever." All the sentences in 10–14 begin *si quis*. I vary the translations to avoid monotony.

must spend two days [109] on bread and water. When someone asserts a falsehood and will not retract, he gets two days on bread and water. [110] If someone contradicts his brothers and does not seek pardon, two days on one loaf. Interrupting an order [111] and thus breaking the rule means two days of one loaf and water. If a monk does a task enjoined [112] but does it sloppily, let him spend two days on bread and water. If a monk speaks badly of his abbot, seven days on bread and water. [113] If

[109] "Bread and water" (*uno paxmatio et aqua*). Here, and in the rest of the paragraph, the penalty is precisely "one loaf" (*paxmatium*). I have dropped the precision for the sake of euphony. But I also begin to wonder if the phrase *should* be translated. In other words, had it become mere code language for "bread and water"?

[110] "Asserts a falsehood" (*contendit mendacium*). This sentence is not as simple as it seems. Does the monk *knowingly* tell a lie? If he does so out of ignorance, does he stubbornly cling to his "difference" (*distinctionem*) after he has been set straight? If all this is deliberate, the penalty seems mild. In fact, in 13.3, the penalty for virtually the same fault is *seven* days on bread and water.

[111] "Interrupting an order" (*interrumpit mandatum*). I have joined Walker with this literal version. Vogüé simply has "viole un ordre." Our version takes *mandatum* as the vocalization of an order. Most disobedience is not quite so crass.

[112] "Does a task enjoined" (*cum iniungitur ei opus negligenter facit*). If I guessed right on the previous number, the difference is that now one carries out an order but actually undermines it by doing it badly. There is a form of passive aggression that appears to be compliance but is in fact subversion. For a hilarious tale about passive aggression from beginning to end, see Jaroslav Hašek, *The Good Soldier Schweik* (New York: New American Library, 1930).

[113] "Speaks badly of" (*detractaverit*). There is a wide range of possible meanings for this verb. Walker has chosen the usual English connotation of *detract* with *slander*. Here, one is taking away from the good name of another, and doing it maliciously, as a lie. But given the heavy monastic ideology of filial obedience ("Let them love their abbot with sincere and humble love," RB 72.10), any disparagement of the abbot is anathema. Hence the whole week of fasting.

someone badmouths his brother, twenty-four psalms. To speak badly of a layman costs twelve psalms.[114] If anyone forgets something outdoors, the punishment is twelve psalms if it is a small item, but thirty psalms for a big one. For something lost or ruined, the penance[115] should be proportionate to the value of the object.

XI. If any monk has an unauthorized conversation with a layman, twenty-four psalms.[116] When a brother finishes his work, he should look for another job and do it unbidden.[117] If he does not, he must chant twenty-four psalms. A double-tongued[118] brother who stirs up the community should spend a day on bread and water. If a monk eats at someone else's house without permission, he should spend a day on one loaf when he returns

---

[114] Since all three of these cases involve *detractaverit*, it looks like the verb does *not* mean deliberate slander. Otherwise, a few psalms are not a very severe penalty.

[115] "Penance" (*paenitentia*). This term can mean either the internal disposition of sorrow and regret for sin or the steps taken to atone for sin. The second meaning seems called for here.

[116] "Unauthorized" (*sine iussu*) is perhaps close to "without permission." Saint Benedict decrees the same gag rule in RB 53.23-24 in regard to guests. Although it may protect the monk from harmful influence, it can also protect the guest from gabby, needy monks. Either way, it is hard to observe in the modern world.

[117] "Unbidden" (*sine iussu*) has a slightly different flavor than in the previous sentence. Whereas in that prohibition the fault is presumption, here it is passivity. In RB 53.18-20, monks are told to be ready for reassignment when they have finished their task. Columban, however, takes this a step further: they are to go *looking* for more work and not wait to be reassigned. This, of course, has its own problems.

[118] "Double-tongued" (*bilinguis*) is an epithet that could have either positive or negative meaning. Obviously, it is no sin to speak two languages, but *bilinguis* often meant deceitful speech, as in Vergil's *Aeneid* 1.661. Because of its trickery of Adam and Eve, the serpent was called "double-tongued" by Saint Ambrose (*De Paradiso* 12.55).

to his own house.[119] If a monk talks about a past sin, one day with one loaf.[120] Or if someone has been out in public and upon return talks about the bad things he has seen,[121] one day on bread and water. If someone is so lukewarm as to agree to keep quiet {in the *culpa*}[122] about someone else murmuring, slandering, or doing something against the Rule, one day on one loaf.

XII. If a monk riles up his brother and later asks forgiveness, but if the brother does not forgive him but sends him to his senior, the one who aroused him must say twenty-four psalms, and the unforgiving one will spend a day on bread and water.[123] When someone wants something but the cellarer

---

[119] "To his own house" (*venerit domui suae*). This unusual expression may simply be used to contrast with *domo aliena*. Vogüé, Règles, 132 n. 4, notes that this prohibition resembles RB 51, but he wonders if the case is the same. Clearly, though, meals were a primary sign of community in ancient times, so absence from the common table was not taken lightly.

[120] "A past sin" (*praeteritum peccatum*). Presumably this means his *own* past sin, but the Latin does not specify. Sometimes it is edifying to relate one's past sins, as with Augustine's *Confessions*. But graphic descriptions of sin (especially sexual ones) can pose a serious source of temptation for others.

[121] "Bad things he has seen" (*de saeculi peccato*). This prohibition is exactly parallel to RB 67.5. But the issue may not be completely transparent. The literal sense of the Latin here is "sin of the world," which could suggest fairly attractive but harmful developments in the world outside the cloister. Yet there are evils outside the monastery that the monks *should* know about if they are to combat them. Naïve ignorance is no great virtue for monks.

[122] "Agree to keep quiet [in the *culpa*]" (*consentit a confessione*). Walker has "withhold confession," and so does Vogüé, but this cannot be a question of the sacrament, for in sacramental confession one confesses one's own sins and not those of others. My own addition "in the *culpa*" is a conjecture, since I do not know if the Columbanian monks had a public confession of faults. The agreement here may have been not to tell the superior. At any rate, *confessione* must mean to make some kind of report.

[123] It is clear enough that Columban considers the refusal to forgive a worse fault than the very fault (provocation) it refuses to forgive. Why

refuses it, if he then runs to the abbot to get it, he gets five days penance.[124] If someone misses the prayers before or after the meal,[125] he must sing twelve psalms. If a brother often falls asleep during the Office,[126] he should sing twelve psalms; if this happens infrequently, six psalms. The monk who does not answer *amen* will receive thirty blows.[127] Should a monk skip an hour of the Office, he must perform the fifteen gradual

---

the provoked brother sends the provoker to the superior is not so clear; probably for a penance.

[124] "He then runs to the abbot to get it" (*et iubet abbas*). Obviously, I am taking liberties with this extremely terse Latin expression. But a literal rendition makes little sense. Actually, I am following Walker's helpful footnote. But it might still be pointed out that classical cenobitic monasticism usually allows the monk to appeal to the abbot if he feels wronged by a subordinate official. Still, when the system is working well, this kind of going over the head of the minor official is detrimental.

[125] "Before or after meals" (*super mensam et post cibum*). Vogüé, Règles, 133, has "before sitting down to table and after the meal." This same fault is punished by exclusion from the common meal by Saint Benedict in RB 43.13-17. In addition to disrupting the prayers, this kind of behavior is damaging to the communal discipline and ethos. The sin is more individualism than just tardiness.

[126] "During the Office" (*dum oratur*). This must refer to public prayer, where dozing is observable and a damage to general morale. If Columban had been talking about private prayer, he would have written *dum orat*. It would not be practical to penalize drowsiness during private prayer, which probably affects most monks. RM 48.10-11 reads, "Now, the reason we have said that the prayer should be short is to avoid falling asleep because the prayer is drawn out, or the devil might set various images before the eyes of those lying prostrate for a long time or insinuate something else into their heart." Notice that here *prayer* is not just psalmody but the silent psalm-prayers that RM wants after every psalm. Lying on the floor certainly could induce drowsiness.

[127] "Thirty blows" (*xxx verbera*). This seems like a disproportionately severe penalty for such a picayune fault. Nevertheless, negligence in liturgical participation can be a sign of a deeper malaise.

psalms,[128] but only twelve if it happens on a winter morning. If a monk does not heed the signal for the Office,[129] twelve psalms. If a brother comes to Mass wrapped in just his night belt and garment, twelve psalms.[130]

XIII. If some brother eats before the ninth hour on Wednesday and Friday,[131] unless he is sick he must [live] two days on bread and water. If someone speaks a falsehood,[132] fifty stripes if he does so unawares. But if he does so knowingly and boldly, he must spend two days on bread and water. If he holds to his lie[133] even in the face of contradiction, seven days

---

[128] "Gradual psalms" refers to Pss 120–34, which are short psalms. But of course it takes much longer to recite fifteen of them than to participate in one of the Day Hours. As for a "winter morning," which Vogüé renders "the hour of matins in winter," no doubt it was tempting to stay in a warm bed in the middle of the night. But the penalty of twelve psalms is a bit puzzling since Matins usually involves more psalms than that.

[129] "Heed the signal" (*non audierit sonitus*). In this case, *audire* means not just to hear but to hear and obey. Ancient monks had no watches, so they were dependent on a bell or some other audible signal.

[130] "Night belt and garment" (*nocturnum cingulum vel vestis circa eum*) shows that these monks slept in different clothes than those they wore all day. It is surprising that Mass was said so early in the morning, if that is what is implied here.

[131] "Wednesday and Friday" are also fast days in RB 41. Except Eastertide, when monks eat at noon, and Lent, when they eat only in the evening, the Benedictine Rule calls for the meal to take place at 3:00 p.m. or thereabouts. In summertime, fieldwork dictates that they eat at noon, but then too they are required to fast until mid-afternoon on Wednesdays and Fridays.

[132] "Falsehood." *Mendacium* usually means a lie, but that cannot be the simple meaning here. For if a person is unaware he is speaking an untruth, it is not normally called a lie. Still, one wonders why there should be *any* penalty for innocent error. Could it be that Columban is talking here about someone who tells a lie for what he thinks is a good purpose?

[133] "Lie" (*mendacium*). It is hard to tell whether this *mendacium* is deliberate or not. The way I read it, someone has refuted (*denegatur*) the *mendacium* with truth/fact, so it is perverse to cling to it.

on bread and water. If a monk[134] sleeps in the same house as a woman, two days on bread and water, but only one day if he does not know it is forbidden. If someone does not shut the church door, twelve psalms.[135] If someone spits and hits the altar, twenty-four psalms; if he hits the wall, six.[136] Someone who forgets to sing a psalm or read, three psalms.[137]

XIV. If anyone comes late to prayers, fifty stripes;[138] who

---

[134] "Monk" (*monachus*). Although I have been using *monk* throughout this translation, for the sake of variety, Vogüé, Règles, 134 n. 4, says this is the only time *monachus* appears in this entire Rule. Probably the monk still receives a light penalty because he should have known but also because he may have given scandal.

[135] "Shut the church door." Both in medieval Ireland and on the Continent, these monks lived in remote and wild places. Open doors are an invitation for wild creatures to wander in. Yet once they are frightened or confused, it is harder for them to wander out. A mountain lion once wandered into the chapel of a monastery in Colorado!

[136] "Spits." Apparently it was all right to spit in church, as long as one didn't hit the altar or the wall. We might find this disgusting, but sensibilities differ according to place and time. The Rule of the Master, which was written about a century before the Rule of Columban, shows the same manners, or lack thereof: "There should not be a great deal of frequent coughing or constant spitting or gasping, because the devil uses all these as a hindrance to prayers and psalms. For what we have said above should be avoided also during the prayers, namely, if the one praying wishes to spit or dispose of filth from his nose, he should get rid of it not in front of him but behind him, because of the angels standing in front, as the prophet indicates when he says: 'In the presence of the angels I will sing your praise; I will worship at your holy temple'" (RM 48.6–8).

[137] Clearly, the reference here is to the Divine Office, and probably to solo parts. Someone who "forgets" his turn is not only causing a disturbance; he is probably showing that he has not prepared his part. Most of these parts were memorized in ancient times.

[138] "Fifty stripes." Most of the peccadillos in this paragraph are punished with fifty blows of some sort. They must have been mostly light blows, because fifty blows of any kind seems excessive. Perhaps an analogy

ever makes a lot of noise, fifty stripes;[139] whoever is slow in doing what he is told, fifty stripes. To speak loudly after the final pax earns fifty stripes.[140] A sassy response brings fifty stripes.[141] If a monk comes into the house with his hood up, fifty blows.[142] If one enters the house without asking a blessing, fifty stripes. To eat without praying, fifty stripes. If he talks with his mouth full, fifty stripes.[143] If he makes noise during prayer,

---

would be the raps on the knuckles meted out with a ruler by old-time teachers.

[139] "A lot of noise" (*plausu*). This word often means hand clapping, but that seems unlikely here. Vogüé translates *bruyamment* = "noisily." This could refer to the Divine Office, but a racket is unwelcome any time in the monastery. *Plausus* also appears in Coen I.7, but there it means "shout."

[140] "Speak loudly" (*sonaverit*). *Sonare* can mean any loud noise, but in regard to humans it usually means loud speech (OLD). The "final pax" appears in the *Bangor Antiphonale* 54 (597B) as the closing ceremony of the day. RB 42.8-11 strictly forbids talking after Compline, except for those caring for guests.

[141] "Sassy response" (*Si contumaciter responderit*). Cassian condemns such behavior in Inst 4.16. The word "sassy" was chosen to render *contumaciter* in the hope of offering readers a vibrant English word for an arcane Latin word. Nevertheless, *contumax* has an excellent monastic pedigree, since it is used by Benedict in RB 23.1 to characterize what he considers reprehensible in a monk. Walker has "stubborn" and Vogüé *avec arrogance*, of which I much prefer the latter.

[142] "With his hood up" (*velato capite*). The Pachomian monks wore their hoods up at meals to avoid seeing their neighbor eating. The meaning of head covering is heavily cultural, as witness recent French attempts to stop Muslim girls from coming to class veiled. But when the American nuns took off their veils, cultural police reacted contrarily. Surprisingly, the punishment for this offense is fifty *blows* (*verbera*), not hand slaps.

[143] "Mouth full" (*locutus est aliquid in ore suo*). Vogüé must understand this differently—*Si l'on dit quelque chose dans sa bouche*—but I don't get his point. This whole section greatly resembles Coen III.7–8. Could the fault here be eating during the Divine Office?

fifty blows.[144] If a brother holds on to anger or sadness or envy against his brother,[145] he will have to do penance on bread and water as long as he persists in this attitude. But if he confesses the first day, he must sing twenty-four psalms.

XV. If a brother loses the Host[146] and does not know where it is, he must do a year of penance.[147] If one neglects the Sacrament to the point that it dries up,[148] is devoured by worms, and becomes nothing, he must do half a year's penance. If a monk neglects the eucharistic element to the point that a worm is found in it, he must do forty days' penance. As for the worm, if it is still intact, burn it and hide the ashes in the ground near

[144] "During prayer" (*dum oratur*). This seems to be the standard expression for the Divine Office; see Coen XII.4. If it is not the Office, then one wonders why such a dire punishment for noise.

[145] "Holds on" (*retinet*). The problem here is not anger, sadness, or envy as such, but its retention. *Tristitia* could be "spleen," as Walker has it. With this prohibition, Columban shows a good deal of psychological penetration, at least in my view. Grudges are extremely corrosive of community. The penance here could be enormous: some people cannot let go of destructive feelings!

[146] "Host" (*sacrificium*). In Coen IV.3 and XII.8, *sacrificium* refers to the Sacrifice of the Mass, but here the term means the sacramental bread. Without daily Mass, early Christians took the Host home with them for private communion. To judge from the following prohibitions, this practice could lead to abuses.

[147] "A year of penance" (*annum paeniteat*). This tremendous penance indicates the extreme reverence Christians have for the Eucharist. Eventually, private retention of the Eucharist was discontinued, but the reservation of the Sacrament became a general practice. Nevertheless, one occasionally still comes across cases where pious Catholics obtain official permission to carry the Host on their person. For example, Elizabeth Kornerup, the spiritual confidant of David Knowles, always carried the Host in her purse. See Adrian Morey, *David Knowles: A Memoir* (London: Darton, Longman and Todd, 1979), 89.

[148] "Dries up" (*siccetur*). This tells us that the eucharistic bread Columban was using was not a cardboard-like wafer. To dry up, it must have had some body to it—it must have looked and tasted like bread.

the altar.[149] If a brother neglects the Host, which is then trans-
formed and loses its taste as bread, he must do twenty days'
penance if it turns red and fifteen days if it turns purple.[150] If the
Host has not discolored but has become sticky, seven days' penance. If someone immerses the Host, he should immediately
drink the water in the pyx; then he should consume the Host.[151]
If it has fallen [152] from a boat, a bridge, or a horse, not through
negligence but by accident, he should do a day's penance. Yet
if he has carelessly submerged the pyx, that is, waded out into
the water [153] without thinking of the danger to the Host, forty

[149] "Hide the ashes." While this may appear a fussy, if not bizarre,
approach to the problem of wormy eucharistic bread, it can also represent Roman Catholic devotion at its most intense. Most Roman Catholic
sacristies feature a *sacrarium*, that is, a drainpipe running straight into the
ground. Extraordinary care is taken that anything that remotely touches
the Body and Blood of Christ—for example, the water that has washed
the cloths used to wipe the chalice—*not* be run down the sewer.

[150] "Purple" (*iacinctino*). Hyacinth is a deep blue or purple, not usually associated with bread. But since we do not know the exact chemical
composition of the communion bread used by these monks, we are pretty
much in the dark. The mere fact that Columban spends so much time on
the details of how not to treat the Host suggests that there were lots of
problems surrounding the custom of private reservation of the Sacrament.

[151] "Immersed" (*merserit*). Presumably someone has accidentally
dropped the pyx into the water and not done so deliberately. The Host,
of course, was in a pyx. While some of these cases seem bizarre, if the
Sacrament is habitually kept on one's person, a lot can happen to it. No
wonder the church keeps the reserved Host in a heavy tabernacle bolted
to the wall!

[152] "It has fallen" (*ceciderit*). Since no pronoun is given, the meaning
could be "if *he* has fallen." But if the person fell, the Host would not necessarily be in danger. Apparently, the monk has dropped it by accident.
Notice there is no talk of diving into the water after it!

[153] "Waded out into the water" (*exierit aqua*). Strictly speaking, the
meaning is "waded out of the water," as Walker and Vogüé have it. But
isn't the negligence precisely to carry the pyx into the water? Maybe the

days' penance. But [154] if the brother vomits his supper on a day of Communion, if this happens because of unusually rich food and the vice of gluttony, [155] twenty days. If this happens because of infirmity, [156] ten days on bread and water.

[He who knows his brother is committing a mortal sin [157] but does not confront him [158] should be considered a transgressor

---

point is that one should check on the pyx when emerging from the water to see if it has taken water.

[154] T. M. Charles-Edwards notes that this sentence presupposes a contrasting "if clause" that apparently has dropped out of Coen ("The Penitential of Columbanus," in *Columbanus: Studies on the Latin Writings,* ed. Michael Lapidge [Woodbridge, Suffolk, UK: Boydell and Brewer, 1997], 217–39, here 227). This missing clause is in fact found in the *Pen Bigotianum* 1.3.1–2 (in Ludwig Bieler, ed., *The Irish Penitentials* [Dublin: Dublin Institute for Advanced Studies, 1963]), which must have been copying from a better text of Coen. The missing clause reads, *Qui sacrificium evomit causa voracitatis, xi diebus* ("If anyone vomits the Host because of gluttony, eleven days' penance").

[155] "Vice of gluttony" (*vitio saturitatis sed stomachi*). I cannot account for the *sed* in this sentence. Walker and Vogüé gamely work with it: "not through the vice of gluttony but of indigestion," which makes little sense to me.

[156] "Because of infirmity" puzzles me. If the monk simply falls ill, why penalize him? *Infirmitas,* of course, can also mean weakness of character, which would lend some plausibility to this harsh penalty.

[157] The extensive bracketed portion from here to the end of Coen comes from the Long Text. "Mortal sin" (*ad mortem*). Every Catholic knows (or knew) this concept: a sin so serious that it would result in eternal damnation unless repented. Whether the author of 1 John 5:16, which is the biblical reference here, meant the same thing is debatable: "This is only for those whose sin is not deadly. There is such a thing as deadly sin, about which I do not say that you should pray." Further, Columban has left out the very crucial word "not" from the quotation before "mortal" (*non ad mortem*)!

[158] "Confront" (*arguit*). This term, drawn from contemporary psychological parlance, seems to express exactly what this sentence wishes to convey. *Arguere* can also mean "accuse," but that is not the point in 1 John 5:16, nor is it appropriate here. The issue is *fraternal correction,*

of the Gospel law. This is the case until he confronts him about whose evil he kept silence and confesses to the priest.[159] As long as his bad conscience kept quiet, that is the extent he must do penance.[160] Let him who overlooked a small sin do penance with a similar rebuke,[161] but not with the same affliction: he should receive thirty strokes or sing fifteen psalms. If in the future he neglects these little things with disdain, he should do penance on bread and water, for the Lord commanded[162] that the sinner be corrected. But he who confronts harshly[163] is to be held guilty until he seeks pardon from the corrected brother, and thirty strokes or fifteen psalms. If someone loudly accuses another of a shameful sin before he has confronted him privately as the Lord commands,[164] he should be punished until

---

which involves private exhortation before any public action is taken. See Matt 18:15, where the Vulgate uses *corripe*.

[159] "Confesses to the priest" (*fateaur sacerdoti*). Grammatically, the subject here could be the original sinner, but the logic of the sentence dictates that the one who must confess to the priest is the one who failed to confront. This interpretation is borne out by the next sentence.

[160] "As long as" (*quamdiu . . . tamdiu*). This looks like a guideline for the priest assigning a penance. Obviously, such a criterion could result in very severe penance. Columban takes fraternal correction very seriously.

[161] "A similar rebuke." I take this as referring to the priest who heard his confession. Vogüé seems to sidestep the issue: "Let him do penance in similar fashion." I don't actually understand "a similar rebuke," though.

[162] "For the Lord commanded." This is meant to render an *ut*-clause, the exact grammatical force of which is unclear to me. Is it a purpose clause? A result clause?

[163] "Harshly" (*non leniter*). A rare occasion where Columban admits that correction is a delicate business where feelings can easily be hurt. Who is supposed to levy the punishment is not very plain from the grammar. Vogüé adds a parenthesis (*lui infliger* = [it is necessary] to inflict on him).

[164] "As the Lord commands." This reference to Matt 18:15 makes it clear that this whole section is based on Matt 18:15-18, which is the bedrock of most ancient monastic penitential systems. Unfortunately,

he makes it up to the one he accused. He should do three days' penance on bread and water.

[If someone disobeys a specific command[165] or the general rule of discipline, he should be barred from table and only received back the next day.[166]

[When a brother engages in a private and familiar conversation with a woman, except in the presence of trustworthy persons, he should remain without food or two days on bread and water.[167] An alternative is two hundred stripes.[168]

[If someone presumes to take a trip [169] without permission of

---

Walker attaches this clause to what follows rather than what precedes. The importance of privacy and discretion in fraternal correction is a matter well understood by Columban. Yet all the discretion in the world cannot take the risk out of this business. To intervene is to court possible rejection.

[165] "Specific command" (*iussio*). By itself, *iussio* means any command, but here it forms a contrasting pair with "general discipline." It is a favorite word of Saint Benedict, occurring no fewer than ten times, and usually as a direct command of the abbot.

[166] This rendition of *maneat expulsus sine cibo ut in crastinum recipiatur* does not square with either Walker or Vogüé. They think this is a complete expulsion and that the subject of *recipiatur* is the expelled monk. For my part, I doubt the expulsion is from anything but the table. The *ut* clause is probably one of result.

[167] "Without food or two days on bread and water." This is a puzzling alternative, since the duration of "without food" is not stated.

[168] "Two hundred stripes." This seems like a huge penalty for a minor offense, but it may be due to a degree of misanthropy in the author. The Romans forbade more than thirty-nine blows (forty stripes less one, 2 Cor 11:24) in a flogging, probably on the grounds that more could be fatal. The term *plaga* could mean a range of blows, from severe to slight. I suspect that the blows here were not particularly severe.

[169] "Take a trip" (*facere ambasciam*). According to Charles Du Cange (*Glossarium Mediae et Infimae Latinitatis* [Paris: Didot, 1840], s.v. *ambascia*), this term, which is not found in the OLD or Blaise, *Dictionnaire*, refers to some kind of delegated journey—i.e., as an ambassador. But the issue here is precisely that the monk has set out on a journey *without* permission.

the superior [170] and sets out freely and without any necessity,[171] he should be punished with fifty strokes.[172] To presume to work for personal profit brings a hundred stripes.[173] When anyone is found to possess anything unnecessary and beyond that which is generally granted to the brothers, it should be taken away, and he should be punished with a hundred stripes. To give or receive anything necessary [174] or lawful without permission earns twelve stripes. But if there is some reasonable defense for this action, then a humble request for pardon will be enough.

[170] "Superior" (*eo qui praeest*). This circumlocution for the superior is typical of Rufinus's Latin translation of the Rule of Basil (Greek) from about AD 400. That was well before western monasticism had developed technical terms such as *abbas* or *prior* for the superior. Columban knew the Latin version of Basil, as he quotes it now and then. But this is the first time the Basilian term for the superior turns up in the Rule of Columban.

[171] "Sets out freely and without any necessity" (*libera et ineffrenata processione absque necessitate*). My translation here is redundant but not as repetitious as the Latin. Yet the larger question is why the monk should feel constrained to make a journey. Of course, if he really was an ambassador (see previous note), he would not be free. But whose delegate could he be but that of the abbot?

[172] "Punished" (*inhibeatur*). This verb can mean "to prevent," but it is clear that this penalty takes place after the delict has been committed.

[173] "Work for personal profit" (*operis peculiaris*). *Peculium* refers to personal gain or interest. Here it could mean a job that one does for one's own profit (Vogüé, Règles) or some private work (Walker). That it is unauthorized is indicated by the additional term *presumptio*. In RB 55.16, the term *opus peculiare* does not refer to work but to private possessions, which the abbot must search out in the dormitory. Conversely, some medieval monks were provided by the cellarer with a *peculium* or small private allowance.

[174] "Necessary" (*necessarium*). One might think it would be enough that an item be "necessary" (or lawful) for the monk to dispose of it. But who is the judge of that? Thus permission is required for all cenobitic transactions. The term *necessarium* in its various forms appears in all three sentences of this unit, thus forming an organizing concept. Since the material traded is "necessary and lawful," the punishment is relatively slight.

[If someone talks while eating,[175] he should receive six blows. Someone whose voice carries from table to table deserves six blows.[176] If a brother yells from the house to the outside, or vice versa, let him receive twelve blows.[177]

[To go out of the house or come into it, or to perform a work, without a blessing and the sign of the cross, is punished by twelve stripes.[178]

[Saying *mine* or *yours* brings six strokes.[179]

[A word simply[180] spoken against the word of another costs six blows. But a word spoken in a spirit of contradiction is visited by a hundred blows or the imposition of silence.

---

[175] "Talks while eating" (*comedens loquitur*). By itself, this prohibition could be against talking with the mouth full, but the next sentence is clearly about silence at meals rather than table manners.

[176] "Voice carries" (*vox obstrepit*). It sounds as if Columban did permit soft speech at table. It is unclear to me if the monk is here shouting to another table, as Vogüé thinks (Règles, 137). As for Saint Benedict, he demands the strictest silence during table reading (RB 38.5). The Rule of the Master also has table reading but encourages questions by the monks and answers by the abbot (RM 24.18–19). Since cenobitic monasteries usually had table reading, this was probably also true for Columban.

[177] "Yells" (*sonuerit*). This may seem an excessive interpretation of *sonuerit*, but normally one must shout to be heard in such circumstances. Obviously, this prohibition does not pertain to fires, although there was an extraordinary occasion when a group of nuns (was it at Arles?) let their convent burn down rather than break the night silence. Since silence is the normal atmosphere in a monastery, yelling tends to shock.

[178] Walker gives the additional words "if otherwise," but Vogüé omits them. Since I do not understand them, I also omit them.

[179] "*Mine* or *yours*" (*meum vel tuum*). Obviously, the words themselves have no intrinsic moral content. Yet they imply an ethos of private property, which was and is strictly out of place for a cenobitic monk. The point is made equally forcefully by Saint Benedict in RB 33.1: "This vice in particular [private property] must be torn up by the roots."

[180] "Simply" (*simpliciter*). Walker has "honestly," while Vogüé has "sans refléxion," which shows this is a fairly complicated issue. Basically, *simplex* means without addition; here the addition would be in a spirit

[If a brother does not observe the proper order in the psalmody, six blows.[181]

[Whoever presumes to speak unnecessarily during the time set aside for silence, give him seventeen stripes.[182]

[If a monk loses or wastes any piece of monastic property through carelessness,[183] he must restore it by his own sweat and additional work.[184] He must do penance according to its

---

of contention. Still, *simpliciter* must have something negative about it or else one could not punish it even with six blows. In traditional society, one did not contradict seniors or superiors. Here, though, it appears that Columban does not want the monk to contradict anybody.

[181] "Proper order in the psalmody" (*ordinem psallendi*). As it stands, this injunction could mean many things. In the context of cenobitic monasticism, it probably refers to the Divine Office. Since the order (series) of the psalms is always set, it is unlikely that an individual would or could change it. Probably the offense here is somehow to disrupt the smooth chanting, and there are many ways to do that.

[182] "Time set aside for silence" (*statuto tempore taciturnitatis*). Monasteries usually try to observe a considerable level of silence at most times and places, but this prohibition shows that Columban did not impose a complete regime of silence. Doubtless the principal "set time" of deep silence was at night, as in RB 42. Even though Benedict threatens offenders with serious reprisals, he acknowledges that certain reasons, such as the needs of guests, can demand talking. The Trappists used to maintain a draconian regime of silence. Thomas Merton somewhere recounts that a monk died during the night; rather than break the night silence the monks left the corpse in the dormitory until morning.

[183] "Carelessness" (*per contemptum*). Contempt is a worse fault than carelessness, but the latter can be the result of the former.

[184] "Sweat and additional work" (*proprio sudore et operis adiectione*). Although the monk cannot make monetary restitution, he can do extra work in his free time.

value in the judgment of the priest:[185] a day of privation[186] or on bread and water. If he loses or breaks something, not by carelessness, but by accident, he shall pay for his negligence in a public manner.[187] When all the brothers have gathered for the Divine Office, he will seek pardon by lying prostrate until the completion of the prayers.[188] He will receive pardon when at the abbot's judgment he is commanded to get up from the floor.[189] The same goes for someone who comes late when summoned to prayer or some other work.[190]

[185] "Priest" (*sacerdotis*). *Sacerdos* also turns up in Coen VIII and XV as a superior of some sort. Unless Columban is implying a double superior structure (prior and priest) à la Augustine's Rule (Praec), this must refer to the prior. Here it appears that "the priest" judges the extent of the damage, not the penance.

[186] "Day of privation" (*superpositione*). See Coen IV notes for *superpositio*.

[187] "By accident" (*casu aliquo*). As in the previous sentence, I have interpreted *contemptus* somewhat benignly. Nevertheless, the logic here is bewildering. Even though the monk is the victim of an accident, he still must do penance—and *public* penance. The same mentality is exhibited in RB 46.1-4, where the slightest gaffe must be atoned for. Although this kind of stern rigor can promote scruples or perfectionism, probably its purpose is to inculcate care for the goods of the monastery.

[188] "Until the completion of the prayers" (*donec orationum consummetur sollempnitas*). Not knowing what to make of *sollempnitas*, I have more or less ignored it, as do Walker and Vogüé.

[189] "He will receive pardon" (*inpetraturus*). This rare use of the future participle is in line with the general awkwardness of this enormous sentence (which I have trisected into three sentences). The ritual of prostration of penitents during the Divine Office also appears in RB 44. In that text also, the abbot orders the monk to arise at the end of the ritual (44.10).

[190] "Summoned" (*arcersitus*). Probably a reference to the signal that calls monks to various exercises. While these elaborate public penances may seem excessive for mere tardiness, the ancient monks did not think so. RB 43 is entirely devoted to this problem, and the ritual of "kneeling out" was observed by latecomers to the Divine Office until the reforms following Vatican II. By the way, it made no difference if one was legitimately detained or not.

[If a brother chants a psalm hesitatingly, or if he responds excessively, harshly, or with arrogance, a day of privation.[191] If one negligently fulfills the obedience commanded, a day of privation. To murmur even slightly brings a day of privation.[192] If one prefers *lectio divina* to work of obedience, a day of privation.[193] If a monk performs the tasks assigned him in a lackadaisical way, a day of privation. Whoever does not immediately return to his cell at the end of the Divine Office is subject to a day of privation.[194] If a monk stops with someone for a moment, a day of privation.[195] If he hides away for a

[191] "Hesitatingly" (*titubaverit*). Presumably this refers to the intonation of a psalm in the Divine Office, where a wavering cantor can mislead the whole choir. "If the bugle gives an indistinct sound, who will get ready for battle?" (1 Cor 14:8, RSV).

[192] "Even slightly" (*vel leviter*). Such a stiff penalty for the least grumbling shows the abhorrence of the early monks toward that fault. Saint Benedict shares that extreme distaste, but he admits at least once that murmuring may be justified (*justa*, RB 41.5). In connection with heavy field work in summer, the abbot must keep an eye on the situation and provide an early meal when needed. Otherwise, the monks have a right to complain.

[193] "Prefers" (*preferens*). Here the term "prefer" should probably have its root sense of "put before." This is not just a bad attitude but a concrete offense. *Work of obedience* just means that the monk is told to do something else during the time set aside for *lectio*. This is an exception, but it must be honored.

[194] "To his cell" (*ad cellam*). The noteworthy thing here is not the demand that the monk return to his cell but that he has a cell. The Rule of Saint Benedict, which was written about fifty years before Columban and his Irish monks arrived in France, has the monks sleep in large, open dormitories where they have little or no privacy. Benedict may have been motivated by a decree of Emperor Justinian (March 17, 535) requiring the monks to sleep in dormitories. Perhaps Columban had not heard of this legislation.

[195] "With someone" (*cum aliquo*). No doubt to "chat" with someone. What seems to us like a trivial and perfectly natural gesture of ordinary good will was unacceptable to the ancient monks. They did not want

moment, a day of privation.[196] If he presumes to chat even a moment with anyone but his cellmate, a day's privation.[197] To hold hands with another brings a day's privation.[198] To pray with a brother who has been barred from prayer brings with it a day of privation.[199]

[If a monk meets with a relative or lay friend[200] or speaks with him without permission, if he receives any sort of letter or presumes[201] to send one without the abbot's leave, a day of

---

a chatty society, and they took severe measures to prevent it. The sixth chapter of Saint Benedict's Rule was written in this spirit. Yet other parts of RB, such as 49.7, which requires *less* chitchat during Lent, imply that the monks engaged in at least some casual conversation.

[196] "Hides away" (*uspiam secesserit*). This text risks making Columban a control freak like the Rule of the Master, whose deans are perpetual watchdogs (RM 11). Yet cenobitic life *is* essentially a public life, with little room for hideaways or days off. Those who need a great deal of privacy probably belong somewhere else.

[197] "Cellmate" (*cellae suae cohabitator*). Again we hear of the cell, but now it is clear that the monk has a roommate. Not only that: Columban expects that the roommates will converse. *Confabulari*, strictly speaking, means to swap stories. Columban probably frowned on that, but he must have known that if you put two compatible people together in a closed room, they will talk about what they please.

[198] "hold hands" (*tenuerit manum*). This reference to male bonding is rare in this Rule (I do not know of another instance) and also in the overall panoply of ancient monastic Rules. Yet Pachomius, the earliest monastic legislator, discusses homosexual issues in Pr 92–97. No doubt the reality had to be faced in every monastery.

[199] "Barred from prayer" (*ab oratione suspensus*). The ordinary term was *excommunicated*.

[200] "Lay friend" (*amicorum saecularium*). Apparently it was all right to visit with monks or even clerics. RB 53.23-24 also forbids any monk but the guestmaster to converse with outsiders.

[201] "Presume" (*praesumpserit*). In this sentence, presumption means neglect of permission. But this verb is also used by cenobitic legislators to register indignation at attitudes and behavior that are not sufficiently docile, e.g. RB 33.2, 6.

penance. If he has prevented anyone from carrying out a necessary deed,[202] a day of penance. Should one of the brothers exceed the norm of religious law[203] because of mental fervor, he deserves a day of privation. If, however, someone presumes, out of his own lack of fervor,[204] to prevent another from a legitimate act of fervor, a day of discipline.

[Spiritual censure proceeds to this point with similar offences[205] so that *the correction of the sinner made by the community*[206] might promote his salvation. Henceforth, he should be more prudent and diligent in correcting his way of life so as to be saved by the good God.

---

[202] "Carrying out a necessary deed" (*necessarii facti expletione*). There is no indication here of what precisely this deed or job or function might be. This kind of vagueness is not typical of this Rule.

[203] "Norm of religious law" (*legitimum religionis . . . modum*). An alternate reading would be "the legitimate norm of religion." An example of the violation of religious law today would be to receive communion many times a day. Here the appendix to Coen indicates that one can err by excess in regard to piety.

[204] "Out of his own lack of fervor" (*teporis sui gratia*). Literally, "his own tepidity." This prohibition seems to be the obverse of the preceding one. Now the problem is not an excess of fervor but a lack thereof. Sometimes common sense must try to temper too much enthusiasm, but here the fervor is "legitimate," so it must not be squelched by a cold lack of piety or cynicism.

[205] "Similar offences" (*in similibus admissis*). This seems to be a summary statement, probably of the whole bracketed section (starting in section XV, all of which comes from the Long Text). There are no more specific offences, at least none beginning with *si* ("if").

[206] "Made by the community" (*fit a pluribus*). In 2 Cor 2:6, where this passage first appears, it must refer to some kind of ecclesial censure. Walker thinks that here it "suggests public confession and open reproof in chapter." Thus the monastic chapter is relieved of the duty of deciding the extent of penances.

[Whoever mixes[207] in a quarrel must do seven days' penance. The brother who shows disdain[208] for his immediate superior[209] or curses the Rule[210] is to be expelled unless he says, "I am sorry for what I said." If he does not humble himself, he must do forty days of penance,[211] for he has been bitten by the serpent of pride.[212]

[The talkative should be punished[213] with silence, the restless with mildness, the greedy with fasting, the drowsy with

---

[207] "Mixes in a quarrel" (*rixam commiserit*). Both Walker and Vogüé have the fault here as "provoking" a quarrel. Undoubtedly it is worse to start a fight than just to participate in it, but I can see no warrant for that in the verb *commiserit*.

[208] "Shows disdain for" (*dispexerit*). Strictly speaking, the verb should be *despexerit*, for *dispicere* has no pejorative connotation. Both Vogüé (Règles, 138) and Walker (167) have *despise*, but that is an internal feeling that is not necessarily perceived by others. Unless it becomes public, it is not punishable.

[209] "Immediate superior" (*praepositum*). As we have seen in Coen VII and VIII, there was a tendency in this community to disrespect secondary superiors. These people usually represent monastic authority "at the coal face," but they lack the prestige of the abbot.

[210] "Curses the Rule" (*regulam blasfemaverit*). This verb usually refers to speech directed against God, and its use here lends a sacred aura to the monastic Rule. Yet the Rule is not sacrosanct (like the Bible), so I have avoided the English "blaspheme." *Blasfemare* is such a Judeo-Christian word that there is no entry for it in the OLD!

[211] "Forty days' penance" (*XL diebus peniteat*). It is hard to see how this penalty is meant, since the monk has just been expelled! This may be a clue that the expulsion was not meant literally. If it was, it would be the first place where this Rule has mentioned it. See the one disputed text with expulsion at the beginning of the addenda (see n. 166 above).

[212] "Bitten by the serpent of pride" (*superbiae morbo detinetur*). I have supplied "serpent" on the grounds that the monk must have been bitten by *something*. Of course, the venom may be that of pride personified.

[213] "Should be punished" (*damnandus est*). This is a rather unusual meaning for *damnare*. It implies that *authority* has judged these faults and sins and decided on certain fitting punishments. Noteworthy here

vigils, the proud with imprisonment,[214] the absentee with expulsion.[215] Let each one receive[216] exactly what he deserves, so that the just might live justly.[217] Amen.

[The rule of silence ought to be[218] kept very strictly in every place, and during every kind of work. Thus we will be cleansed

---

is the careful choice of a penalty meant to counter the fault. Up to this point, the penalties have almost been generic, not specific. As Walker notes, this paragraph is an exact copy of Paen A12, another collection of Columbanian penalties.

[214] "Imprisonment" (*carcere*). This is the first sign that Columban even had a prison! But prison cells became common in early medieval monasteries. For example, Caesarius's *Rule for Monks* 23 (sixth century) and *The Rule of Fructuosus* 16 (seventh century) both arrange for a prison cell. See Terrence Kardong, "People Storage: Mabillon's Diatribe against Monastic Prisons," CSQ 26, no. 1 (1991): 40–57, here 46–47.

[215] "Absentee with expulsion" (*distitutor*). *Distitutor* is an exceedingly rare word, which I found only in Jacobi Facciolati and Egidio Forcellini, eds., *Totius Latinitatis Lexicon*, 4 vols. (Padova, 1771), which claims that *distitutor* is the frequentative form of *distare*, "to be apart." Although it may seem redundant to threaten a wandering monk with expulsion, this may mean that the *distitutor* will be denied the possibility of return.

[216] "Receive" (*sentiat*). The basic meaning of *sentire* is "to feel" or "experience." It seems clear that this paragraph is a summary of the penalties that came before it (basically the whole document), so "what he deserves" must refer to penalties. The philosophy of punishment enunciated here is unexceptionable, but it is hardly adequate as an expression of Christian or monastic ethics, for it leaves no room for mercy. Statements like this have gained Columban a reputation for fierceness, but as a very successful monastic founder he must have known how to temper strict justice to the exigencies of community life.

[217] "Justly" (*iuste*). This could be either a purpose or a result clause. Presumably it refers to the exemplary nature of this whole penal system: it is meant to promote upright monastic behavior by strictly punishing faults.

[218] "Ought to be" (*censetur*). *Censeo* normally means to "think over" or "to estimate," but here it seems simply to lend a note of solemnity to the sentence. Vogüé uses it as I do, but Walker, 168, tries to give it its

of vice[219] as far as this is possible for human fragility. For we are accustomed to plunge into vice through our unbridled tongue.[220] Proper speech will help us to edify[221] our neighbors, for whom our Savior Jesus shed his holy blood. (This is much preferable to) ripping into them in absentia with our secret thoughts and idle words, for which we will surely have to pay the price before the Just Judge.

[I have thought it good to lay down these rules[222] for those who wish to take the high road leading to the heights of heaven.[223] They are also meant for those who, though they are

---

classical meaning, with poor results. But he is right that the "rule of silence" probably refers to Columban, Reg II.

[219] "Cleansed of vice" (*mundemur vitio*). This is the first (negative) result clause dependent on keeping the rule of silence, which is the main clause. Obviously, there is much more to moral purity than restraint of evil speech.

[220] "Plunge into vice" (*ad vitia praecipitari*). Here the author seems to locate all evil in the tongue, which cannot be justified by the Bible or any other ethical system. Nevertheless, other monastic texts such as RB Prologue take the same route. This and the following five sentences are all part of an enormous periodic sentence requiring extensive editing to arrive at a comfortable modern English rendition.

[221] "Edify our neighbors" (*aedificationem . . . proximorum . . . ore promamus*). Here is the second (positive) result of keeping the rule of silence. But notice that this clause is also followed by another long attack on sinful misuse of the tongue.

[222] "I have thought it good to lay down these rules" (*Haec . . . statui visa*). Ten English words to render three in Latin! This highly formal structure frames a long, complex sentence that I have bisected for the comfort of modern English readers.

[223] "High road leading to the heights of heaven" (*superum . . . iter tendens alti ad fastigia summa*). This formulation is reminiscent of the Epilogue (chap. 73) of Saint Benedict's Rule, except that Benedict does not claim that his Rule will lead one to highest heaven. For that, one needs to turn to Scripture and the Father for tutelage.

surrounded by the dark crimes of crude men,[224] mean to cleave
to the one God, who was sent to earth. They will certainly receive the reward of immortality, with a supreme joy that will
never cease.

[Here ends the Cenobitic Rule of Saint Columban the Abbot.
Thanks be to God.]

---

[224] "Dark crimes of crude men" (*rudiumque . . . flagitiis atro*). This
could refer to the rough Merovingian nobility that drove Columban and
some of his monks out of Francia. But no doubt life in Lombard Italy was
also very primitive in the seventh century. The word *atro* seems to be the
analogue of *alti* in the first member. It could refer to hell as opposed to
heaven. Why it is ablative case is not clear.

Penitential

(Paenitentiale)

Here begins the *Paenitentiale*.[1]

A1. True penance is to not commit faults that must be repented but to weep for faults that have been committed.[2] But because this principle is broken by many, not to say all,[3] out of weakness, we think it necessary to publish the measures of penance. Thus a system of these measures is handed

---

[1] This translation is based on the critical edition with facing-page English translation of G. S. M. Walker, *Sancti Columbani Opera* (Dublin: Dublin Institute for Advanced Studies, 1970), cited in footnotes below as Walker. Walker's emendations from the Long Text appear in the text below in brackets; my own clarifying insertions are in curly brackets. A French translation appears in *Règles et pénitentiels monastiques*, trans. Adalbert de Vogüé with Pierre Sangiani and Jean-Baptiste Juglar, Aux sources du monachisme colombanien vol. 2, Vie monastique 20 (Bégrolles-en-Mauges, France: Abbaye de Bellefontaine, 1988), cited below as Vogüé, Règles.

[2] "To not commit" (*non admittere*). This is a rare meaning of *admittere* but the only one that makes sense here. Both Walker and Vogüé have "not to commit," which looks more graceful but gives the wrong impression. Why would anyone think true repentance is to commit faults? The point is basic: repentance means to stop sinning (future) and to repent (past) sins. Vogüé, *Vie de Saint Columban*, 161, notes that this maxim is in fact quoted from Gennadius, De eccl dogm 54. Cassian, Conf 20.5.1 has a close version of the principle.

[3] "Not to say all" (*ut non dicam omnium*). This probably means that everybody breaks the law of penance. Perhaps the grammar could allow "I do not say all," but Christian theology would not.

down by the holy fathers[4] so that the length of the penances might be established according to the gravity of the faults.[5]

2. Therefore if someone sins in his heart by desiring[6] to kill a man or to fornicate or steal or to secretly eat and get drunk,[7] or certainly to strike someone or to desert or to do some such thing, and has planned in his heart to carry these things out,[8] he must repent of the greater sins for half a year, and for the lesser by forty days on bread and water.

3. If anyone is so carried away[9] as actually to commit these sins, that is, if he commits murder or sodomy, his penance is ten years.[10] If a monk fornicates only once, he should

---

[4] "Holy fathers" (*sanctis . . . patribus*). Presumably this refers to the whole Irish penitential tradition, some of which is listed by Vogüé in "Le 'Pénitentiel' de Columban et la Tradition Anterieure," in his *Histoire Littéraire du Mouvement Monastique dans l'Antiquité*, 11 vols. (Paris: Éditions du Cerf, 1991–2006), 10:253–66.

[5] I have omitted the word "also" (*etiam*), which seems to have led Walker astray: "so that in accordance with the greatness of the offences the length also of penances should be ordained" (169).

[6] "Desiring" (*concupierit*). Sins of desiring are not as serious of those of commission, even though Jesus condemns them in the Sermon on the Mount (Matt 5:21-28). Yet they can be very hard for individuals to judge in their own case: when do I pass from a mere velleity to full-blown desire?

[7] "Secretly eat and get drunk" (*clam commedere et inebriari*). These look like monastic sins; they are hardly on a par with murder or theft. "To desert" also looks like a monastic sin, probably referring to the community.

[8] "Has planned in his heart to carry these things out" (*paratus ad haec corde complenda*). Now it is no mere velleity but coldly premeditated sin.

[9] "So carried away" (*peccatis praevalentibus*), literally, "the sins overcoming." These are the sinful *thoughts* mentioned in the previous number. Now they are put into action (*facto*).

[10] "Sodomy" (*sodomiticum*). This rare word could stand here for all sorts of sins against the sixth commandment, but it probably means what it says: anal intercourse. The only Latin dictionary that even lists

do three years' penance.[11] If he does this more often, the penance is seven years. If a monk leaves the monastery and breaks his vows,[12] he must do 120 days[13] of penance if he repents and immediately returns. But if he only comes back years later, the penance is three years.

4. If anyone has committed theft, his penance is one year.

4a. The penance for perjury is seven years.

5. Should a monk strike his brother in a quarrel and draw blood, three years' penance.

6. Should one get drunk and vomit, or if he vomits the Host after overeating, forty days' penance.[14] But if he vomits the

---

this adjective is *Totius Latinitatis Lexicon*, ed. Jacobi Facciolati and Egidio Forcellini, 4 vols. (Padova, 1771), but the term is biblical and routinely used by ancient commentators.

[11] "Only once" (*semel tantum*). The idea here is not to minimize monastic fornication but to contrast a single occurrence with multiple occurrences. The latter are dealt with in the following sentence. Because the term *monachus* occurs in the apodosis ("he should do") and not the protasis, Walker has "he should do three years penance *as a monk*" (169). Vogüé, *Règles*, 162 interprets it as I do and thus implies that all this applies to monks.

[12] "Leaves the monastery" (*discesserit*). I have supplied "monk" and "monastery" because they are clearly implied. This penalty applies only to religious with a vow of stability.

[13] "120 days" (*tribus quadragesimis*), literally, three times forty days, or "quarantines" in archaic language. The word *quadragesima* meant not only forty days but forty days of *fasting*. As such, it could apply to Advent, Lent, or the forty days after Pentecost (Theodore of Tarsus, Penit XIV.1, quoted by Walker, 171, and Vogüé, *Règles*, 162). Ordinarily, however, *quadrigesima* referred to Lent.

[14] "The Host" (*sacrificium*). This is Columban's usual word for the Holy Communion bread. Since ancient Catholics fasted for hours before Communion (even from water), the gluttony must have occurred after Mass. But it must have occurred soon after Mass, with the Host as yet undigested.

Host because he is sick, seven days' penance.[15] If someone loses[16] the Sacred Host, he must do penance for a year.

7. If a monk pollutes himself,[17] he must do penance for a year if he is a junior.

8. Whoever knowingly bears false witness[18] must do two years of penance together with loss or restitution of the thing in question.

What precedes concerns serious lapses;[19] what follows is about minor offenses.

[15] "Because he is sick" (*per infirmitatem*). The person vomits through no fault of his own, yet he must still do light penance. This shows that all penance is not punitive, nor even educative; some penance is ritual gesture.

[16] "Loses" (*perdiderit*). It was the custom at that time, at least among the monks of Columban, to carry the Host in a pyx (*chrismal*) around one's neck for daily Communion. The community prayed Mass only on Sunday. For more on this issue, see Coen XV and nn. 34, 74.

[17] "Pollutes himself" (*se ipsum coinquinaverit*). Although this could refer to any kind of defilement, the long penance suggests moral pollution. And since it is clear that the monk does it to himself, the obvious implication is masturbation. Presumably a young monk would have more trouble with this problem than an old one, so the penance for the young is less (only a year!).

[18] "Bears false witness" (*falsum testimonium testificatus*). Although the ninth commandment can refer to any form of lying, here it looks like a legal context. The extraordinarily formal *testimonium testificatus* certainly suggests a courtroom. What a monk would be doing there is less clear, especially since it seems to be a fight over property. Yet medieval abbots spent a lot of time in court defending community property, and they sometimes used unsavory means to gain their ends.

[19] "Serious lapses" (*causis casualibus*). I base my translation entirely on Vogüé's *les cas de chutes* (Règles, 163). Walker has "ordinary cases," which better renders *casualibus* but makes no sense to me. The second half of the sentence, "minor offenses," suggests that the first half is about serious offenses. Actually *minutis morum inconditorum* means "minutiae of awkward behavior."

9. If a brother does something on his own without consultation,[20] or if he says, in a contradictory tone, "I won't do it!" or if he murmurs—if it is serious,[21] three days of privation; if it is trivial, one day. A word simply[22] spoken against the word of another is to be punished by fifty blows.[23] If it is intentionally done, however, it merits the imposition of a day of silence;[24] if a quarrel develops, one must do a week of penance.

10. The monk who slanders someone, or who listens to slander with pleasure, must spend three days in penitential privation; if the slander is against the superior, the slanderer must do a week of penance.

11. The brother who shows disdain for his immediate superior or curses the Rule is to be expelled unless he immediately says,[25] "I am sorry for what I said." If he does not humble himself, he must do forty days of penance, for he has been bitten by the serpent of pride.

----

[20] "Without consultation" (*sine interrogatione*). This is a bit different from "asking permission," as Vogüé has it. In a cenobitic community, much conflict can be avoided if people consult before undertaking a new initiative.

[21] "If it is serious" (*si grande sit*). But were we not just told this section was to be about trivial faults?

[22] "Simply" (*simpliciter*). Walker has *frankly*, and Vogüé has *sans réflexion*. Since the next sentence contains *ex intentione*, *simpliciter* must mean a spontaneous, and perhaps thoughtless, reaction. The idea here is to prevent quarrels by nipping contentious speech in the bud. See Coen XV.

[23] "Fifty blows" (*plagis*). In Coen XV, the same offense merits only six blows. In Coen XV the worse offense is *ex contentione* instead of *ex intentione*, but they probably mean about the same thing here.

[24] "A day of silence" (*silentii superpositione*). *Superpositio* does not specify the content of the penance but the length. Albert Blaise, *Dictionnaire latin-français des auteurs chrétiens* (Strasbourg: Le Latin Chrétien, 1954), s.v., says the penance "lasts to the next day (and not to such and such an hour)."

[25] "Immediately" (*confestim*). This word does not appear in the (almost) identical paragraph at the end of Coen XV.

12. The garrulous person ought to be punished by a regime of silence;[26] the agitator should be healed by gentleness,[27] the big eater by fasting, the drowsy one by vigils, the proud by imprisonment,[28] and the deserter by expulsion.[29] Let each one experience precisely the penalty he deserves, so he will live justly as a just man.[30]

B. The various kinds of faults ought to be healed by various penitential remedies.[31] For medical doctors also concoct

---

[26] "Regime of silence" (*taciturnitate*). Although *taciturnus* can mean either the fact of saying nothing or the habit of silence (see OLD, s.v. *taciturnus*), it is clear that the first is meant here. This paragraph is found verbatim in Coen XV, where I comment on it more extensively.

[27] "Healed by." All of the clauses in this series are based on *damnandus* ("ought to be punished"), but it is not very useful to translate it as "punished" in every case. In this case, it is not helpful to speak of an agitator's being punished by gentleness. I avoid this problem hereafter by simply leaving out the verb, as does the Latin.

[28] "Imprisonment" (*carcere*). At this point the pattern of correcting vices with opposed virtues breaks down, since incarceration has no obvious relation to pride. Of course, in the monastic world, where humility is exalted, pride is a heinous crime. As for the jail cells, many monasteries had them in the Middle Ages.

[29] "Expulsion" (*repulsione*). Expulsion is hardly the antithesis of desertion, but at a certain point the community has to be able to exclude very dysfunctional individuals. Medieval European society did not permit monks to leave the monastic life, so the monastic prison cell was invented.

[30] "Justly" (*iuste*). In the context of condign punishment (exactly fitting the crime), *just* has a limited meaning. But this sentence also functions as the finale and summary of section A of the *Paenitentiale*, so it probably has a broader meaning.

[31] "Ought to be healed." The Latin verb is the cryptic *facit* (makes), which leaves a good deal to be explained. The sentence is really an explanation of the whole Irish/Columbanian tendency to catalogue sins and penances. This eventually became one of the preoccupations of Roman Catholic moral theology.

the medicines[32] in various ways, depending on whether they are treating wounds, sicknesses, swelling, bruises, gangrene, blindness, fractures, or burns. So likewise spiritual doctors should use various kinds of cures to heal the wounds of the soul, sicknesses, faults, sorrows, pains, and infirmities. But few possess this gift, that is, to know how to cure all things at their root[33] and how to restore the weak to their original state of health. Therefore, let us propose a few things according to the traditions of the elders and according to our own partial understanding. "Our knowledge is imperfect, and our prophesying is imperfect."[34] First we will legislate on capital crimes,[35] which are also punished by the law itself.[36]

---

[32] "Medicines" (*medicamenta*). The following rather extensive list of possible human ailments does not mean that Columban had formal medical training. Before the advent of scientific medicine, everybody had to have a rudimentary knowledge of medical treatment. This would surely apply to religious superiors. See RB 27 and 28, where medical jargon abounds, without scientific significance.

[33] "At their root" (*ad purum*). This is an obscure phrase, but I think Vogüé, Règles, 164 must be closer to the mark with *à fond* than Walker, 173 is with "to a nicety." Apparently the idea is to deal with the real causes of sickness and not just surface symptoms.

[34] "Imperfect" (*ex parte*). Both Walker ("partial") and Vogüé (*partiellements*) hew closer to Jerome's Latin than to the Greek original of 1 Cor 13:9 (*ek merous*). It is clear, however, that Paul is simply talking about the limits of human knowledge, and so is Columban.

[35] "Capital crimes" (*capitalibus . . . criminibus*). Walker has "mortal sins," which is no doubt also true but seems an unnecessary interpretation. On the other hand, it is clear enough that most of the crimes listed below were not punished by death in any ancient society. Vogüé (Règles, 165 n. 15.1) thinks that the Law in this case is the Mosaic Law and not the civil law.

[36] "Punished by the law itself" (*legis animadversione plectantur*). Walker has "by the cognizance of the Law," but I prefer to stay with Vogüé's simpler locution. *Plectantur* is certainly a rare word for "punished."

1. If any cleric has committed murder and killed his neigh-bor, he is to do penance by ten years of exile.[37] After that time, let him be received back into his native land if he has done his penance properly on bread and water according to the testimony of the bishop[38] and another priest with whom he did penance and to whom he was committed. He must make satisfaction to the relatives[39] of the person he killed. He must take the place of their son by going to them and saying, "Whatever you want, I will do it." But if he does not satisfy the neighbor's relatives, he should never be received into his homeland, but be a wanderer or fugitive in the land like Cain.

2. If any [cleric] falls into the greatest ruin[40] by begetting a child, he must do seven years' penance as a pilgrim living on bread and water. He should then be restored to the altar[41] at the judgment of a priest.

Animadversio can mean just "notice," but it often refers to the scrutiny of the law into someone's affairs.

[37] "Exile" (*exul*). No doubt this meant "off the island" in the original Irish context. The term *patriam* (native land) could mean many things in seventh-century Continental Europe.

[38] "Bishop" (*episcopi*). Presumably this means the bishop (and priest) to whom he was entrusted in the place of exile. Notice that this process is handled by the church according to her own law. Eventually, secular governments took over the punishment of serious crime. A vestige of this system continued until Vatican II in the exile of clergy and monks to some monastery for problems such as alcoholism.

[39] "Relatives" (*parentibus*). I am not aware of any civil or canon law that makes such a demand. Some murderers, of course, do express real remorse to the family of the victim.

[40] "Greatest ruin" (*ruina maxima*). I doubt if Columban means that this is the greatest of all sins. Rather, it is worse for a priest to beget a child than just to have intercourse. To judge from Paen B8, the Irish clergy were required to take a vow of celibacy at ordination.

[41] "Altar" (*altario*). Walker, 173 has "restored to communion," but I think the obvious sense here is restoration to the priestly ministry.

3. If [a cleric] [42] fornicates as the Sodomites did, he must do ten years' penance. The first three years are to be done on bread and water, and for the next seven he is to abstain from wine and meat. He must live alone forever more. [43]

4. If anyone fornicates with women but no child results and the thing does not come to public notice, if he is a cleric, [44] he must do three years of penance; if a monk or deacon, five years; if a priest, seven years; if a bishop, twelve years.

5. Should anyone lie under oath, he must do seven years' penance, and he must never swear again. [45]

6. Should anyone destroy [46] by black magic, he must do three years' penance with bread and water by measure. And he should abstain from wine and meat for another three years. Then finally in the seventh year, let him be received back into Communion. But if someone uses magic to excite love [47] but kills no one, the penalty is a whole year on bread and water for a cleric. Half a year for a layman, two years for a deacon, three years for a priest. But if this causes a

---

[42] "Cleric." As in the previous number, I assume the reference is to a priest. Otherwise, we have to conclude that the ancient Irish church, or at least Columban, was afflicted with extreme homophobia. I have added the word *cleric* to some items that seem to demand it.

[43] "Forever more" (*in aeternum*). It appears to me that the issue is homosexual concubinage. The priest would be required to live as a hermit.

[44] "Cleric" (*clericus*). Here the term is used in its former technical sense of any Roman Catholic man who received tonsure and thus minor orders. In Paen B1 (above), *cleric* seems loosely to mean a priest. That is the way I used it in B2 and B3. Nowadays, Rome has abolished minor orders, but once upon a time Italy was full of men called clerics, who were church officials but not priests.

[45] "Swear" (*iuret*). This must refer to public testimony with legal implications. Apparently, one strike and you were out.

[46] "Destroy" (*perdiderit*) no doubt means "kill" here but does not exactly mean to murder. Still, the result is fatal.

[47] Probably this means the use of an aphrodisiac to further one's sexual agenda.

woman to miscarry,[48] one should add 240 days, lest he be guilty of murder.

7. If some cleric[49] steals something, that is, if he steals a cow or a horse, a sheep, or some other animal[50] from his neighbor, if this is his first or second offense he must first return the beast and then do penance for a whole year on bread and water. But if he does this regularly and cannot make restitution, he must do penance for three years on bread and water.

8. Should a cleric or a deacon or a clergyman of any grade who has been a layman with sons and daughters in the world after his conversion[51] know his servant woman[52] again and beget another child with her, he must know that he has committed adultery.[53] He has sinned no less than if he had been a cleric from his youth and sinned with another woman. For he has sinned after his vow,[54] after

---

[48] "Cause to miscarry" (*partum deceperit*), literally, to fool into giving birth. It appears that this miscarriage is an indirect result of the aphrodisiac mentioned above.

[49] "Cleric" (*clericum*). Here the term probably means anyone in holy orders, not one in minor orders. See n. 44 above.

[50] "Animal" (*animal*). The Irish clergy were typically farmers. Actually, there were almost no towns in ancient Ireland.

[51] "Conversion" (*conversionem*) seems a very strong word for the choice to become a clergyman. But given the fact that the Irish clergy had to take a vow of celibacy even at this early date, it was indeed a momentous step for anyone.

[52] "Servant woman" (*clientelam*). Another meaning given by the OLD is "devotee." Walker, however, has "wife," which is certainly plausible, given that the text has *iterum* (bis), thus indicating that this is the same woman who previously bore him children.

[53] "Adultery" (*adulterium*) and not just fornication (Paen B3), because when one has taken a vow before God, one is married to God. At least that seems to be the reasoning, which continues to find quite a bit of mileage today.

[54] "Vow" (*votum*). This is the reason the whole thing is taken so utterly seriously: one is lying to God.

he consecrated himself to God, and thus voided his vow. Therefore, let him do seven years' penance on bread and water.

9. If any cleric gets into a fight with his neighbor and spills blood, he must do a full year of penance. A layman must do forty days for the same offence.[55]

10. If someone has defiled himself with his own hand[56] or had sex with an animal, he must do two years' penance if he is not in clerical orders. But if he is in orders or religious vows, he must do three years' penance unless his age makes that impossible.

11. If any [cleric] desires[57] a woman but cannot have her because she won't have him, let him do a half-year of penance on bread and water. He must also abstain for a year from wine and meat, and also from communion at the altar.

[55] The fact that Columban demands nine times more penance for a fighting cleric than a layman shows that he thought it grossly inappropriate ecclesiastical behavior. Nevertheless, it must have happened often enough that he needed to mention it. Certain races, including the Scots-Irish, are famously quick to settle quarrels with their fists.

[56] "Defiled himself with his own hand" (*per se ipsum fornicaverit*). This is Walker's rendition, which seems unavoidable. Yet two or three years of penance for masturbation also seems unhinged, especially since it is placed on the same level as bestiality! If this draconian approach to sexuality was actually practiced by the Irish church, one wonders if many people practiced regular auricular confession.

[57] "Desires" (*concupiscit*), but this must involve an actual proposition; otherwise, the reference to rejection by a woman makes little sense. It would seem the offender must be a cleric, since proposition (and rejection!) is an ordinary part of courtship. Could it be that these fanatical views of sexual purity had a part in shaping the core of Catholic morality in the European church? It must be remembered that these lists were the earliest form of a confessor's manual for private confession.

12. If anyone loses the Sacred Host,[58] he must do a year's penance. If he vomits it because of drunkenness or gluttony [59] and carelessly casts it aside, he must do 120 days' penance on bread and water. But if this happens because of illness, seven days of penance are enough.

    But these things have been said in a random manner[60] about clerics and monks. The rest concerns laymen.

13. Whoever commits a homicide, that is, kills his neighbor, must spend three years in exile and unarmed,[61] living on bread and water. After three years, he should return home and pay his due of duty and piety to the family of the slain man.[62] After he has made satisfaction, he can be joined to the altar at the judgment of the priest.

---

[58] "Sacred Host" (*sacrificium*). Not only did the early Christians preserve the eucharistic bread after its consecration at Mass, but they also carried it (if they so wished) in a pyx hanging around their neck. Needless to say, this could sometimes result in accidents. Nowadays, Catholics are not permitted to indulge in such practices.

[59] "Drunkenness or gluttony" (*ebrietatem aut voracitatem*). This is also a form of carelessness, but now the Sacred Host has been ingested. Communion can also be desecrated by unwise drinking and eating afterward. This was also probably one of the reasons the Catholic Church used to require strict fasting regulations before Communion.

[60] "In a random manner" (*mixtim*). Walker has "collectively," which has much to be said for it, since Paen B1–12 do include both groups. Yet all twelve numbers cannot pertain to clerics and monks since they are explicitly mentioned only in some numbers.

[61] "Unarmed" (*inermis*). A curious glimpse into life in medieval Ireland. The assumption, of course, is that everybody went about armed; not to do so would be considered a hardship. Moreover, someone who has committed one homicide was probably deemed a good candidate for another. Notice that the church is dealing with a crime of this magnitude; apparently there was virtually no civil law.

[62] In Paen B1, the duty to make personal amends to the family of the victim was spelled out in rather dramatic form. Perhaps it was

14. If any layman fathers a child on another man's wife, that is, commits adultery by violating his neighbor's bed,[63] he must do three years' penance. During that time, he must abstain from juicy foods and also from his own wife.[64] He must pay the price of chastity[65] to the husband of the violated wife. Then let his guilt be cleansed by the priest.[66]

15. But if a layman fornicates in the Sodomite manner, that is, sins with a man by means of feminine intercourse,[67] he must do seven years of penance. The first three years must be done with bread and water and salt, with dry fruit[68] from the garden. The remaining four years he must avoid wine and meat. Thus let his guilt be removed from him, and so let him be joined to the altar.[69]

16. If a layman fornicates with unmarried women, that is, widows or girls, he must do one year's penance if it is with a widow. If it is with a girl, he must do penance for two years and pay her parents the price of her humiliation.[70]

---

expected that a priest would be more articulate in expressing remorse than a layman.

[63] "Bed" (*toro*). This unusual term for bed is derived from the word for *thong*. Thus the marriage bed is a frame with a web of thongs strung on it.

[64] "Own wife" (*propria uxore*). So the innocent wife must share the penalty of the guilty husband.

[65] "Price of chastity" (*praetium pudicitiae*) was no doubt a standard fine in Irish society.

[66] "Cleansed" (*abstergatur*). No doubt through the sacrament of penance.

[67] "Feminine intercourse" (*coitu femineo*). Perhaps this refers to the passive partner in the sexual transaction, but more likely it is simply a sexist slur on both parties. Walker has "effeminate," which is an odd thing to say about an action involving no woman.

[68] "Fruit" (*fructibus*) can refer to either fruit or vegetables: whatever the garden produces.

[69] "Joined to the altar" (*iungatur altario*), that is, restored to communion after seven years of excommunication.

[70] "The price of her humiliation" (*humiliationis eius praetio*). This is a technical term, defined in the *Ancient Laws of Ireland*, ed. W. Neilson

But if he has no wife and fornicates with a virgin, let her become his wife, if her parents agree. But they must both do penance for a year before their marriage.

17. If some layman has sex with a donkey, he must do a year of penance if he is a married man. If he has no wife, his penance is half a year. Moreover, if a married man commits masturbation,[71] he must do penance.

18. Should some layman or woman smother[72] their child, they must do penance on bread and water for a year. And they should abstain from wine and meat for another two years. Only then may they be admitted to Communion[73] at the judgment of a priest, and then such a husband may lawfully use his [marriage] bed.[74] For penance should not be halved.[75]

19. If a layman commits a theft, that is, if he steals an ox or a horse or a sheep or any animal belonging to his neighbor,[76] if he does it once or twice, he should first compensate

---

Hancock, 6 vols. (Dublin: Alexander Thom; London: Longman, Green, et al., 1865–1901), 1:133, as a "shekel and a marriage gift." See Walker, 177 n. 2.

[71] "Masturbation" (*propriis membris se ipsum violaverit*). This translation assumes that *membris* refers to the hand, as an ablative of agent. But *membrum* can also mean genitals, as a dative of reference.

[72] "Smother" (*oppresserit*). It is not clear to me whether this is a case of deliberate infanticide. In ancient times, families often slept in one big bed. It was possible for small children to be inadvertently lain upon and smothered, especially during parental intercourse. See 1 Kgs 3:19.

[73] "Admitted to Communion" (*altario . . . iungantur*). As before, "joined to the altar" is the literal meaning.

[74] "Use his [marriage] bed" (*suum torum . . . cognoscat*). Apparently the sinner was expected to abstain from intercourse for three years.

[75] "Penance should not be halved" (*demedia namque paenitentia non debet esse*). The meaning of this enigmatic saying is that the penitent is barred from both Communion and intercourse.

[76] This number is a good illustration of how utterly rural medieval Ireland was. In such a place, "theft" meant theft of livestock. Before the invention of the barbed-wire fence, rustling was a serious problem,

his neighbor for his loss and then spend 120 days doing penance on bread and water. If, however, he is a habitual thief and cannot make restitution, he must do penance for one year plus 120 days and then promise never to do it again.[77] Thus let him return to Communion on Easter of the second year, that is, after two years. But first he must give alms to the poor from his labor and a banquet[78] to the priest who judged his penance. So the guilt of his evil habit is remitted.[79]

20. If a layman commits perjury, especially out of greed, he must sell all his goods and give them to the poor. He must convert wholeheartedly to the Lord, entirely reject the world, and receive the tonsure,[80] and serve God unto death in the monastery. But if he perjures himself not out of greed but from fear of death,[81] he must do three years' exile

---

especially if times were hard. For most people at that time, the loss of an ox or a horse was catastrophic.

[77] The penance for habitual theft, to the point beyond restitution, seems comparatively mild. But we should remember that this society probably had no jails. Since the *Paenitentiale* was a manual for confessors, not a law book, the part about promising "never again" makes sense. After all, every penitent in private confession makes the same promise. But surely in that peasant society habitual theft, especially of cattle, was more roughly dealt with!

[78] "Banquet" (*epula*). Walker, 177 n. 3 says that a similar feast is mentioned by Finnian of Clonard, PenF 35. Walker adds that baptismal and marriage feasts, as a fee to the clergy, occur in *Ancient Laws of Ireland*, 3:19.

[79] "Guilt" (*culpa*). Unfortunately the evil habit itself is not so quickly or easily eradicated. For that, counseling and hard moral labor are required.

[80] "Tonsure" (*tundatur*). No dictionary at my disposal gives this meaning, which comes from Walker. The standard rendition is to beat or pummel, which does not work very well here.

[81] One is taken aback by these tremendous penalties against perjury, even in the face of death. Perhaps the oath was especially sacred in what was primarily a verbal culture. Every society will defend its dearest values with stern penalties.

unarmed and on bread and water. He should do two more years of abstinence from wine and meat. Then, offering a life for his own life, that is, freeing a servant or maid-servant from the yoke of slavery and giving lavish alms for two years (he can licitly use all foods except meat during this time), he may communicate again after the seventh year.

21. If some member of the laity sheds blood in a brawl,[82] or wounds or incapacitates his neighbor, he must make recompense for as much harm as he has done. But if he is unable to pay the fine, he should do his neighbor's work as long as he is laid up. He should call in a doctor, and after his healing he must do forty days' penance on bread and water.

22. If any layman drinks himself drunk, or eats or drinks to the point of vomiting, he must do a week of penitence on bread and water.

23. If a layman wishes to commit adultery or fornication with a married woman, and if he desires his neighbor's wife but cannot have his way with her because she won't have him[83]—but he is quite prepared to fornicate—he must confess his sin to the priest and do forty days' penance on bread and water.

24. If a layman eats or drinks near the pagan temples,[84] if he does this out of ignorance, he must promise to never do it

---

[82] "In a brawl" (*per scandalum*). This is a rare meaning for *scandalum*, but it does occur also in Gregory of Tours, Mir 2.5. See Blaise, *Dictionnaire*, s.v. s*candalum*, 4. But Du Cange, s.v. *scandalum*, cites *only* medieval usages of the word meaning quarrel.

[83] Perhaps Columban goes to some length to make his point here because some people cannot easily grasp the point that when it comes to moral culpability, intention counts for a lot, if not for everything.

[84] "Near the pagan temples" (*iuxta fana*) could also be translated "according to the pagan temples," but Walker, 179 has *near*, and he is

again. He must also spend forty days' penance on bread and water. But if he does this out of contempt, that is, after the priest has advised him that it is a sacrilege, and he eats[85] at the table of demons—if he does this or repeats it only[86] because of the vice of gluttony—he must do 120 days' penance on bread and water, but if he does it to worship the demons or to honor their images, he must do three years' penance.

25. If a layman communicates, out of ignorance, with the followers of Bonosus or other heretics,[87] he must stand among the catechumens at Mass, separated from other Christians for forty days. He must expiate the guilt of his unclean association for another eighty days in the lowest order of Christians, that is, in the order of penitents.[88] If, however, he has done this out of contempt,[89] that is, after the priest has denounced the sect and warned him not to befoul himself

---

probably right. *Fanum* can be any temple, but Blaise, *Dictionnaire*, s.v. *fanum*, says it usually means pagan temple. Apparently the Irish Christians avoided these places—if they knew where they were.

[85] "Eats" (*communicaverit*) could also be translated as "shares." The point here is not to call what went on in pagan temples "communion" in the sense of the Catholic Eucharist. But ancient people all considered a shared meal a lot more than juxtaposition of the participants.

[86] "Only" (*tantum*) is used here not in an absolute sense but in a relative one: gluttony is bad, but not as bad as idolatry.

[87] "Bonosus" (*Bonosiacis*). According to the *Oxford Dictionary of the Christian Church*, s.v. *Bonosus*, this bishop of Sardica denied the perpetual virginity of the Blessed Virgin Mary. His great offense, however, was to persist in his error after being condemned by a church council. Then he formed a sect that continued down to the seventh century.

[88] "Order of penitents" (*inter paenitentes*). Columban makes a clear distinction between catechumens and penitents. The former were not permitted access to Holy Communion, whereas the latter were.

[89] In this number, as in the former (24), Columban seems to want to make sure people understand that intention is the key determinant in assessing moral guilt. Obviously contempt is a sign of bad will.

by communing with it, he must do penance for a full year, plus 120 days. He must also abstain from wine and meat for two years, and so let him be restored to communion by the imposition of hands by the Catholic bishop.

Finally, we must add some minor ordinances concerning monks.

26.   If someone has left the compound[90] gate open at night, he must fast for a whole day.[91] If he does this in the daytime, he receives twenty-four blows if others were not following behind.[92] If someone has gone out immediately before him,[93] he still must fast for a whole day.

27.   If a monk seeks cleanliness[94] but bathes alone, he must do a whole day of penance. But if he does this standing before the brothers in the correct way,[95] except where there

---

[90] "Compound" (*vallum*). Probably, Columban is thinking about his own monasteries, situated in the forests of medieval France and Italy. They were like rural estates, with many small buildings enclosed in a surrounding palisade (*vallum*). African monasteries are still built this way.

[91] "Fast for the whole day" (*superpositione*). This technical term does not specify the kind of penance, just the length. It could also have been a day of silence. See Coen IV n. 39.

[92] Obviously, one would leave the door open for those following right after. Apparently they could not risk leaving the gates of the stockade open for any length of time. Wild animals or brigands were a constant worry.

[93] "If someone has gone out immediately before him" (*Si quis hunc ipsum absolute praecesserit*). Walker has, "If someone has gone out immediately in front of himself," which makes no sense to me. Maybe the Irish use of "himself" is a stumbling block to me here? My conjecture is that even though another person has left the gate open in front of someone, the second person must still close it behind himself.

[94] "Cleanliness" (*lumentum*). Walker, 181, translates this word as "bath," which it must mean in the next number. But here I think it is less specific. Of course, light (*lumen*) and cleanliness are not far apart.

[95] "Correct way" (*licito*). Apparently the brothers had to wash together, but in a modest way. Exactly how they accomplished this is not so clear to me.

is need to wash the dirt more fully, he should be corrected with twenty-four blows.

28. But if someone sitting in the bathtub[96] uncovers his knees or arms, without the necessity of washing off dirt, he must not wash for six days, that is, the shameless[97] washer shall not wash his feet until the following Sunday. It is all right, however, for a monk standing apart[98] to wash his feet. An old monk, however, may have his feet washed by someone else as he stands in public.

29. Every Sunday, before the sermon, all the members are to gather together, except for certain necessities.[99] That way, no one will be missing from the number of those listening to the teaching except the cook or the doorkeeper. And even these latter should do their best to be present when the gospel bell is heard.[100]

---

[96] "Bathtub" (*lumento*). Now the term must refer to some kind of receptacle in which the bather can sit. This is a rare word that is not found in standard dictionaries, even ones covering the Middle Ages (Du Cange; Facciolati and Forcellini).

[97] "Shameless" (*inhonestus*). Exactly why the exposure of the knees and arms should be a source of shame is a mystery to me, but every age and place has its own sensibilities. When one lives in unheated buildings, there is little incentive to disrobe. Apparently these monks washed their feet only on Sunday, whether they needed it or not.

[98] "Apart" (*secrete*). The extreme modesty of the Irish monks seems to have made even the washing of feet a touchy point. This is something foreign to the Rule of Benedict (see RB 35 and 53).

[99] "Except for certain necessities" (*exceptis certis necessitatibus*). The author will go on to mention the cook and the porter. But in an average monastery, there are many other duties (e.g., harvesting) that can keep people away from church. No ideal monastic schedule can keep all these demands at bay.

[100] "Gospel bell" (*tonitruum evangelii*). Presumably this refers to the summons to the sermon (*praedicationem*) that must have been given before Mass. This kind of bizarre scheduling was not unusual before Vatican II, and it always threatens the integrity of the Mass.

30. Confession must be made carefully,[101] especially of bad thoughts,[102] before going to Mass. Otherwise, one might approach the altar unworthily, that is, having an unclean heart. For it is better to wait until the heart is healed[103] and free from scandal and envy[104] than boldly to approach the judgment of the throne. For the altar is Christ's throne; his body with his blood is there to judge those who approach unworthily. Therefore, just as we must beware of capital[105] and fleshly sins before we communicate,[106] so too we must refrain from and be cleansed from interior vices and sicknesses of a torpid[107] spirit. {We must do this before we approach[108]} the assembly of true peace and the union of eternal salvation.[109]

[101] "Must be made" (*dari . . . praecipitur*). Literally, "it is commanded that. . . ." This unusually formal construct may have some special connotation, but I do not know what it is. Perhaps it is a reference to Irish church legislation.

[102] "Bad thoughts" (*commotionibus animi*). Walker, 181 has "mental disturbances," but these are not sinful in themselves. Therefore, I take this as a euphemism for carnal thoughts, especially those that are dwelt on.

[103] "Healed" (*sanum fuerit*), that is, by the sacrament of confession. If it were not for the previous sentence, one might think the advice here is simply to let the passions subside before communicating.

[104] "Scandal and envy" (*scandalo ac invidia*). This proves that not all the "bad thoughts" were of a sexual nature.

[105] "Capital" (*capitalibus*). This may refer to the seven Capital Sins, but it could simply mean major sins. Since the text goes on to contrast interior sins with sins of passivity, this probably refers to blatant public sins—which would be scandalous for a monk.

[106] "Before we communicate" (*antequam communicandum sit*). I suspect that the correct form would be *communicetur*. As it is, we have the curious spectacle of two passive periphrastics in the same sentence.

[107] "Torpid" (*languentis*). Maybe this means sins of omission? Walker has "sicknesses of the drooping spirit," which looks like the famous monastic sin of *acedia*.

[108] My addition to break up this enormous, awkward sentence.

[109] "Union of eternal salvation" (*aeternae salutis conpaginem*). I take this to refer to Mass or Holy Communion. Although *conpago* can mean any gathering (*con+paganus* [villager]), the topic here is sacramental purity. "Assembly of true peace" is a synonymous expression.

Rule of Walbert
(Regula Walberti)[1]

Chapter 1. What Kind of Person the Abbess Ought to Be.[2]

1. The abbess of the monastery ought to be noble, not so much in parentage as in wisdom and sanctity.[3]
2. Thus she should not contradict by her actions the conferences she crafts[4] to instruct souls by pious[5] learning,
3. for subjects imitate the form of acted example more than they obey[6] teaching.

---

[1] This translation is based on the Latin text given in Lucas Holste, *Codex Regularum* (Graz, Austria, 1759; reprint, 1957), 393–404. I was greatly aided by the French translation and notes of Lazare de Seilhac and M. Bernard Saïd, trans., "Règle de Walbert," in *Règles Monastiques au Féminin*, Vie Monastique 33 (Bégrolles-en-Mauges: Abbaye de Bellefontaine, 1996), 55–95. I cite this work in the footnotes as Seilhac and Saïd.

[2] This title resembles that of RB 2, yet the word order is inverted: *Abbatissa monasterii qualis esse debeat.*

[3] As a matter of fact, the monastery for which Walbert wrote this Rule (Eboriac) was governed by a daughter of the nobility. For that matter, so were most of the medieval monasteries of women and men.

[4] "Crafts." *Lucubrat* literally means to write deep into the night. The general meaning is to labor over a manuscript. Apparently superiors at Luxeuil and other Columbanian monasteries were expected to put serious work into their conferences.

[5] "Pious" is one of the meanings given by Albert Blaise (*Dictionnaire latin-français des auteurs chrétiens* [Strasbourg: Le Latin Chrétien, 1954]) for *justus*. None of the other meanings seems to fit this context.

[6] "Obey," literally, "attune their ears to" (*aurem accommodant*). The point here is not just listening but obedience.

4. She must join holy works to holy words, so that whoever imitates the teaching of her words will also imitate the education[7] of her works,

5. for if her acts contradict any of her words, her teaching will have no effect.[8]

6. So therefore, let her be distinguished in speech and deed so that her action squares with her talk and her talk with her actions.[9] She should be adorned[10] with the flower of continence and chastity, so that everybody can praise her and she can be imitated as an example for the desires of everyone.

7. Let her be decked out with the benevolence of charity so as to gladden the hearts of all the faithful.[11]

8. In regard to the care of pilgrims and guests, she should be directly involved.[12] In regard to the care of the sick, she

---

[7] "Education" renders *cultum*. Another possible meaning could be "fruit," as we find in Columban's Reg II.1 n. 7. Indeed, *fructus* appears in the very next verse as *fructus vocis*.

[8] In this sentence, I have simplified the florid Latin: *fructus vocis non obtinere valeat effectum.*

[9] There are overtones of the Rule of Benedict throughout this section on the abbess. Thus RB 2.12 tells the abbot that his deeds must match his words. And RB 19.7 wants our minds to be in harmony with our voices at the Divine Office.

[10] "Adorned" renders *compta*, the participle of *comere*, to make tidy or beautiful.

[11] This verse is reminiscent of RB 64.7-19, which presents the abbot as generally benevolent and very pastoral.

[12] The next three sentences all begin with *Erga* (In regard to), followed by a genitive and an accusative. At the end of the sentence comes an imperative. "Directly involved" renders *praesto*, probably meaning that the abbess should not leave the ministry of hospitality entirely to her subordinates.

should be full of care.[13] In regard to aid for the poor and the weak, she should be very generous.[14]

9. She should correct the listlessness of the negligent so as to lead flighty and tired minds back to religious fervor.

10. She should distribute the gifts of goodness in a merciful manner. But she should not feed the fires of sin through an excess of goodness.[15]

11. So she should be good to the good by means of reward but bad to the bad with the whip, which must be handled carefully[16] according to the prayer of the psalmist, which says, "Lord, teach me goodness, discipline, and knowledge" [Ps 119:66].

12. In both cases, the abbess must be careful not to foster vice in the hearts of her subjects through excess kindness, nor to spoil by harsh correction or by too much austere discipline[17] those things that should have been healed by a gentle reproach.

[13] One is reminded of RB 36, where the abbot is told to see that the sick are being properly taken care of.

[14] "Very generous" translates *opulenta*. The charity of the monastery should not be stingy. Actually, medieval monasteries were the primary sources of aid for the poor and the weak. There were virtually no other social services. Thus the total suppression of the monasteries of England by Henry VIII left the poor of the country destitute.

[15] Perhaps this is an overinterpretation of *facinorum fomenta non nutria*, but RB 2.23-28 urges the superior to deal harshly with the first signs of evil.

[16] "Carefully" renders *scientiam* from Ps 119:66. This unusual meaning is an attempt to interpret the idea of whipping in a "knowledgeable" way.

[17] Harsh correction or too much austere discipline seems to be pleonastic, although correction and discipline are not exactly the same thing.

13. She should approach the careless with such gentle persuasion that she effects a cure by somehow applying an antidote to their troubles.[18]
14. Let her offer these things[19] by exhorting those of healthy morals to bring to completion and improvement what they have begun to do,
15. for it profits nothing to have begun if they do not strive to persevere in the good work they have begun.
16. Therefore she should consider herself mother of as many souls as she has daughters under her care.
17. Likewise she will know how to restrain the vices of all according to the habits of all.[20]
18. Let there be such providence toward all that neither benevolence remove discipline nor discipline remove benevolence.[21] She must take care of all so that from the profit of all she may receive the reward of interest.[22]
19. Thus when she has been snatched from the corruption of this present life, she may receive a reward for as much labor as she offered as help to the defenses for conquering the enemy.[23]

---

[18] The Latin is *ut eorum saniei antidote quodammodo medendo curam infundat*. I am not sure I have captured all the nuances of this phrase. As far as I can see, *antidote*, *medendo*, and *curam* are essentially synonyms. Like many noblemen and monastic superiors, Walbert probably knew some rudimentary medicine.

[19] "These things" (*ea*) probably refers to the cures of the previous verse.

[20] I take this to mean that the abbess must know the manner of life of the whole group if she is to prevent and eliminate bad habits.

[21] "Remove." *Locum tollere* seems clear enough, but why the objects should be in the dative case escapes me. The overall need for both strictness and gentleness is no doubt the thrust, as it has been throughout this chapter on the superior.

[22] "Interest" is but one of the possible meanings of *merces*; I chose it because it seems to jibe with "profit" (*profectu*).

[23] The last phrase is obscure. "Offered" (*praebuit*) seems to refer to past action by the abbess. Presumably the enemy (*inimicum*) in question is the devil. But the whole idea is unclear to me.

Chapter 2. What the Prioress of the Monastery Ought to Be Like.

1. To be named prioress of the monastery, a nun should be mature[24] in her manners more than in age.

2. Many accrue a surfeit of years,[25] but the shame of an idle life reduces them to the immaturity of infancy through lukewarmness.

3. So the qualities of a good prioress are being serious in manner, skillful in speech, strong in character, alert to the needs of others,[26] vigorous in movement,

4. dutiful in correction,[27] moderate in discipline, chaste in her action,[28] not extreme in her lifestyle,[29] evenhanded in her dealings with the sisters, splendid in her humility,[30] patient, gentle, not restless,[31] not given to anger,

[24] Literally "aged" (*senili*) but here it must refer to maturity, not years.

[25] "Many accrue a surfeit of years" renders *Multas etenim prolixitas annorum attolit.* Thus the grammar is backward: "A surfeit of years adds up for many."

[26] *Consideratione vigil.* Admittedly a free translation, but at least it takes account of both words.

[27] "Dutiful" could also be "gentle." *Pia* has a wide range of meanings. I chose "dutiful" over "gentle" because the next phrase is about gentleness.

[28] *Actu casta* could also mean "objective" as opposed to "partisan." But I have settled on the ordinary meaning for *casta,* namely, "chaste."

[29] "Not extreme" renders *sobria.* English "sober" is no longer understood this way.

[30] *Humilitate ornata* is actually a nice oxymoron, since *ornata* implies a certain flair, but *humilitate* wants to keep its head down.

[31] *Non turbulenta* ("not restless") is also found in RB 64.16 concerning the abbot. In fact, many of the requirements given here for the prioress are reminiscent of RB 64 on the abbot. *Non turbulenta* probably comes from Isa 42:4, the highly significant Song of the Servant.

5. not scarred by the vice of pride and arrogance, not a free spender,[32] not too talkative,[33] but distinguished in every act of religion,

6. who knows how to prop up those who are fainting and fire up the listlessness of the lukewarm.

7. Over her the abbess should be confident that[34] she will never deviate from her orders.

8. But subject in all things and restrained by the order of the seniors, she should do nothing contrary to the will of the abbess, nor order such to be done. She should ask the abbess's permission for everything, according to the text, "Ask your father and he will tell you, your elders and they will guide you."[35]

9. One must always ask that the souls of the subjects differ in no way from the counsel of the seniors;[36] the sheep should not go aside from the will of the shepherd.

10. For Roboam spurned the advice of the seniors but followed that of the young men.[37]

11. The truth of Scripture tells what an occasion for loss this was for Roboam, who lost control of eleven tribes. He

---

[32] "Free spender" could be more soberly translated "not wasteful." *Prodiga* is a term from Benedict's treatise on the cellarer (RB 31.1, 12), which is based on RB 64.16.

[33] *Non garrula* summarizes RB 6 on taciturnity. Also, RB 7.61 quotes Sextus, Enchir 145: "The wise man is known by his few words."

[34] Strictly speaking, the *ut* clause here is probably one of result, but it seems to work better as a noun clause.

[35] Deut 32:7. The mention of *majores* here may seem to undercut my argument (see n. 36), but I think the reference is to the abbess of the previous sentence.

[36] "Seniors" (*seniores*). One wonders how to understand this term here. Generally speaking, all the superiors are "seniors," as are all elderly monks. But in the Benedictine system, the abbot is above the seniors, and so are the deans. Perhaps the Columbanian system was different?

[37] See 1 Kgs 12:8.

avoided a cruel death but spent the rest of his life under great pressure with but one tribe under him.[38]

12. Indeed, the prioress ought to provide for all necessities of body as well as soul. Thus she should offer help[39] for present necessity and by constantly urging arouse the hearts of the subjects to express praise for the Creator.

13. She should promote to a higher position of honor those who are humble subjects on account of Christ.[40] But she should demote with the whip of punishment[41] to a lower rank those who puff themselves up.

14. Let her take such good care of the things of the monastery, whether vessels or bedding, that they in no way be found darkened by the shadows of negligence.[42]

15. Thus when she has applied all the care of holy labor, may she receive the reward of her labor from the Almighty.

16. Every Saturday after the Hour of None, the prioresses should visit the beds of all the sisters, whether they be seniors or juniors. They should investigate their possible

---

[38] Roboam paid a terrible price for his foolish stubbornness: the loss of the northern tribes plus Benjamin. Actually, Roboam's sin was not in consulting the young men; it was to reject all advice that went against his own perverse inclinations.

[39] "Help" (*subsidia*) no doubt means material aid "of body" (see previous sentence). The next sentence takes care of spiritual needs.

[40] The notion that a prior can promote another monk is not something mentioned by Saint Benedict in his chapter on the prior (RB 65). Indeed, Walbert seems to entrust the prioress with many of the powers found in Benedict's abbot and cellarer.

[41] "The whip of punishment" (*castigationis flagella*). It is not clear to me whether this phrase was meant literally or not. The Columbanian monks certainly used corporal punishment, and I do not doubt that the women did as well. But the context here seems to be demotion of rank, a subtler but longer-lasting punishment.

[42] "Darkened by the shadows of negligence" is a somewhat free rendering of *negligentiae tenebris . . . fuscata*. Whether this refers to physical dirt is questionable.

negligence,[43] or if something has been found stored illicitly and without leave.[44]

17. Likewise they should inspect the beds of all by torchlight after Compline. That way they may recognize those whose senses are awakening and who are tiring of prayer.[45]

18. This should be done at all the Night Offices[46] so they may know who rises for the Office out of zeal and who out of tepidity. Those whom they find culpable of tardiness and laziness they should admonish or whip, as befits their fault or age.

Chapter 3. The Portresses of the Monastery.

1. The portresses or doorkeepers of the monastery ought to be sisters who, at a mature age, build up the treasure of all, and of such an age that the world no longer means much to them.[47] They should no longer desire present baubles.

---

[43] *Faciant propter earum negligentias inquirendas.* Although the Latin grammar here is a bit murky, the meaning is plain enough. In RB 55.15-16, the abbot inspects the mattresses.

[44] *Sine commeatu.* The term usually means provisions or food, but it can mean permission. In the RB, and for all early cenobites, storage of personal items was forbidden. Moreover, they had no place to hide them—except in the mattress.

[45] "Awakening" and "tiring" translate *expergiscentem* and *tepescentem*. They are a good example of Walbert's exceptional vocabulary: he was a learned man. It does seem, however, that he was a bit of a zealot. Yet we should also recall that he was a young man when he wrote this Rule. A verse like this smacks more of the rigor of Columban than the balance of Benedict.

[46] The term used here for the Offices is *cursus*. The Columbanian monks rose at midnight and again early in the morning (Reg VIII).

[47] This version depends on the unusual translation of *merces* as "treasure," not "reward." The key element here is the old age of the portress. This may be based on RB 66.1, which wants the porter to be a *senex sapiens*.

2. But they should cling to their Creator with all the affection of their heart, saying, "It is good for me to cling to God, to place my hope in God" [Ps 73:28].
3. For what could they desire from present ornaments who have despised passing things and begun to love Christ? By mental contemplation they have understood that the highest good consists in remaining in Christ.
4. They should be very solid in their religious identity: [48] "Turn aside our eyes lest they see vain things; make us live in your ways" [Ps 119:37].
5. Let them show such an example to those arriving that the name of the Lord might be glorified by the strangers standing outside.[49] This is in accord with the Lord's saying: "So let your light shine before men that they may see your good works and glorify your Father who is in heaven" [Matt 5:16].[50]
6. So let them prepare within {for themselves}[51] the gain of reward from their sister companions, since it is in the name of all that they take care of their external needs.[52]

---

[48] "Religious identity." I have taken great liberties with *mentis suae statu* because I think more is at stake here than just mental balance. As the following verse from Ps 119:37 shows, the portress needs to be invulnerable to various kinds of flattery and corruption.

[49] There may well be here some influence from RB 66.3: "As soon as anyone knocks or a poor person cries out, he should respond 'Thanks be to God!' or 'Bless me!'" Note the joy at the arrival of the guest.

[50] The primary role of the portress is to offer hospitality, but this verse from the Sermon on the Mount refers to the Christian as witness to the Kingdom of heaven. Sometimes visitors meet no one *but* the portress, so the impression of the monastery they carry away derives mainly from her.

[51] As is true here, my additions are marked by inclusion in curly brackets.

[52] An alternative version for this difficult sentence might be, "Let them thus prepare the gain of a reward within their companions while they in

7. Thus they should be cautious in their manners with humility, the mother of virtues,[53] showing the soft words of perfect patience in their agreeable conversation.[54]

8. They should never converse with one or two without a third party as a witness.

9. They should never raise their eyes to look intently at laymen or clerics.[55] Let them have the necessary conversations with the face humbly lowered and eyes cast down.

10. Among all their duties, they have care of the poor, pilgrims, and guests, for in them Christ is received. He himself said, "Whatever you have done to these little ones you did it to me" [Matt 25:50].

11. Without the permission of the abbess they should absolutely not give anything out, minister to anyone,[56] or receive anything from outside.

12. Whatever they receive in the way of outside gifts and alms from others, they should not carry it to the storeroom before they deposit it before the oratory. There the whole community should pray for the donor.[57]

13. They definitely should not entertain the stories they hear at the gate from laymen or anyone else.[58] If they hear them

---

turn care for their external needs." There seem to be two contrasts here: (1) inside and outside the gate; (2) in the soul and the body.

[53] "Mother of virtues" (*mater virtutum*). In RB 64.19, discretion is called *matris virtutum.*

[54] In RB 66.1, Benedict says the porter "should know how to listen to people and also how to speak to them." Obviously an uncouth porter gives a bad impression of the community.

[55] An alternative translation could be "If laymen or clerics look boldly at them." Either way, flirting is forbidden.

[56] "Minister" (*ministrare*). Perhaps this refers to medical assistance. The portress is ministering generally to everyone who comes to the gate.

[57] "Donor" represents *Qui hoc exhibuit*. That could the portress, but that would make little sense.

[58] "Entertain" translates *accommodent*. "Entertain" was traditionally applied to "bad thoughts," which are not sinful unless one dwells on them.

unwillingly and understand them, they should certainly not relate them to the sisters.[59]

14. If they violate these matters we have mentioned, they should be visited with the punishment of the Rule.

15. If they manifest {their fault} with humble satisfaction, the fault should be judged according to the humility of the one confessing.[60]

16. If, however, the crime of contumacy occurs, that will increase the level of penance.[61]

17. They absolutely must not keep the keys of the gates or doors on their person overnight. They should bring them to the abbess at night and receive them back in the morning after the Second Hour.[62]

18. The cellarers and bakers and cooks should try to do the same, so that at sunset or when the necessary work is done, the abbess shall retain the keys until the Second Hour.

19. But if some necessity turns up, they should retain the keys at night, and then they should be given out again after the Second Hour.[63]

[59] "Certainly not" stands for *nullatenus*, which Walbert uses four times in the last few verses. In general, his treatise on the portresses has a rather negative, scolding tone. The portress has a sensitive job, and I believe she deserves more trust than Walbert gives her.

[60] As far as I can determine, the meaning of this clumsy sentence is as follows: the portress who spreads gossip must confess it in chapter. The gravity of her fault should be determined by the sincerity of her confession.

[61] Contumacy (*contumax*) or insolence is one of the chief faults punished by the Rule of Saint Benedict. In fact, it is one of the first words in the penal code (RB 23.1).

[62] "Second Hour" (*Secunda*) is a liturgical hour said in the dormitory. In contrast to Benedict's porter, who lives at the gate (RB 66.2), the portress at Faremoutiers returns to the cloister at night.

[63] If they already have the keys overnight, the distribution of the keys after Secunda must have been a ritual gesture as well as a necessity.

20. From the signal for Vespers to the end of the Second Hour, the doors of the gate should never be opened, nor should they admit any entry from outside. But if it becomes necessary to have a conversation after Vespers, this should be done entirely through the window that is in the same door.[64]

21. If the needs of guests or travelers make it impossible for the portresses to eat with the sisters at the hour for the meal, they should eat later with the cooks and servers,[65] or whenever they find time to eat.[66]

22. The vessels and other utensils that they use for serving the guests, they should control and protect as if they were consecrated to God.[67] Otherwise their neglect will mean that they receive no reward from him whose goods they did not protect from despoliation.[68]

23. They should permit no man or woman to eat or drink within the walls or gates of the monastery. They should

[64] No doubt this was a large gate that would be hard to open and close, and the window opening would be less exposed to danger.

[65] This is the so-called "second table" that is customary in monasteries with a formal dining arrangement.

[66] The provision that the portresses eat whenever they find time suggests that this is one of the most demanding, and occasionally chaotic, jobs in the monastery. It can require extreme flexibility.

[67] "Vessels and other utensils" (*vasa et reliqua utensilia*) seems to be drawn from RB 31.10 on the cellarer. This is especially true of the term *sacrata*, and it conveys the idea that in the monastery ordinary things are an object of reverence. It is also true that in ancient times, all metal objects were expensive and rare.

[68] The general value lying behind this verse is stewardship: care and responsibility for the goods of another. RB 64.20-22 applies this idea to the abbot, quoting Matt 24:47. The reward in that verse is promotion over the whole estate of the landlord. The mention of a reward (*merces*) recalls what they receive from the *consodales* earlier in this chapter.

attend to the guests who arrive outside in the guesthouse,[69] as their rank demands and the abbess orders.[70]

24. We declare that only those who have made vows of holy religion to God and are bound in the unity of obedience under one Rule should eat and drink within {the monastery}.[71]

25. Portresses should always preserve the spirit of the Rule since they have zeal for God in all things. Thus they will receive a full[72] reward for their diligent and careful labor.

Chapter 4. What the Cellaress of the Monastery Should Be Like.

1. The cellaress of the monastery should be chosen from the whole community; she should be wise and pious.[73] In her distribution, she should not serve herself or her desires

2. but the whole community impartially and dutifully.

---

[69] "Guesthouse" is *hospitale*. That can be misleading to a modern Anglophone reader, but it does give us "hospitality." That this facility be outside the gate was emphasized more in female monasteries than male.

[70] "As their rank demands" does not resonate with the modern sensibility. But ancient class distinctions could not be ignored by the monks— even though they did not live by them themselves. Nobility arrived with an entourage that had to be accommodated (sometimes ruinously).

[71] This would seem to exclude all persons but the local community from the refectory. The "abbot's table" of RB 56 seems less restrictive. The Latin text begins with *intus* and ends with *censemus*, the mirror opposite of my English.

[72] "Full" is my free version of *incorruptam*, but this may be a reference to the heavenly reward that "neither moth nor rust consumes" (Matt 6:19-20). For the third time in this chapter, we meet the term *merces*. A remarkable display of merit theology.

[73] This opening sentence is clearly based on RB 31.1, especially the verb *eligenda*. The stipulation that the cellarer be a monk from the community is not a given. There may be a need for outside expertise in a modern monastic business office, but there remains a need for monastic wisdom.

3. Neither should she try to please in this direction and that, thus bringing herself into the ruin of sin or others to the harm of transgression by consent.

4. That is, she should distribute nothing beyond the proper measure because of any special attraction; she should distribute according to merit. She should know that "the just God loves justice forever; his face sees the upright" [Ps 11:7].[74]

5. She must be pleasing to all in her just arrangements.[75]

6. She should be mature in her behavior, frugal, not a glutton, arrogant, violent, unfair, stingy, or wasteful.[76] She should be well balanced in all matters.[77]

7. She ought to care for the whole community, that is, the seniors as well as the juniors, with affection like a mother.[78]

8. She should take good care of all the things committed to her

9. but not to presume to do anything without the abbess's leave.[79]

---

[74] Ps 11:7 in the RSV has "The upright will see his face."

[75] "Pleasing to all" is from *omnibus grata*, which should not be misunderstood. In fact, it is not possible to please everybody, and someone who worries too much about that will not make a good cellarer.

[76] This verse is an exact quotation from RB 31.1, in my 1996 translation from *Benedict's Rule*, 258. As I explain in my notes on this verse, the term *non turbulentus* is taken from Isa 42:4, the Song of the Servant. The nonviolent quality of the cellarer is brought out in the rest of the chapter. This term is also found in Benedict's description of the ideal abbot in RB 64.16, although not in Walbert's description of the prioress.

[77] "Well balanced" stands for *bene composita*. It could also refer to self-control.

[78] "Like a mother" (*materno ordine*). Even the abbess is never called mother in chap. 1, although she has *filias*. For his part, Benedict's cellarer is to be "like the father [= abbot]" (RB 31.2). I don't know what to make of *ordine*.

[79] Although this is not a verbatim quotation of RB 31.3-4, the meaning is the same. *Omnibus* could refer to persons as well as things.

10. She should disturb neither the senior sisters nor the juniors.

11. If one of the sisters makes an outrageous demand of her, she should deny the irrational petition calmly and with a gentle voice.[80]

12. She should minister to the sisters in the infirmary with diligent care and manifest affection.[81]

13. Likewise, she must take good care of the poor.

14. She should demonstrate the fear of the Lord in all things,[82] well aware that she will have to answer to him if she does not do all things to fulfill his precepts. She should always be mindful of him who said, "Whoever serves me must follow me" [John 12:26].[83]

15. We should join the fear of the Lord to every good work we do.

16. So she must be careful not to incur damnation through negligence. She must entirely flee the plague of avarice and cupidity.[84]

17. Just as she is not avaricious, she must not be wasteful.

[80] Here again a passage of RB 31 (v. 7) is reworked, but the substance is retained. My term "outrageous" renders *irrationabiliter.* It may be a bit of overtranslation, but I think the issue is violence more than just imprudence. The cellarer should return good for evil, à la Isa 42:4.

[81] Chapter 15 will deal specifically with the infirmary, which has its own nurse (*ministra*). No doubt the cellarer's job is to supply the infirmary, but Walbert wants her to take a personal interest in the patients.

[82] "Fear of the Lord" is a favorite theme of Benedict, but he does not mention it in regard to the cellarer. RB 31.9, however, tells the cellarer to be mindful of Judgment Day.

[83] "Serves me" actually translates *mihi ministrat.* Of course, *ministrare* fits the cellarer well. Jesus, however, is talking about Christian discipleship and its ultimate demands.

[84] RB 31.12 also warns the cellarer to avoid avarice. But a more trenchant critique of avarice is found in RB 33, which is based on Cassian's *Inst* 7. Cassian claims that avarice is insatiable: it can never have enough. Therefore, it must be completely eradicated like some noxious weed.

18. That is, just as she must not detract from the gift of God by hiding it under the vice of avarice,[85] just so she should not rob the community's substance by lending too much without proper management.[86] She must consider all these things carefully, tempering them with discretion.[87]

19. And if she does not have the wherewithal to give what is asked of her, let her respond gently, without any bitterness. Sweetness of heart and voice should be noticeable in her response.

20. For it is written, "Good words are like a honeycomb" [Prov 16:24], and "A good word is better than a good gift" [Sir 18:17].[88]

21. She should know that the work committed to her will bring a reward[89] if she strives to do everything with humility and care.

22. Even if she does not have something she is asked for, she must not say that. Rather, let her say with a confident voice, "the Lord will provide."[90]

---

[85] As I interpret it, the cellarer must not obscure the goodness of God by miserliness. To put it positively, she must, by her generosity, witness to the divine generosity.

[86] "Lending too much" (*nimis faenerando*). Strictly speaking, *faeneror* means to lend at interest. Certainly, this could not be done to monks, who have no money. I have never heard of cellarers lending to outsiders, but perhaps they did.

[87] "Discretion" (*discretio*) is a favorite virtue of Saint Benedict, who mentions it thrice. Here it is reinforced with a virtual synonym, *temperare*. But religious discretion is not enough in a cellarer. She must also have business sense, and that may require outside consultation.

[88] These verses transmit in so many words RB 31.13-14. However, Walbert has added Prov 16:24, which just redoubles Sir 18:17.

[89] "Reward" (*merces*) appears over and over again in this chapter, presumably referring to heavenly reward. But it is hard to ignore the earthly reward that good business management should bring. Of course, humility and piety do not guarantee a good economy.

[90] "The Lord will provide." This may not be too consoling to someone who needs a pair of shoes, but at least it is better than a blunt "No!" Cellarers can cause deep wounds by saying harsh things at sensitive times.

23. What must be given must be given promptly. Otherwise an occasion for scandal or a case of offense may come about by this tardiness.

24. She should remember the precepts of the Lord, who does not want any of his little ones to be scandalized.[91]

Chapter 5. On Loving One Another, or Obeying One Another.

1. The Lord shows in the gospel of John with what zeal the nuns in the monastery ought to love one another in Christ when he says, "This is my commandment, that you love one another. No one has greater love than to lay down his life for his friends" [John 15:12-13].

2. And there is also this: "In this all will know that you are my disciples, if you love one another" [John 13:35].

3. So we are commanded to love one another that we might save each other[92]

4. and to imitate by mutual love "him who loved us, and washed us from our sins in his blood" [Rev 1:5].

5. If therefore a sister would love a sister on account of Christ, she should not drive Christ away by worldly love.[93]

---

[91] "Scandalized" (*scandalizati*) here could have a very specific meaning. If the cellarer takes her time providing the nuns with necessities, they may be tempted to take matters into their own hands. RB 55.18: "But to completely root out this vice of private ownership, the abbot must provide people with everything they need."

[92] "We might save each other" (*ut invicem salvemur*). Although Blaise does not give a deponent form from *salvo*, that must be what we have here. The idea of Christians' saving each other is also somewhat unusual, but true if properly understood. The causality is obviously secondary.

[93] "Worldly love" (*temporalem dilectionem*). This is an unusual expression, which probably refers to what were later called "particular friendships." This topic is expanded in this chapter, which is not based on the Rule of Saint Benedict. Benedict never discusses particular friendships, much less homosexuality.

6. For love that is true and Christly does not work to the harm of the neighbor.
7. Therefore the sister who is our neighbor should be loved not with carnal affection, but with holy love.[94]
8. She should be loved with purity, piously, gently, and with all charity.[95]
9. So Christ should always be found in every love, and let love remain according to God, not the world.[96]
10. Thus the Lord commanded, "You shall love your neighbor as yourself" [Matt 22:39].
11. Now if a sister loves a sister as herself, she will never incur the guilt of sin, but adorned with the practice of tenderness and charity she will receive the eternal rewards.[97]
12. So let love remain always in your heart so as to extinguish the poison of the ancient enemy.
13. Through him, death opened up an entrance in the first deceived person.[98] As it is written, "By the envy of the devil, death entered the world" [Wis 2:24].

---

[94] "Holy love" represents *pietatis ministerio*. Granted that this is a rendition of "dynamic equivalence," anything literal would be misleading. The clear reference here is to Christian love.

[95] The term *diligatur* is repeated four times in the Latin, but modern English is not so fond of repetition.

[96] Although Walbert has used *dilectio* for love up to this point, in this sentence he twice uses *amor*. Although some authors like Anders Nygren think *amor* is too carnal to be Christian, Saint Benedict did not scruple to use it eight times, e.g., RB 4.21; 4.72; 5.16; 7.34; 7.69; 63.13; 72.3; 72.9.

[97] "Adorned with the practice of tenderness and charity" (*cultu pietatis dilectionis*) is hard to decipher, but at least it is clear that holy love of neighbor is a *practice* and not just a passing fancy.

[98] "The first deceived person" (*in primordio protoplasto*), that is, Adam. Unlike the modern medical term, *protoplastus* was a common name for Adam among the Church Fathers.

14. The sister is to be loved lest the cruel blot of hatred turn into the crime of murder, for the apostle John testifies, saying, "Whoever hates his brother is a murderer" [1 John 3:15].[99]

15. The sister is to be loved, lest by some recent encouragement of discord one is not absolved from the chain of one's own crime. So the Lord testified, saying, "If you do not forgive men their sins, neither will your heavenly Father forgive you your sins" [Matt 6:15].

16. Let us forgive our neighbors so that we might be forgiven by the Almighty. "Give, he says, and it will be given to you" [Luke 6:38].

17. O what a fair exchange! O what tender mercy: to receive in giving, and to give in receiving!

18. No increase of quarrels or promotion of them is allowed.[100]

19. Thus the apostle exhorts us, saying, "Be kind to one another, and merciful. Give to one another as God gave to you in Christ" [Col 3:13].[101]

20. We are commanded to give nothing but what we asked be given to us.[102]

---

[99] "Murderer" (*homicida*). The First Letter of John is marked by extreme language, but in fact monks and nuns are quite capable of hatred and even murder. Some of the Frankish princesses who joined seventh-century convents had seen enough violence that it was quite familiar to them.

[100] "Promotion of them" is a stab at *nutrimenta*. Neither is *retineantur* crystal clear. The English translators of Donatus's Rule (RDon) take *nutrimenta* literally as meaning "food" ("The Rule of Donatus of Besançon," trans. Jo Ann McNamara and John E. Halborg, in *The Ordeal of Community: Hagiography and Discipline in Merovingian Convents*, by Jo Ann McNamara [Toronto: Peregrina Publishers, 1990], 83).

[101] This quotation has been shortened to an unintelligible degree. The RSV reads: "If one has a complaint against another, forgiving each other; as the Lord has forgiven you, so you must forgive."

[102] That is, forgiveness.

21. So we pray, "Forgive us our sins as we forgive those who sin against us" [Matt 6:12].
22. In forgiving sinners, we are freed from debt.
23. We, therefore, free our neighbors by kindness and love, so that God frees us from our sins by his compassion and love.

Chapter 6. On Making Constant Confession.[103]

1. Confession is to be made with frequent and wise care, as the tradition of many Fathers, according to their many writings, shows.
2. Confession is to be constantly made so as to guard the aging state of the mind,[104] which is darkened and made rude by the daily enticing shadows of sin.
3. As Scripture teaches, "Guard your heart carefully, for from it proceeds life" [Prov 4:23].
4. Likewise blessed David prayed thus to the Lord: "I have made my sin known to you, and I have not hidden my injustices. I said, I will confess against myself my injustice, and you have forgiven the iniquity of my sin" [Ps 31:5].
5. A pure and timely confession is so effective that it brings a sure response.[105]
6. Having confessed[106] that he has been in opposition, so as to throw off the weight of sins, he weeps over himself in confessing, and he gives glory in receiving forgiveness.

---

[103] "Constant." *Assidue* means without cease. Walbert means this literally, as the following verse amply shows.

[104] "Aging state of the mind" (*vetescentem mentis statum*) is a curious turn of speech, and I have no idea why the aging of the mind should require frequent confession.

[105] "Response." The Latin term is *impetratio*, which means a successful petition.

[106] "Having confessed" (*confessus se adversum*), that is, that he has been in opposition. McNamara and Halborg take *confessus* to be a noun

7. Grieving makes plain the sin and restores hope by giving {forgiveness}.

8. He did not anticipate the confidence of hope because he remembered that once upon a time he was illuminated by the Lord to say through the Holy Spirit, "For with you is forgiveness, and I have rested in you, Lord" [Ps 130:4].[107]

9. And again, "For there is mercy with the Lord, and with him the fullness of redemption" [Ps 130:7].

10. He says continual mercy is with Him, and an abundance of redemption as well.[108]

11. Let us therefore seek mercy where we already know copious redemption dwells.

12. May sorrow increase after ruin so the medicine of fault may be found.

13. Let us confess our faults to one another,[109] so the Almighty may forgive us our sins.

14. So Scripture exhorts us, saying, "Confess your sins to one another, and pray for each other" [Jas 5:16].

15. We learn how extensive is the tenderness of the gentle Judge toward us: what sin only bound together through strenuous acts is now loosed by mutual prayer![110]

(= *confession*), which makes sense, but it is sanctioned by no dictionary that I have seen. On the other hand, my version isn't much better. Why *confessus* should be masculine, I do not know.

[107] RSV (Hebrew) Ps 130:4 reads: "But there is forgiveness with Thee, that thou mayest be feared."

[108] It is not clear to me why Walbert repeats the ideas of the previous verse.

[109] "To one another." Walbert is proposing that the nuns confess their sins to the abbess, not a priest. Actually, the practice of private confession was only beginning at this time on the European continent. The Irish monks were instrumental in this change. But whether Walbert was leaning toward private sacramental confession I do not know.

[110] "Bound together . . . loosed" (*contractum . . . solvatur*). These verbs could be rendered less literally as "brought about . . . forgiven." The idea that sinning is more strenuous than forgiveness is at least interesting.

16. Therefore let the consolation of mutual prayer be given so that protection be sought by praying together.[111]
17. For indeed more fruit is gathered when the healing of sins is gathered from self-revelation.[112] The psalmist says, "Reveal your way to the Lord, and he will nourish you" [Ps 36:5; 54:23].
18. If the soul is nourished by revealing sins, so let them be revealed by daily effort through confession so that wounds may be healed by daily medication.
19. But now we must indicate at what hours sins are to be daily washed away.[113]
20. Some time after Compline, the mind and body lose their facility for the dark night, and this is to be carefully expiated by means of confession after the Hour of Secunda.[114]
21. When, however, a nun sins by laxity during the day by sight, hearing, or thought, it is to be expressed for purgation at the end of the Office of Nones.[115]
22. If the mind attracts any filth after Nones, it is to be confessed before Compline.[116]

[111] About the only insight I have into this opaque sentence is this: The nuns should pray together because that will encourage them to pray together!

[112] That is, the revelation of one's sins to another. Since this sentence corroborates the previous one ("for indeed," *etenim*), the "mutual prayer" urged there must be confession.

[113] Probably the author wants to say "at what hours each day." Actually the Latin has "at what appropriate" (*congruentibus*), which is hard to put into English.

[114] *Secunda* was an hour of the Divine Office that was recited in the dormitory about 7:00 a.m. (the second hour). Thus it resembled Prime of the Benedictine Office. See n. 62.

[115] "It is to be expressed by purgation" (*ut purgetur censendum est*) is a circumlocution for confession.

[116] "Attracts any filth" (*Quidquid . . . maculae attraxerit*) is a strong expression that I have translated literally. McNamara has "whatever stains the mind," which is less jarring but also less accurate.

23. However, the abbess should see to it that when she enters the hall[117] after Secunda when the prayer is over, she should not permit anyone to leave before she has made her confession. The same should be done after Nones and again before Compline.

24. But those Sisters who are barred from confession because of grave sin should not stand in church with the others who are communicating. Rather, they should sing the Office apart in the other church.

25. And when the Office is finished, they must stand in front of the church in which the communicants are finishing their Office.

26. When the community exits, they should prostrate themselves on the ground and pray the Lord that the grave sins they have committed be erased by their contrition of heart.[118]

27. They remember the sayings, "God does not reject a contrite and humble heart" [Ps 51:17] and

28. "The Lord was mindful of us in our humility" [Ps 136:23].

29. Let the penitent prostrating in prayer[119] always say, "Turn your face away from my sins and wipe out all my evil deeds" [Ps 51:4].

30. This is to calm by the sentiment of a pious mind the wrath of the accusing Judge and the one ready to retaliate.

---

[117] "Hall" is my version of *schola*. Seilhac and Saïd have *salle* (French), which can mean any hall.

[118] This arrangement of the penitents standing publicly in front of the church indicates that the Franco-Irish were still partly operating in the old system of public penance. For this was precisely the routine for public penance in the early church.

[119] "Prostrating in prayer" (*in oratione posita*). I assume this is a continuation of the discussion on the prostration of the penitents outside the church door.

Chapter 7. On Not Broadcasting the Confessions of the Sisters.

1. The abbess or the prioress, or any of the sisters who are delegated by the abbess to receive confessions,[120] should in no way divulge minor or major sins, except to the just Judge, who cleanses the sins of all who confess them,

2. for she who humbly confesses her wounds does so not to receive a reproach but to restore her health, for she has God as her just witness, and she awaits[121] healing from him.

3. The senior sister who receives {confessions} should keep them very modestly to herself with sobriety and moderation,[122] lest in pouring medicine into the wound of another she sully the purity of her own mind.

4. No nun is to presume to receive confession or give penance without the order of the abbess. Otherwise, the sin committed may be hidden from the abbess; everything should be done with her knowledge.[123]

---

[120] According to Jonas's *Life of Columban* (Miracles of Eboriac) II.19 and 22 (21), only the abbess heard confessions. But Seilhac and Saïd, 72, think Jonas was concentrating his attention on the foundress, Burgundofare.

[121] "Awaits." *Exspectare* is a term that needs careful handling. The English "expect" connotes a certain presumption when it comes to the relation of creature and Creator. "Await" should imply hope that God faithfully will fulfill his promises.

[122] At this point, the text becomes rather overloaded: *cum gravitate et moderatione penes se occultando honestissime teneat.* As far as I can see, the author is trying to discuss the problem of how the confessor can deal with certain sins without being corrupted by them herself. For example, she can advise a penitent that there is no need to go into detail about sexual sins.

[123] This could be taken to mean that the abbess has to know about every sin committed in the monastery. But, as Seilhac and Saïd note (72 nn. 4–5), this would contradict verse 1 on the "seal of confession." I would suggest that "everything" here refers to confession, not sin. But that still leaves us with the troublesome verse "otherwise," etc. That may refer to sins against the community (Seilhac and Saïd). So the church's demand

5. But should some nun be found who tries to violate[124] this statute of the Rule, she should be corrected with a severe penance.[125] For she wished to hide a den of iniquity from the abbess.[126]

Chapter 8. How We Should Rise at the Signal for the Work of God.[127]

1. Whenever the signal sounds[128] for the Work of God, whether by day or night, we should rise immediately with the greatest haste.[129] It is like when the king's herald sounds

---

that religious superiors not hear the confessions of a subject *unless requested by the subject* (Canon 630.4) looks all the wiser.

[124] "Tries to violate," along with "wished to hide" (*occultare*), suggests a deliberate campaign of concealment. While it is clear enough who is being kept in the dark (the abbess), it is not so clear who is doing the hiding (sinner or confessor?).

[125] "Severe penance" is literally "knowledge of a grave penance." Seilhac and Saïd, 72, have *la rude expérience de la pénitence* = "the rough experience of penance."

[126] "Den of iniquity" is my stab at fathoming *delicti fomitem*. Seilhac and Saïd have *foyer de péché*, which is literally a "furnace or hearth of sin." My translation has no fire but tries to account for concealment.

[127] "Work of God" (*dominicum*), literally, "of the Lord." *Dominicum* can also refer to Sunday, the Lord's Day, but the context shows that this is not what is under discussion here. Nor does it refer to Mass, the Supper of the Lord, but to the Divine Office.

[128] "Signal sounds." As I explain in *Benedict's Rule*, 353, the issue here is not so much promptness as obedience. Listening for a summons is different from watching a clock, or even setting an alarm.

[129] The first part of this chapter is clearly based on Benedict's chapter 43. He too wants people to respond with alacrity to the signal for the Divine Office.

the call[130] and one must put aside whatever one has in one's hands.[131]

2. So let nothing be put ahead of the Work of God.[132] But we should hurry, with mind attentive to the cry of the herald and eager for the Work of God.

3. We should hasten with all gravity and modesty[133] to sound forth the glory of his majesty and give thanks for his goodness.

4. And if anyone moves so languidly and sluggishly[134] as to arrive after the end of the first psalm of the Office, she should know that she will be removed from her place until the end of the Office.

[130] "King's herald" (*praeco regis*). This refers to an official, but it almost seems to refer to the sound he makes with his trumpet. Benedict just talks about the sound (*sonitus*), the herald of the king.

[131] The spectacle of the monk dropping his work at the signal for the Divine Office was a commonplace in early monastic literature. In Inst 4.12, Cassian tells of a monastic scribe leaving a letter (perhaps omega?) unfinished.

[132] This very famous saying is lifted bodily from RB 43.3. It should be kept in context, however; in RB 72.11, Benedict says nothing should be preferred to *Christ*.

[133] "Modesty" (*mansuetudine*). The basic meaning is gentleness, but I wonder if Walbert is not responding to Benedict's *scurrilitas*, which probably means "silliness." Monks racing each other to choir is not as implausible as it sounds.

[134] "Languidly and sluggishly" (*morose et segniter*). The word *morose* may or may not imply bad will. In fact, there are two different *morose* words in Latin, one meaning reluctance and the other just slowness. See OLD, s.v. Curiously, Saint Benedict (RB 43.4) wants the first psalm said slowly (*morose!*), precisely so that those who move slowly will not be late. Compared to him, Walbert is less tolerant of tardiness.

5. She will be put in the last place, that is, in the place set aside for such negligent people. Let her wait there in shame and fear.[135]

6. And after the Office ends, she should make prolonged satisfaction before the community of sisters as they file out.[136]

7. They should not be completely set apart outside, for fear that they might go back to bed. That would give the Devil an occasion for mischief.[137]

8. If they come inside, they won't lose all that has been begun,[138] and they will be shaken by shame and fear because they are seen by the others.[139]

9. When the Office is complete and the others have exited, they should stay in church for their tardiness and sing in order twelve psalms more than the regular number.[140]

[135] "Shame and fear." Shame (*verecundia*) was an important element of ancient culture. Life was lived much more publicly than we know it today in the northern countries. People expected to be publicly honored or dishonored, depending on their deserts. See my article, "The Healing of Shame in the Rule of Saint Benedict," *American Benedictine Review* 53, no. 4 (2002): 453–74.

[136] Although Walbert does not say exactly *how* they make their "prolonged satisfaction" (*prolixa venia*), it was probably by prostration. Until recently, a common penance was to "kneel out" during the final oration.

[137] Walbert is still copying RB 43.8-9, but he omits the phrase "or sit themselves down outside and gossip."

[138] That is, by those who arrived on time. People who habitually come late seem to assume that it is the responsibility of others to start the Office.

[139] Walbert here has chosen to repeat the idea of shame and fear from v. 5 instead of Benedict's laconic "and will improve for the future."

[140] "Regular number." I could have translated *cursus* as Office, but that would be repetitive. Presumably, the latecomer (*ipsa tarditate*) has sung the bulk of the Office with the choir.

10. But if she misses a whole Office (especially the Night Hours), which no other work may replace,[141] she should be subject to a day of penance.[142]

11. The sister who has been appointed for this task ought to arrange[143] the Hours for the Office according to the wishes of the abbess. She should be someone of a careful and balanced mentality, suitable for this work. Thus the Work of God will not be delayed.[144]

12. If for any reason the Office is displaced from the proper time, and the Hours are not done in their right order, she should be subject to a day of penance.[145]

Chapter 9. How the Rule of Silence Ought to Be Kept in the Monastery, whether at Daily Work or at Table. How They Should Read at Table.

1. The Holy Scriptures[146] declare that the rule of silence ought to be observed at all times when it says through the prophet, "Justice will bring about silence and peace."[147]

---

[141] "Replace." Literally, "threaten" (*impendit*). The Night Hours at Luxeuil were twelve psalms at nightfall, twelve psalms at midnight, and twelve psalms at early morning (Reg VII). ·

[142] "Punishment" is *suppositio*, a special word from Luxeuil, found throughout the Rule of Columban. It seems to mean a day of extra fasting or silence. See Coen III.9.

[143] "Arrange." *Procurare* has a more general meaning than Seilhac and Saïd's *annoncer*. Yet it is true that this verse and the next one are about the *time* for the Hours.

[144] In an age before alarm clocks, indeed before *any* reliable clocks, rising for the midnight Office cannot have been easy.

[145] Again, *suppositio*.

[146] Literally, the "texts of Holy Scripture" (*sanctarum scripturarum series*). Following the lead of Seilhac and Saïd, 74, I have omitted *series*.

[147] The Latin is *cultus justitiae silentium et pax*. This is in fact an adaptation of Isa 32:17: "Justice will bring about peace; right will produce calm and security" (NAB). The absence of the word *silence* in this verse

2. Clearly one must avoid telling idle, useless, smutty, depraved, or wicked stories.[148]

3. Of these, the prophet prayed, saying, "Lord, place a guard at my mouth, and a door of protection over my lips. Do not incline my heart to evil words."[149]

4. Certainly we should cease telling idle tales; otherwise we will incur the damnation that comes from the sloth of an undisciplined mind,

5. for we will have to render an account, not only for smutty and hurtful talk but, according to the Lord's precept, for idle chitchat.[150]

6. What else should the nun seek but God alone, on whom she has fixed her desire? She should do this by devoting[151] to this same God the words of her mouth and the desire of her soul.

---

is not surprising since the OT has no spirituality of silence. Perhaps the monk Jerome introduced it into his Vulgate translation. Isa 32:17 is also quoted in Reg II.1, which is also on silence. But Walbert wisely avoids Reg's long string of adjectives describing improper speech.

[148] This verse is probably drawn from RB 6.8: "As for crude jokes and idle talk aimed at arousing laughter, we put an absolute clamp on them in all places." The words *otiose* and *scurrilitas* are reused by Walbert. But he has avoided some of Benedict's rather obscure teaching on the avoidance of *good* talk, a teaching that the Italian abbot drew from the Rule of the Master 8–9. See my overview in *Benedict's Rule*, 124–29.

[149] An exact quotation of Vulgate Ps 140:2-3.

[150] Seilhac and Saïd, 74, propose the following teaching of Jesus: "I assure you, on judgment day people will be held accountable for every unguarded word they speak" (Matt 12:36, also quoted in Reg II.3 on silence). For his part, Saint Benedict in RB 6 wants to suppress not just evil or loose talk, but *all talk*. Happily, he drops this dangerous ideal of the Rule of the Master from the rest of his Rule.

[151] "Devoting" accounts for *vacare*. The implied object here is *se*, herself. Already, by this teaching that talk should follow desire, Walbert surpasses RB 6 in depth and richness.

7. Therefore, during all the hours of the day, except for meals, from the Second Hour until Compline, one should say whatever the utility of the Holy Rule demands,[152] by permission of the abbess.

8. But from the Hour of Compline, when the prayer for a peaceful night is said,[153] no one should presume to speak at all, unless the great necessity of the monastery demands it.[154]

9. She who has care for others should speak when she is ordered to do so by the abbess, or even by the prioress.[155]

10. At table, absolutely no one besides the abbess, or whomever the abbess commands, should presume to speak for the common good of the sisters.[156]

11. But all should intently give thanks to the Creator in their hearts as they enjoy a good measure of food and drink.[157]

---

[152] "Utility of the Holy Rule" (*utilitas sacrae Regulae*). This probably is to be understood broadly, as is the reference to abbatial permission. These sisters engaged in necessary talk.

[153] The traditional formula is, "May the Lord grant us a peaceful night and a perfect end. Amen."

[154] Somewhere in medieval history, perhaps regarding the Gilbertines, it is recorded that a convent of nuns let their convent burn down around their ears rather than break the night silence by calling for help. Surely, that was a case where "the great necessity of the monastery" demanded it! This prescription hews close to RB 42.8 and 10 without copying it.

[155] This sentence could be construed differently, with the "responsibility for others" going with the prioress. But I think the reference here is to the guestmistress.

[156] "At table" (*Ad mensam*). This could be a reference to RB 38, which calls for silence on behalf of table reading. Yet RB 38.9 permits the abbot to "make a brief remark for edification." That was probably aimed at RM 29.26–37, which arranged for regular discourses at meals by the abbot. But it is doubtful that Walbert wants discourses at table, by the abbess or anybody else.

[157] "A good measure" is from *solidae mensurae largitione*, so it could be rendered more expansively. Although this may look like an offhand

12. As for the portress, when she asks permission from the abbess to speak for necessary reasons, let it be granted her.[158] This only pertains to an occasional necessity that admits of no delay.

13. Before the meal they read aloud one or more chapters of the Rule, should it please the abbess.

14. That way the soul will be fed by reading just as the body is nourished by food.[159]

15. All this should be done in a serious spirit and with gentle moderation, so the Lord will be delighted with the whole procedure.[160]

16. On feast days of the Lord, however, that is, the Nativity of the Lord, or the Easter Solemnity, or Epiphany or Pentecost, or if there are other feasts of the Lord or the holy martyrs to be celebrated, we do not deny permission to speak at table, if the abbess gives her permission.[161]

---

comment in a treatise on silence, it may show us that the Irish asceticism was not excessive—at least as regards food and drink.

[158] At this point, one wonders if Walbert is talking about the behavior of the portress during the night or day. Chapter 3 indicates that the portress does not spend the night at the gate. But it also seems unlikely that the portress would seek permission to speak each time someone arrived at the door. At least RB 66 makes spontaneous welcome an important part of the gatekeeper's task.

[159] This neat formulae was a commonplace among the old monks, starting with Augustine, Praec 3.2. In my estimation, table reading needs some such justification, since it is a somewhat unnatural practice. Table conversation is a profoundly humane practice.

[160] "Delighted" (*delectetur*) may be a clever play on the "delights of the table." The sisters should enjoy their food, but in a restrained way and not raucously (or piggishly). Then the Lord will enjoy their enjoyment! There is no trace here of anti-materialistic shame.

[161] "Permission to speak at table." I am not aware of any other traditional monastic Rule that allows conversation at meals. In the days before the reform of monastic life (ca. 1968), Benedictine monasteries usually

17. But they should speak in a restrained manner, and not carelessly. For if they burst out in loud or excessive voices, it will be a sign of dissipation rather than of joy.[162]

18. This conversation should be drawn from the Bible; then it will be for the profit of the soul and not for its damnation.

19. Those, however, who have received a penance demanding silence[163] should guard it all around; then they will merit to receive the reward of true mortification.

20. No matter where they find themselves, two sisters should not presume to converse without a third party as witness.

21. They should always discuss necessary questions in groups of three.[164]

---

allowed for table talk on a few feast days. Caesarius, Reg Virg 5.71.3, does provide for festal meals, but that is unusual.

[162] An interesting case of disciplined table talk is seen with Saint Augustine of Hippo. For his monastery, he prescribed table reading (Praec 3.2), but when he became bishop he allowed the clerics at his table to engage in conversation—but not just any conversation; he absolutely excluded gossip, going so far as to carve on the table these words: "Whoever slanders the name of an absent friend may not at this table as guest attend" (Possidius, *Life of Augustine* 22).

[163] The Cenobitic Rule of Columban has a few penalties calling for silence. Coen V imposes a day of silence for someone who shouts. Coen IX penalizes chatting with three hours of silence, or the time between two Hours of the Office.

[164] "Groups of three." This regulation obviously flies in the face of the modern drive for privacy, but before the past century, almost all of life was lived in public. Certainly poverty was a major determinant. Fear of sexual liaisons may have been a factor, but a greater worry was a "particular friendship" that could erode community.

Chapter 10. How the Diet Is to Be Administered and Observed.[165]

1. It is up to the abbess's judgment how to handle the administration and observance of the diet with justice and sobriety.[166]
2. The religious spirit should prevail in all these matters, as befits the servants of God.[167]
3. Thus you should distribute drink and food to all in equal measure,[168] as the time demands, whether it be a solemnity, a day of abstinence, or an ordinary day.

---

[165] *De ratione mensae qualiter administrandum vel observandum sit.* Literally, "Concerning the table-system: how it is to be administered and observed." Seilhac and Saïd, 76, interpret the gerundives concretely: "to be served and not exceeded."

[166] *Mensae administratio vel observatio quanta aequalitate vel sobrietate percurrere debeat, Abbatissae scientia est trutinandum: ut in omnibus, sicut decet Dei ministras, religionis vigeat fomes.* The exact grammatical structure of this verse is not perfectly clear to me. Apparently, the first part, *Mensae . . . debeat,* is an indirect question. The verb *percurrere debeat* probably means "ought to work, run," but even that is swallowed up in my rather free translation. I suspect Walbert himself is somewhat led astray by his own title, which also involves an indirect question. The obscurity of this verse can be seen in the fact that it takes Seilhac and Saïd thirty-one French words to translate fourteen Latin words. I myself use twenty-one English words.

[167] "Servants of God" (*Dei ministras* = religious). Blaise, *Dictionnaire,* s.v. *ministra,* has "deaconesses," but here that is not quite appropriate. The point is that religious should maintain a religious attitude toward food.

[168] "In equal measure" (*aequali libratione*). Obviously, everybody does not need the same amount of food and drink. I wonder if *aequali* might not mean "just" measure, with each nun getting what she needs. That is the ideal of RB 34. This matter is clarified in v. 5 below.

4. For ordinary days, we think two dishes[169] are enough, except for gifts of fruit;[170] these dishes should consist of[171] beans or pulse, or perhaps some kind of grain porridge.

5. The food should be distributed to all in equal measure, unless weakness of old age or bodily illness or recent arrival[172] makes it impossible for someone to bear this regime; that is dependent on the judgment of the abbess.[173]

6. The usual amount of fermented drink, that is, beer,[174] should be made available.

7. If it is the wish of the abbess, and it is respectfully demanded[175] because of hard work or a feast day or the arrival of a guest, a portion of wine should be given in addition.

[169] "Two dishes" (*duo fercula*), much in the sense of "two courses." In a typical French meal, this might mean soup and bread.

[170] "Gifts of fruit" (*pomorum donis*). Does this mean the nuns did not go out to pick fruit? In RB 39.3, Saint Benedict has "and if fruit or fresh vegetables are available, a third may be added."

[171] "These should consist of" is a spelling out the colon in the Latin original, in other words, a suggestion as to the content of the "two dishes."

[172] "Recent arrival" is a simplified rendition of the more florid *novellae conversationis novitas improbata* = "the untested newness of new conversion." In other words, it took time to get used to the diet. Probably most of the recruits to Eboriac were nobles, who were used to a richer diet.

[173] A dramatic example of this is found in the life of Saint Pachomius. One time the abbot was lying sick in the infirmary, and lying near him was another monk who was even sicker. Although he was skin and bones, the attendants would not bring him the meat he requested—the Rule did not permit it! Pachomius, the legislator, upbraided them for their rigid adherence to the Rule. See "First Greek Life" 53, in *Pachomian Koinonia I*, trans. Armand Veilleux, CS 45 (Kalamazoo, MI: Cistercian Publications, 1980), 333.

[174] "Beer" (*cervisia*). Since Eboriac (and Luxeuil) were not in the European wine zone, the standard drink was beer. Potable water was a rarity. The term *sicera*, liquor, was a Hebrew one meaning "any fermented drink except wine" (Blaise, *Dictionnaire*, s.v. *sicera*).

[175] "Respectfully demanded" (*pia precatio exagitaverit*). Strictly speaking, these ideas do not go well together. *Exagitare* means to "stir up or

8. If they have two meals on a given day, the same rule[176] is to be observed, except for the ration of wine.[177]

9. But on feast days,[178] out of reverence for the holy solemnity, they should be served[179] more dishes, that is, three or four courses.

10. This should be done, however, with smaller dishes,[180] even if they be more numerous.

11. That way, the body will be refreshed by necessary food and not damaged by overeating.[181]

---

disturb," which must be aimed at the abbess. But of course one must also approach her respectfully.

[176] "The same rule" probably refers to all that preceded in chapter 10. Still, one suspects this is a reference to the times for the meals. Although Walbert has not yet said so, no doubt their standard practice was what is described in RB 41: on ordinary days, the monks ate one meal a day, at ca. 3:00 p.m.; on fast days, they ate only at Vespers; on festal days, they ate at noon and again at evening. But even on a two-meal day, there was no total increase of food served.

[177] "Ration of wine" (*potium vini*). Why should he mention wine, which was not their standard drink? Why not beer? Perhaps it is assumed that any two-meal day is festal, and therefore vinous.

[178] Seilhac and Saïd, 77, point to Caesarius, Reg Virg 5.71.3, as another monastic Rule that provides for festal meals. No doubt this had considerable influence on convents in early medieval Francia.

[179] Literally, "their bodies should be refreshed." It is hard to get this into graceful modern English, but it does indicate that they ate for nourishment, not for entertainment. The same point is made more forcefully in the next verse.

[180] "Dishes." Here Walbert uses the term *cibaria* for the courses. In the previous verse he used *cibus* and *fercula* for the same item, a sign of his considerable Latin culture.

[181] *Damnare* could also have a theological meaning: "judged for overeating." Strictly speaking, *nimis satietate* would mean "too much overeating," a pleonasm.

12. But when the sisters sit down at table, no one should raise her eyes to watch another eating.[182] Nor should she look disapprovingly[183] at the amount of food or drink consumed by another person.

13. When food is brought to the table, no one shall commence eating before the sign for blessing sounds forth.[184]

14. For her part, the abbess should give the signal[185] as soon as the food is served; when they hear the signal, all should ask with one voice for the blessing.

15. Then the abbess should answer them, saying, "May the Lord be so kind as to bless us!"

16. This same ritual is to be observed when each course is served,[186] including those of fruit and drink.

17. We especially decree that no one presume to give any food from her portion to another sister, nor accept any from

---

[182] This rule also appears in Pr. 31 of the Rule of Pachomius, where the diners wear their hoods up during meals precisely so they cannot see others eating. Heinrich Bacht, *Das Vermächtnis des Ursprungs II* (Wurzburg, Germany: Echter Verlag, 1983), 147 n. 136, thinks this rule was so they would not know who was fasting and who was not.

[183] "Look disapprovingly" (*iniqua consideratione*). The common expression is a "dirty look," which lets the eater know that the other person disapproves of her behavior.

[184] "Sign for blessing sounds forth" (*signum ad benedicendum insonet*). The next verse will explain this somewhat elaborate procedure for prayer at meals.

[185] "Give the signal" (*signum tangere procuret*). The literal meaning seems to be "take care to touch the *signum*." Could this refer to a little bell such as is commonly used on the abbot's table? Seilhac and Saïd, 77, leaves it generic, so I do the same.

[186] "Course" (*fercula*). These were family style meals, with waiters bringing the courses. The whole process emphasizes mutual service and communal charity.

another.[187] Only the abbess may do that, or the prioress, if she has been told to do so by the abbess.

18. If, however, anyone violates any of the rules we have laid down above, out of either inexperience[188] or carelessness, she should be corrected with the discipline of the Rule for the boldness of her presumed carelessness.[189]

Chapter 11. The Proper Hours for Meals in Winter or in Summer.

1. From the beginning of the most sacred solemnity, that is, the beginning of the holy season of Easter, when the Resurrection of the Immaculate Lamb is celebrated, until the sacred solemnity of Pentecost, when the Holy Spirit was poured out, that is, a space of fifty days, they should eat at noon.[190]

2. Likewise, they should have supper in the evening. For the nature of the sacred season requires that no one in the church should look sad.[191]

---

[187] The intention here is to block any form of private patronage or special gift-giving relationship. The same is found in RB 54, which deals with the handling of gifts from outsiders. In the cenobium, everyone receives what she needs from the community, through the agency of the superior or her delegate.

[188] "Inexperience" (*novitas*). Strictly speaking, this could refer to a new regulation, but that is unlikely. It probably refers to a new monk.

[189] "Carelessness" (*temeritas*). Here, Walbert reveals himself as something of a rigorist who always presumes the worst in the motives of others.

[190] Like RB 41, Wal 11 begins with the Easter Season, which is theologically primary for Christians. Unlike the laconic RB 41.1 ("From Holy Easter to Pentecost, the brothers should dine at noon and have supper in the evening"), Walbert's opening verse is more expansive. He achieves this by florid language and a description of Easter and Pentecost. From what we know, the Romans ate their main meal in the evening, with a lighter one at noon. Frankish custom was probably similar.

[191] The thinking here is exemplary: Christians must show forth their joy at the resurrection, and one way to do this is by taking their meals

3. But from Pentecost to the beginning of Lent, they should eat a single meal at Nones,[192] unless heavy labor demands an earlier meal or the arrival of guests necessitates some change of the mealtime.[193]

4. They should eat twice a day when great feast days occur[194] or heavy work requires it.

5. From the beginning of Lent until the most holy solemnity of Easter, except for Sundays, they should eat in the evening.

6. But this meal should be finished before nightfall, while there is still light.[195]

7. When it comes time to serve the meal, one sister should arise at each table[196] and proceed calmly to the window of

---

earlier in the day than usual. This presumes that it was, and is, a hardship to wait until 3:00 p.m. for the first meal of the day.

[192] "Nones" (*nonam*), the ninth hour of the day, was at 3:00 p.m. on average. This would be somewhat earlier in winter, given the shorter days, but later in summer. In RB 48.6, Benedict has Nones said at about 2:30; they have already eaten and napped, and now he wants them to get to work.

[193] Neither "demands" (*exigat*) nor "necessitates" (*cogat*) has an object in the Latin, so I have supplied them. No one can do much heavy labor on an empty stomach, but historically women's monasteries had laymen to work in their fields. As for guests, if they come in off the road or need to get back on the road, true hospitality means feeding them promptly.

[194] "Great feast days" (*magnarum sollemnitatum eventis*). These are liturgical festivals and do not imply huge meals. In fact, some food was held over for supper from the noon meal. Still, the previous chapter (10.9) shows they had more variety of diet on feast days.

[195] "While there is still light" (*cum statione lucis*). In the region of Eboriac, twilight in March occurs about 6:00 p.m. RB 41.9 wants evening meals done by daylight, not candlelight. In his *Dialogues* (2.20), Pope Gregory describes Abbot Benedict eating by candlelight. Either this is an exception that proves the rule or Gregory had not read the rule carefully.

[196] "At each table" (*singulae ex singulis mensis*). Unlike Benedict's arrangement, where the table waiters seem to be a separate crew. Otherwise, why should they eat a snack an hour earlier as in RB 35.12? Traditionally, those servers ate *after* the main body at something called "second table."

the kitchen. This should be done without any loud stamping of feet or clatter of dishes.

8. They should all serve the senior table first,[197] and only then should they carry the dishes to the table where they sit.

9. The leader of the table[198] should decide how they ought to serve one another, either by turn, or by the youngest in age if there be such.[199]

Chapter 12. How They Should Do Manual Labor on Ordinary Days.[200]

1. They should work all the time[201] except feast days so as to take care of their own needs and also have something to give to the poor.[202]

---

[197] "Senior table" (*seniorum mensam*), presumably, the table where the abbess eats, and probably elders or community officials as well. Traditionally abbots dined alone, but modern abbots often abandon this inhuman custom.

[198] "The leader of the table" (*praeposita mensae*). The context shows that the reference here is not to the second-in-command but to the head of each table. Walbert may have gotten this idea from Caesarius, Reg Virg 18.4. He did not get it from Benedict.

[199] "Youngest in age" probably means that some tables of old folks need young folks to help during the meal.

[200] Seilhac and Saïd, 79, have "weekdays," but *quotidianis diebus* is the counterpart to "feast days," as is clear from v. 1.

[201] "All the time" (*omni tempore*) should not be taken literally, which would be a violation of monastic balance. Rather, it could well be an expression of concern that the nuns not behave like ladies of leisure. Since most of them were from aristocratic backgrounds, this may have been a temptation.

[202] This is a classic expression of monastic economy. Already in the Egyptian desert, we read of a monk who worked enough to earn two coins: one for his own sustenance and one for the poor. Note that he did not just work to stay out of mischief, or even to atone for his sins. Healthy monastic work should have a practical purpose.

2. Yet we must cease work lest the fruit of *lectio* be lost.[203] First we should apply ourselves to work for a set time, and then be free for *lectio divina*.[204]

3. Manual labor should begin from the Second Hour[205] and continue until the ninth hour.[206]

4. From the ninth hour, it is customary to do *lectio*.[207]

5. If someone needs to do some personal work like sewing or washing clothes, she should do it with permission of the abbess or prioress.[208]

---

[203] The implication seems to be that some people may be tempted to work without pause. This is, in fact, the tendency with a certain type of high-energy, production-oriented personality. Walbert knows that a balanced monastic life must set limits to such workaholism.

[204] "Free for *lectio divina*" (*lectioni divinae vacetur*). This is precisely the vocabulary of RB 48, which is the basis for the beginning of this long chapter. For a long time, translators rendered *vacare* as "apply themselves" to *lectio*. This translation is all right insofar as it shows that *lectio* demands focus. But *lectio* is not just work, either. As indicated by the expression "fruit of *lectio*," it is more a matter of holy leisure than productive work.

[205] This is not 7:00 a.m., but a brief liturgical hour (*secunda*) prayed in the dormitory. See Wal 6.20 and 9.7, with notes. Walbert uses the elegant turn of phrase *sumat exordium*, "take its beginning," and then *finem accipiat*, "accepts its end."

[206] Seven unbroken hours of manual labor are a great deal for a group of people who have already spent considerable energy at Morning Prayer. No doubt some food and rest were also in order, as will be clear from what follows.

[207] "It is customary" (*usitetur*). Walbert will immediately allow an exception to this. But considering v. 2, he hardly wants the exception to become the rule.

[208] The fact that one had to secure special permission to perform routine personal maintenance shows how regimented the life of these sisters really was. In my novitiate (1956) there was a fifteen-minute period called *utilis occupatio*. The senior monks did not live on such a tight schedule. Caesarius, Reg Virg 29.2, also provides *utilis occupatio*.

6. And if some pressing work turns up[209] so they have to go to work earlier, or if there is a heat wave, the abbess should take this into consideration.

7. If the time requires it, or the burden of the work, they should stop work at noon if the abbess thinks that is warranted.

8. After some rest and nourishment, they should work until evening.[210]

9. Above all, if the abbess is present,[211] or if the prioress replaces her, she must see to it that absolutely no nun engages in idle chatter, except for necessary questions. During the work of the hands, they must also be mindful of the work of God.[212]

10. For while the hands are outwardly occupied with work at the proper time,

11. inwardly the mind and tongue are sweetened by meditation on the Psalms and recollection of Scripture.[213]

---

[209] For example, the need to harvest crops or tend farm animals. Sometimes, though, monks need to protect their horarium in the face of demanding customers. The customer does not always come first.

[210] Notice that no provision is made for *lectio* on such a day. Certainly, such days occur in the typical monastery. But it also looks as though Walbert is not concerned here with the ideal monastic horarium as in, say, RM 50 or RB 48. Walbert discusses exceptions without emphasizing that they are exceptions.

[211] Apparently "present" refers to the work site. This implies that the nuns of Eboriac worked together. Given the general outlook of Walbert, and probably of Abbess Fare as well, the superior's presence would not be primarily for surveillance.

[212] "The work of God." Given the context, *opus Dei* here does not refer to the Divine Office, as in RB 8–18. Rather, the reference is probably to the whole monastic life, as in Basil, RBasil 7. The next verse explains.

[213] This is a very nice description of the practice of early nuns and monks. Because they had so much Scripture by heart, they could ruminate on it during work. This implies that the work was usually simple enough to allow such a practice.

12. If any violator of this rule indulges in chitchat,[214] she is to undergo the penalty of silence.
13. If there be penitents in the community, they must tend the fire,[215] two by two and a week at a time.
14. The penitents must prepare for the hair washing of the sisters each Saturday and for the baths on solemn feasts.[216]
15. If there are other lowly jobs to be done, the penitents should do them. They will be cleansed[217] more rapidly of their sins by the mercy of Almighty God if they do this work with a humble and contrite attitude out of the fear of God.
16. On the way to work,[218] they should sing this psalm verse: "May the splendor of the Lord be upon us. Direct the work of our hands! Direct the work of our hands!" (Ps 90:17).

---

[214] "Indulges in chitchat" (*fabulatione delectetur*). This penalty is not aimed at occasional whispering but at habitual chattering. To "delight" in something is to do it often. See RB 4.68: "Not to love quarrelling."

[215] "Tend the fire" (*focos facient*). Seilhac and Saïd, 80, have *dans le dortoir*, but I am not sure why. Is that the way they take *in schola*? I interpret this as "in the community." Perhaps they reason that people in seventh-century Francia would only keep a fire going at night. Of course, there was no central heating.

[216] "Prepare." No doubt this meant the considerable task of heating tubs of water for a group of people. One reason people in pre-modern times did not wash very much was the sheer labor of this operation. Roman baths were equipped for comfortable washing, but medieval monasteries were not. The washing of hair is also arranged for in Reg V.2 and Coen IX, where hair is washed every one or two weeks. See Seilhac and Saïd, 80 n. 14.

[217] "Cleansed." After doing the dirty work in the monastery for a term, the penitents are now morally cleansed themselves. Monasteries traditionally had the novices do the scut work, but with the shortage of new recruits nowadays, senior monks do the cleaning. Nobody has died from it yet.

[218] "On the way to work." This could sound as though they had to walk some distance to work, as in the fields. But that is probably reading too much into *ad opera eundum est*. Pachomian monks marched to work (Pr Prol.58) but maintained silence as they did so.

17. At the end of work, they should say this verse: "May God our God bless us. May God bless us, and let all the ends of the earth fear him" [Ps 67:7-8].

18. Let the bakers take turns[219] at their common task. Since they will need to talk, there should never be fewer than three of them.[220]

19. If they must linger in the bakery, there should not be fewer than four of them. The senior among them, with a reputation for holiness, should be in charge.[221] She has permission to speak.

20. The senior among them should show the bread they make in their shift to the cellarer. That way they will not be found blameworthy, since they are in safe hands.[222]

21. Likewise, regarding those who work in the brewery,[223] the senior should be in charge. She should watch over everything according to the rule of the bakery.

---

[219] "Take turns" (*alternatim per vices*). Large-scale baking is hard and burdensome work. Bakers often work in the middle of the night, and the work can be hot, heavy, and dusty. It is the same today.

[220] Walbert fears private conversations, as he has already noted in chaps. 3.8 and 9.21. Thus the aim is not so much silence as openness and candor.

[221] Since v. 21 will lay down similar rules for the brewery, it does not appear that the bakery was a special spot. Perhaps the difficulty was that both places were isolated and thus a temptation for intrigue. "Be in charge" (*praeposita*). Although this word is capitalized in M. Brockie's edition (*Codex Regularum* [Vienna, 1759]), it is clearly not an official title here.

[222] "Since they are in safe hands" (*omni custodia tutae*). The sense here is opaque, at least to me. Does *tutae* refer to the nuns or the loaves of bread? At any rate, the system of having two levels of surveillance, namely, the *praeposita* and the cellarer, indicates a problem. Were people making off with loaves of bread?

[223] "Those who work in the brewery." This is a simplification of *quae in braxatorium ad cervisiam faciendam inhabitaverint. Braxatorium* is a Late Latin word, found in Du Cange, *Glossarium*, s.v., but not in the OLD.

22. The cooks should cook a week at a time. Each week three sisters should be assigned to cook, or more if necessary.[224]
23. If we do not assign work carefully, the result will be murmuring instead of gaining a reward.[225]
24. Those beginning their shift[226] should beg the whole assembly of sisters for their prayers.
25. During the Divine Office, they should pray, "Our help is in the name of the Lord, who made heaven and earth" [Ps 123:8] and "Help us, O Lord our savior" [Ps 78:9].[227]
26. When they complete their shift, they should wash the feet of all the sisters.[228]
27. They should return to the *praeposita* all the pots and pans they have used; these should be returned clean.[229]

---

[224] "Three." In a modern monastery, one person can cook for about twenty-five people. By this standard, Eboriac had more than fifty nuns.

[225] The Latin is more elaborate: *ne impositus sine discretione labor, unde mercedem mercari debuit, inde murmurationis fructum reportet.* The basic idea, that careful planning can preclude undue grousing, is one that is spelled out clearly in RB 53.18. Even though Benedict hates murmuring, he admits in RB 41.5 that it may be justified if people do not get the help they need to do their work.

[226] "Those beginning their shift." The Latin has one word, *ingredientes*, and I am sure it is based on RB 35.17-18.

[227] RB 35.17-18 locates this little ceremony on Sunday morning after Lauds. In that text, the psalm verses are said three times and repeated by the wide choir. Probably Walbert assumes a similar litany.

[228] The powerful ritual of foot washing is based on Jesus' own example of service in John 13. In ancient times, this was a practical matter since nothing was paved and feet got dirty. This rite is clearly based on RB 35.7-9. Benedict also has his monks wash the feet of guests in RB 53.13. Of course, people could wash their own feet, but to wash the feet of another was considered a work of extreme humility.

[229] This stipulation is a specific instance of the general principle of RB 32 that all tools must be returned after use, clean and in good condition. The *praeposita* in this verse could be the prioress or the head of the kitchen work crew. "Pots and pans" translates Latin *vasa*.

28. Likewise, they should request prayers at the Office[230] thus: "O Lord, you have helped me and consoled me" [Ps 85:17].[231]

29. On weekdays, the cooks and the cellarer should receive the punishment of twenty-five slaps on the hand for each of their transgressions.[232] This is to prevent them from sliding down the slippery slope from small offenses to big ones.

Chapter 13. Concerning the Utensils and Furniture.

1. It is the job of the abbess to arrange the utensils of the monastery and whatever else is needed for the common work.[233]

2. Let there be chosen sisters in the community who have a strong sense of responsibility[234] and whose uprightness is well tested.

---

[230] As in v. 25, I have interpreted *oratio* to mean the Divine Office. In modern Benedictine monasteries, the prayers for both those exiting and those entering kitchen service are said after Sunday Lauds. Actually, RB 35 places the blessing for those exiting before those entering. In reversing the order, I think Walbert is less logical.

[231] This would be a fitting prayer for table waiters in all ages. Typically, they must rely too heavily on tips because their wages are so low. And they absorb a lot of guff from finicky diners.

[232] Saint Columban, *Règles et pénitentiels monastiques*, trans. Adalbert de Vogüé with Pierre Sangiani and Jean-Baptiste Juglar, Aux sources du monachisme colombanien vol. 2, Vie monastique 20 (Bégrolles-en-Mauges, France: Abbaye de Bellefontaine, 1988), 28 n. 8, refers this kind of penalty to the Irish *Rule of Tallaght* 39 (ninth century). Apparently Walbert got it from Luxeuil, where every fault had a specific penalty attached to it. These slaps were administered before the daily meal.

[233] As with Saint Benedict's superior, Walbert's abbess has responsibility for the material elements of the monastery as well as the spiritual. As is clear from Wal 4, the cellarer is delegated a great deal of authority in these matters, but the abbess still has the ultimate say.

[234] "A strong sense of responsibility" is my guess for *solicitude animi viget*. Seilhac and Saïd, 82, have *d'un grand zèle*, another more or less

3. They should be given the job of distributing to each one the necessities required in a given situation.[235]

4. They should provide[236] these utensils or whatever else has been entrusted to them by the abbess with care inspired by fear.[237]

5. If they do this, they will receive the reward for the charge committed to them[238] and not incur the judgment of damnation.

6. They should keep in mind this saying: "Cursed be the one who does the Lord's work negligently" [Jer 48:10].

Chapter 14. How They Ought to Sleep in the Dormitory.[239]

1. Religious and souls dedicated to God always keep their minds focused on God during the night as well as the day hours.

---

informed guess. Given the context, it can hardly mean "care for souls." *Animi* refers to the mind, not the soul. *Solicitudo* characterizes a careful person.

[235] "In a given situation" (*opportunitate exigente*). Seilhac and Saïd have *selon ce que requièrent les circonstances*. The Latin literally means "convenience demanding." This could mean that people are to make their requests at the proper time, as in RB 31.18-19. But here it seems to mean "give people what they need; judge each case by its merits." Are these people cellarers?

[236] "Provide." This translates *gubernentur*, which does not refer to personal use but to provision for others to use.

[237] "Care inspired by fear," literally, *solicito timoris studio*. This is pleonasm because *solicito* and *studio* mean essentially the same thing. This leaves *timoris* unexplained. Is it fear felt by the administrator, or fear she should inspire in those with whom she deals? What follows indicates the former. This paragraph is heavy on ambiguous genitives that the translator must interpret to make sense in English.

[238] "For the charge committed to them" (*commissae curae*), that is, for fulfilling the charge committed to them.

[239] "Dormitory" (*schola*). This meaning for *schola* is found in Du Cange, *Glossarium*, s.v., with reference to the Council of Tours, II.14.

2. Although the body is weighed down with sleep, the soul should remain always watchful and vigorously intent on the praises of the Creator,

3. as it is said, "I sleep, but my heart is awake" [Song 5:2].

4. Careful watch, however, should be kept; otherwise the sisters may suffer the penalty for their weakness because of lack of maternal solicitude.[240]

5. For this reason we decree[241] that they should sleep two to a bed, except for the sick and the aged.

6. They should do this, however, in such a way as not to speak together or look on each other face to face. They should lie down to sleep with their backs to one another.[242]

7. This will prevent the Ancient Enemy, who wants to wound souls with his greedy bite,[243] from hurling any kind of confusing dart.[244] It will also prevent the Devil from arousing deadly desires through pillow talk.

[240] This verse demands rigorous surveillance of the dormitory by the abbess ("maternal solicitude"), which seems to imply that the dorm was not divided into cubicles. It also implies that individuals were not much concerned for privacy. In fact, medieval people rarely had separate beds, much less private rooms.

[241] "We decree" (*decernemus*). This special declaration is probably meant to bolster innovative legislation. In fact, Caesarius (Reg Virg 9.1) and Donatus (RDon 65.1) assign the sisters to separate beds. We will see, however, that Walbert is cautious about the new rule.

[242] "Backs to one another." This piece of laughable over-legislation is more like the Rule of the Master than anything else. Does Walbert expect people to stay in the same position all night?

[243] "With his greedy bite" (*ore libenti*). *Libens* usually means "willing," but here there must be a sinister connotation.

[244] "Hurling any kind of confusing dart" (*aliquid fraudis jaculando imitate*). Besides descending into the realm of mixed metaphor, Walbert here indulges in unusual prolixity. Perhaps he fears that things can happen when people are drowsy.

8. It should be arranged that one of them is always a senior sister whose maturity is well attested.[245]

9. We absolutely forbid young sisters from lying down together, for fear that they might be swept away by some passionate sin in the carnal battle.[246]

10. If possible, all the sisters should sleep in one dormitory,[247]

11. unless weakness or extreme old age demands that they be kept in a separate room. The same holds for someone being punished or too newly arrived.[248]

12. All the sisters should sleep clothed, with a belt around them.[249]

13. A lamp should burn all night long in the dormitory.

14. When they rise with haste for the Divine Office,[250] they should make the sign of the cross on their foreheads. They

---

[245] RB 22.7 has the same arrangement, though there is no verbal connection. Of course, older people are not inherently chaste, but the "maturity" (*religio*) mentioned here is the key. *Religio* here probably refers to psycho-sexual development, not piety. Or is that anachronistic eisegesis?

[246] "Swept away by some passionate sin in the carnal battle" (*ne in aliquot carnis adversitate aestu delicto rapiantur*). I know what Walbert wants to say; I just wish he had used fewer words in saying it.

[247] "One dormitory" (*una domus*). This is an unusual meaning for *domus*, but the context demands it. In the title, the sleeping room is called *schola*; is Walbert avoiding the term *dormitorium*? In RB 22.3, Benedict makes essentially the same demand for a single room, but if no room is big enough to house the whole community, then they should at least sleep in tens and twenties. Medieval dorms could easily accommodate fifty or a hundred persons.

[248] "Too newly arrived" (*novitas probata non fuerit*), literally, "not proven." Was dormitory life sometimes trying, or did they hesitate to allow anyone in the dorm whom they did not know well?

[249] One wonders if this stipulation was not mainly symbolic. As becomes clear in v. 14, there was emphasis on making haste to the Night Office. But Luke 12:35 speaks of having girt loins and lighted lamps to meet the returning Christ at the Parousia.

[250] "Divine Office" is *cursum* here. This was an early medieval term, no doubt based on the series (*cursus*) of psalms chanted in the Office.

should say silently, "God, come to my aid; Lord, hasten to help me" [Ps 69:2].[251]

Chapter 15. How to Care for the Sick.

1. The very words of the Master[252] tell us how to care for the sick when he says, "Whatever you want people to do for you, you should do for them" [Matt 7:2].[253]
2. Although we must do this[254] for everybody, this precept is to be especially applied in the care of the sick,
3. for the Lord said, "I was sick and you visited me" [Matt 25:36].
4. Therefore we must try to care for the sick as if we imagined[255] we were ministering to Christ himself in the sick person.[256]
5. In fact, she who offers care to the sick on behalf of Christ ministers to Christ himself in the sick one.

Columban's Reg VII is titled *de cursu*, which is apparently where Walbert got the term.

[251] This psalm verse (69:2) is used three times (RB 17.3; 18.1; 35.17) within the Divine Office itself. Walbert does not legislate for the Divine Office.

[252] "The very words of the Master" (*proprietas Auctoris*). It is hard to imagine a more stilted or obscure way of expressing a perfectly simple and straightforward idea. In fact, this verse is a model of convoluted Latinity. One gets the impression that Walbert is trying to impress someone with his sophistication.

[253] At first we might be surprised that this generic command is given instead of Matt 25:36 on sick care. But the subsequent verses show this is part of a larger pattern.

[254] That is, the Golden Rule cited in the preceding verse: Do as you want done to you.

[255] "Imagined" (*putetur*). Seilhac and Saïd, 84, have *believed*, which is not literally accurate. But of course faith is the whole basis of Matt 25.

[256] "Christ himself." Actually, *himself* is not in the Latin. But one of the most powerful themes of the brilliant parable of the sheep and the goats (Matt 25:31-46) is the astonishment of the protagonists. They have no idea that they are serving Christ—or not.

6. The abbess should take care that they have separate rooms with everything necessary.[257] That way, she who is paying the penalty of frail flesh will not have to feel extra pain.[258]

7. If the season requires the other sisters to modify their lifestyle, as in Lent, the sick should always be served a more generous portion of drink and food.[259]

8. The use of baths or medical treatments should be granted without any hesitation.[260] This should be conceded less readily, however, to the healthy, and especially to young people.[261]

---

[257] "Everything necessary" (*cum omnibus opportunitabus*). This could be translated in many ways. The fact is that there were very few "opportunities" in ancient medicine, where even a private room was a luxury. Nowadays, the opposite is often the case in the Western world: people are kept alive more or less against their will.

[258] "Extra pain" (*exteriorem laborem*). Strictly speaking, this means "external pain," but I have trouble seeing how that could be the case here. The sick person is already suffering "external pain"; by offering her decent health care, we can at least spare her *extra* suffering. But no dictionary thinks *exterior* can mean "extra," and neither do Seilhac and Saïd, 84.

[259] "More generous," that is, than fasting. The church has never held the sick to its fasting laws. The "First Greek Life of Pachomius" 53, in *Pachomian Koinonia I*, tells of when the saint was sick in the infirmary. He became indignant when the brothers denied another patient meat-broth. The Rule does not apply to starving persons! (See n. 173 above.)

[260] "Without any hesitation" (*summo . . . studio*). Here I follow Seilhac and Saïd, 84: *le plus grand empressement*. Since the bathing of monks and nuns was carefully restricted, of course there would be "hesitation"! But sickness demands different rules. Although Walbert follows RB 36 in general, he seems quicker than Benedict to grant baths. Two hundred years later, Benedict of Aniane tried to get rid of monastic bathtubs. Many abbots ignored him.

[261] In ancient times, bathing was a big part of ordinary urban life. The Christian ascetics, however, came to see it as a source of spiritual decadence. It was feared as a stimulation of the passions, especially for youth.

9. The abbess should give the sick the kind of care she herself hopes to receive from the Lord.[262] She should see to it that[263] the sick feel no neglect from the cellarer or the nurse.

10. Those weighed down with great age[264] should be so cared for that they suffer no neglect.

11. As seems necessary in each case, and according to the judgment of the abbess, there should be tender consideration made for their weakness.[265]

12. These people cannot bear the full force of the Rule;[266] rather we should treat them with affectionate tenderness.[267]

[262] "She herself hopes to receive." This unusual reference to the personal feelings of the abbess may be a subtle way of making sure she takes a personal interest in the care of the sick. It does not mean that she is the direct caregiver; that is the *ministra* (nurse) of the next line. Yet the ultimate responsibility for the sick still lies with the superior.

[263] "She should see to it that" is represented in Latin by the tiny word *ut*. This conjunction ties the following sentence to what precedes as a result clause.

[264] "Those weighed down with great age" (*decrepita vero aetate fessis*). Despite the fact that Walbert is writing for a young community, he remembers that one day, sooner or later, they will grow old. Up to now in this chapter Walbert has been using RB 36, but it does not discuss the aged, so now he consults RB 37, which does.

[265] "Tender consideration" (*consideratione pia*). Walbert evidently shares Benedict's conviction that nature itself has a soft spot for the aged (RB 37.3). Although we do not abandon our old folks on an ice floe, we sometimes forget them in our nursing homes.

[266] "Full force of the Rule" (*Regulae tenori*). This may risk overtranslation, but *tenor* means an uninterrupted flow. Usually, monasteries have an infirmary where there is a mitigated observance.

[267] "Affectionate tenderness" (*pietatis . . . affectus*) rather than cold efficiency, or even worse, condescension.

Chapter 16. On Accidents That Happen by Negligence or by Chance.

1. The abbess should take into careful consideration faults of negligence, which are often the cause of accidents,[268]
2. as when someone has broken or ruined or negligently abandoned something in the dining room or in whatever activity.[269]
3. Everything should be judged according to its gravity and corrected with a view to the age of the culprit—young or old or in the prime of life.
4. For if the vice of negligence is not corrected in small matters, the person who has been weakened[270] by small faults will fall into greater ones.
5. If a sister has an accident, and if she immediately makes a sincere confession to the abbess or the prioress, and if it is found that it really was an involuntary accident,[271]

---

[268] "Which are often the cause of accidents" (*qua pre multos casus in multis delinquitur*). I must confess I am unclear what this clause really says. I am basically following Seilhac and Saïd, 85: *qui est en bien des occasions l'origine de bien des fautes.*

[269] The template for vv. 1–2 is probably RB 46.1-2. Although the vocabulary is somewhat different, Benedict's chapter also contains a list of negligent behaviors and another list of where these faults can occur.

[270] "The person who has been weakened" (*mens vitiata*). *Mens* is mind or spirit, which is a more literal rendition. "Weakened" may not be strong enough, since the root of *vitiare* is *vitium* = vice. But the idea here is gradual undermining. Negligence at work is dealt with in Coen II, III, and XV.

[271] For our affluent society, this great stress on satisfaction for mishandling tools and breaking things can seem strange. But in ancient times tools were much more costly. Further, negligence in these matters can be a serious problem in a cenobitic community where nobody owns anything.

6. it will be sufficient if she does not deny what she did wrong, if that is possible,[272] and that she make satisfaction by a prostration.[273]

7. Yet if the fault is found out not by her own confession but by the denunciation[274] of another sister, she should be subjected to a penance if the seriousness of the fault demands it.

8. That is because she did not manifest the fault by sincere confession.[275]

9. But if she commits one of the great faults, which bring serious damage to the soul, she should reveal it secretly and willingly to the abbess.[276]

[272] "If that is possible." I do not understand this remark, and neither do Seilhac and Saïd—if that is possible!

[273] "Prostration" (*veniae*). *Venia*, singular, means "indulgence, pardon, forgiveness." But Du Cange, *Glossarium*, s.v. *veniae*, says that this word, which is apparently a nominative plural, means prostration. Seilhac and Saïd, 85, have "prostration." Yet *veniae satisfactione* looks to me like a genitive singular and an ablative singular.

[274] "Denunciation" (*proditio*). The dictionaries give "betrayal" for this word, but it does not look as though Walbert considers it a fault in this sentence. In some monasteries, monks were encouraged to mention the faults of others in the weekly *culpa*. I have never heard a good word about this practice from anyone who lived through it. Yet in RB 46.4, Saint Benedict approves of this denunciation.

[275] "Sincere" (*pura*). Probably the implication is that some confessions are contaminated by self-serving calculation. Yet it is not so easy to eliminate all self-interest from our confessions. The church demands not *pure* confession but rather a contrite heart.

[276] This sounds much like sacramental confession. Before we reject the idea of a non-ordained person, and a woman to boot, hearing confessions, we should remember that at this point (ca. AD 640), the church *had* no regular practice of private, auricular confession. There are indications in some of the early monastic Rules of unordained monks hearing each other's confessions.

10. Otherwise, by blushing to lay open the fault of her soul while there is still time she may conceal the face of the devil within her because of the guilt of her fault.[277]

Chapter 17. That No Sister in the Monastery Ought to Claim Anything as Her Own.[278]

1. In the monastery, nothing is to be considered[279] personal property; rather, in the name of the Lord everything should be held of little account.[280]
2. For what can she claim as her own from the world, this faithful soul "to whom the world is crucified and she to the world" [Gal 6:14]?[281]
3. Why would she who has died to the world once for all begin again to live for the world out of some consuming interest in worldly affairs or wretched desire?[282]

---

[277] This verbose sentence is actually half as long in the original Latin. The basic idea is simple (and clever): when we do not make a clean breast in confession, we give Satan a place to hide in our hearts.

[278] Walbert bases this chapter on RB 33, but his title is clearer than Benedict's. Walbert makes it explicit that the issue here is more one of attitude than of physical use; *vindicare* = to claim. Benedict uses the ambiguous verb *habere*, which can mean either "possess" or "consider." See Kardong, *Benedict's Rule*, 273, note.

[279] "Considered" (*habendum*). See previous note.

[280] "Held of little account" (*contemnenda*). This is the least problematic construal of *contemnenda* I can think of. Obviously, this verse could seem to promote an antimaterialist dualism. But "God don't make junk!" Perhaps that is the ultimate meaning of "in the name of the Lord."

[281] The fuller text of Gal 6:14 shows that this statement about the Christian is based on the crucified Christ. Still, it is well to remember that Christ was not crucified by material goods, but by sin. As such, "worldly goods" are not sinful.

[282] "Wretched" (*aerumnosum*). This word is so close to *aerumnorum* ("pertaining to money") that I wonder if Walbert's pen slipped here.

4. She has already begun to live for God, having turned her back on the world.[283]

5. Therefore this vice must be torn out by the roots in every nun;[284] that is, she must not claim for herself or as her own any clothes or shoes or anything else.

6. The exception is when she is commanded by the abbess to keep possession of something. But then she must do so as if guarding the goods of another and not as mistress of her own possession.[285]

7. After that she must not presume to give or lend to anyone what has been committed to her by the abbess, that is, for her present necessity, whether of clothing or anything else: only if the abbess orders it.[286]

8. For what could she give of the world's goods to another sister, since she has entirely given her own will[287] into the power of the abbess on behalf of Christ?

---

[283] "Turned her back on the world" (*contempto mundo*) refers to monastic profession, with heavy overtones of Christian baptism. Again, the close association of sin and material goods must be kept from becoming ideological.

[284] "In every nun" (*ab omni monacha*). It is not clear to me whether *ab* here means "from" or "by." My version "in" leaves it vague, as does that of Seilhac and Saïd, 86: *chez toute moniale*. Perhaps Walbert wishes to keep this ambiguity, which is also in RB 33.1.

[285] Vv. 5 and 6 form one long Latin sentence. Still, it is done in very concise Latin. What I have rendered in seventy English words is done in forty-five Latin words.

[286] At this point, the text has become very repetitious. This could be due to various reasons: (1) the author wants to hammer home a point; (2) this precept of cenobitic dispossession has not been well understood; (3) the principle has been violated. The effect here is to create a chapter that is even more didactic than RB 33, which is very stern indeed.

[287] "Her own will" (*suas voluntates*). The argument here is *a fortiori*: whoever has given over her will entirely to another should hardly cling to extrinsic goods. Saint Benedict makes the point thus: "That is because they have neither their bodies nor their own wills at their disposal" (RB 33.4).

9. Therefore let all things in the monastery be common to all, as we read in the Acts of the Apostles [4:32]: "All things were common to them."[288]

10. This commonality should be thought of[289] as follows: no one shall presume to give or receive anything without the permission of the abbess.[290]

11. Otherwise, she may be numbered an associate of Judas the Traitor, who fell into the evil trap of greed and rashness.[291]

12. If one of the sisters is caught indulging[292] in this vice, and if she refuses to reform after a first, second, and third warning, she will undergo the regular discipline.

[288] Although a surface reading of Acts 2 and Acts 4 might suggest that the first Christians practiced radical communism of goods, that is highly unlikely. No other New Testament text claims that, and Acts 4:32 itself presents the case of Barnabas as an ideal example, not a norm.

[289] "Thought of" (*habenda*). Here again, stress is laid on attitudes rather than physical possession. In fact, it is impossible to live without at least using physical things.

[290] Repetition of the point made in v. 7.

[291] The gospels accuse Judas of venality as well as treachery (see Matt 26:14-16, 20-25). They at least imply that greed led him to betray Jesus. It seems a bit of a stretch to claim that an infraction of monastic poverty makes one a "Judas"! But RM 13.13 also calls a rebellious priest-monk a "Judas." See Kardong, *Benedict's Rule*, 509.

[292] "Indulging" (*delectari*). The point seems to be frequency more than enjoyment. The mention of multiple warnings also indicates that this is a case of a habit of possessiveness and not just an isolated instance.

Chapter 18. Excommunication for Faults.

1. If one of the sisters, at the devil's prompting,[293] shows herself impudent,[294] proud, disobedient, or a murmurer, or if in some case she is even tempted[295] and falls[296] into violating the precepts of the elders or a regulation of the Holy Rule,
2. according to the Lord's precept, she should be admonished once or twice in secret by the seniors [Matt 18:15-16].[297]
3. If she does not want to improve, she should be scolded by the whole community together.[298]

---

[293] Walbert bases this chapter on RB 23, but he has added this clause to the text. It recalls Caesarius's Rule 23.1. Up to this point in his Rule, Walbert has mentioned the devil in 5.13, 7.7, 14.7, and 16.10. For his part, Benedict rarely mentions the devil, although RM does so frequently. See my articles "The Devil in the Rule of the Master," *Studia Monastica* 30 (1988): 41–62; "The Demonic in Benedict's *Rule*," *Tjurunga* 37 (1989): 3–11.

[294] "Impudent" (*contumax*). This person refuses to accept correction. In fact, all of the four negative characteristics that identify a sister subject to excommunication are *attitudes* rather than acts. RB 23 is the introduction to Benedict's extensive penal code (RB 23–30, 43–46).

[295] "Is . . . tempted and falls" (*lapsa . . . tentaverit*). Strictly speaking, the order is reversed in the Latin: "falls and is tempted." This is what Seilhac and Saïd have (87), but it makes no sense to me.

[296] "Is tempted" (*tentaverit*). One of the things that complicates this sentence is the ambiguity of *tentare*, which can mean to "try" or "be tempted." Seilhac and Saïd have the former (*elle tente de violer*), but I fail to see the logic of it. See previous note. Admittedly, one is on thin ice in making a sentence say what it *must* mean. Yet one can hardly leave the reader with an absurdity.

[297] This arrangement of fraternal (sororal) correction by increment was taken by Saint Matthew directly from Jewish rabbinical practice. What it does very well is to allow the accused to save face and thus be open to correction.

[298] "Scolded by the whole community together" (*simul ab omni Congregatione objurgetur*). Although Walbert is following RB 23 closely (he quotes *objurgetur*), he changes the penal procedure. Benedict has the culprit chided in front of (*coram*) the whole community, not by everybody. This seems more realistic.

4. And if even then she does not want to improve, as the magnitude of the fault demands, she should be judged according to the Rule: that is, if she is already of mature understanding,[299] she should undergo excommunication.[300]
5. But if she persists with the stubbornness of a hard heart[301] and clings to her wicked fault, then she will suffer corporal punishment.[302]

Chapter 19. What Excommunication Should Consist Of.

1. Those who know how to render[303] just judgment determine the measure of excommunication by the gravity of the fault.
2. A slight punishment should be applied to a slight fault, and a hotter[304] condemnation is fitting for more serious ones.[305]
3. The abbess should think carefully about this:

[299] "Already of mature understanding" (*antea intellectus viguit*). In RB 23.4, Benedict puts it a bit differently: "If he understands the penalty," which makes it sound like a question of age. It may have been that for very young monks, but there is more than intelligence involved here. Unless a person appreciates community, excommunication means little.

[300] "Excommunication" (*excommunicatio*). This is claustral, not ecclesiastical, excommunication. It normally involved exclusion from choir and/or table, not from Holy Communion. But the worst-case scenario could demand expulsion from the community, as in RB 28 and Wal chap. 20.

[301] This verse is overloaded with adjectival material: *obstinata et durae mentis tenacitas culpae et improbitatis perseveret*. Although it is not easy to sort out the syntax, it is clear enough that what merits a beating in this system is stubborn intransigence.

[302] "Corporal punishment." RB 30 also prescribes this for children who cannot understand excommunication.

[303] "Render just judgment" (*justum . . . librare judicium*). The image is of balancing a scale by fine adjustment. Of course, jurisprudence is trickier than merely sliding the weights on a pair of pans.

[304] "Hotter" (*ferventior*). No doubt this is meant in a moral sense, but it is hard not to think of the fires of Gehenna. Yet those fires too have to be understood in an extended, spiritual sense.

[305] What looks like a crashing truism may not be so. After all, the death penalty was used against petty theft in seventeenth-century England.

4. if some sister is found guilty of slight faults, she should be kept away from table until a time indicated to her.[306]
5. But for the correction of serious transgressions, a longer term of days, weeks, or months should be laid down.[307]
6. This will be the arrangement: if the sentence of excommunication runs for more than seven days,[308] as long as the term of penance is in force,
7. a sister who is excluded from her place at table is also set apart in church. This means that she is not to sing a psalm in the rank[309] she had before, or have a place in the *statio*.[310]
8. This arrangement should last until she has merited[311] pardon from the abbess or from the seniors through humble satisfaction and heartfelt satisfaction.

On the other hand, Southern juries routinely acquitted white men for lynching black men.

[306] In RB 24.6, the procedure is spelled out: if the community eats at noon, the culprit eats at 3:00 p.m. If the community eats at 3:00 p.m., she eats at 6:00 p.m. She does not eat less; she eats later.

[307] "Term . . . should be laid down" (*definitio . . . finiatur*). The subject and the verb form a tautology, but a mild one. Walbert's insistence that a *term* be established for serious punishments is an astute addition to RB 25, which does not mention such limits. The modern criminal justice system puts a limit on most sentences, probably to give prisoners some hope.

[308] Because Walbert is ready to implement and specify his philosophy of long and short penances, we should credit him with considerable originality. Not only has he carefully studied Benedict's rather detailed penal system; he has also added an important detail that makes the system more coherent: a major penance is one that lasts more than seven days. Serious penitence is also dealt with in Wal 6.24–30 and 12.13.

[309] "The rank she had before" (*in loco in quo antea fuit*). Here I am following Seilhac and Saïd, 88, but the word *loco* could also mean "place" in choir. Rank for psalmody will also be discussed in Wal 22.12.

[310] "Place in the *statio*" (*nullum ordinem*). This could refer to one's choir stall or one's place in processions, as well as various official roles such as acolyte or table reader.

[311] "Merited" (*mereatur*). While the English term *merit* usually means "deserve," the Latin term often means *both* deserve and receive a reward.

9. As long as an excommunicated sister under grave penalty is confined to a cell[312] or separated from the company of the community,

10. absolutely no one is to comfort[313] her by conversation or a visit, unless the abbess has commanded it.[314]

11. If anyone violates this rule, she will suffer the penalty of the Rule.[315]

Chapter 20. Concerning Those Who Have Been Frequently Corrected by Careful Admonishment[316] but Refuse to Improve.

1. A sister who refuses to improve after frequent admonition should be corrected[317] by excommunication according to

---

[312] "A cell" (*cellula*). It is tempting to translate this as *her* cell, meaning her room. That is, or was, common parlance among monks and nuns up until quite recently. But seventh-century nuns had no private rooms; this was a detention cell. Indeed, it could be seen as an early witness to monastic prisons. See my article, "People Storage: Mabillon's Diatribe against Monastic Prisons," *Cistercian Studies* 26, no. 1 (1991): 40–57. Excommunication for grave faults is also discussed in Wal 6.24 and 16.9. Reclusion in a separate cell occurs in Caesarius, Reg Virg 5.34.1, 65.1–3. See Coen VI.2–3 and RDon 2.10; 5.9; 73.9.

[313] "Comfort" is an attempt to render *fruatur* adequately. Walbert uses this intransitive verb as a transitive. Strictly speaking, it means to enjoy, and it takes an ablative object.

[314] RCes V.34.1 mentions sisters who are charged with caring for the excommunicated.

[315] This verse applies to the person who illegally visits an excommunicated sister. For the penalty of those who consort with the excommunicated, see Coen XV.10g.

[316] "Careful admonishment" (*sedulam correptionis curam*). This elaborate expression is hard to put into bearable English because *sedulam* and *curam* seem to say the same thing. At any rate, this remark is aimed at the superior: she must keep after the wayward, whether they respond or not.

[317] "Corrected" (*corrigatur*). Since warnings (*correptio*) have had no effect, the superior must move from words to actions. Although Walbert

the gravity of the fault. If the correction of admonishment achieves nothing, then she will undergo the penalty of blows.[318]

2. But if even then she refuses to improve but becomes puffed up enough with the tumor of pride[319] as to defend the works or acts for which she is being corrected,[320]

3. then she must be corrected by the expertise of the abbess,[321] for it is written, "Miserable is he who rejects discipline" [Wis 3:11].

4. Guided, therefore, by her expertise, she should apply a cure for draining the abscess.[322]

---

bases this chapter on RB 28, he does not follow it slavishly. Benedict moves quickly to beating stubborn culprits. Perhaps because he is writing for women, Walbert is slower to resort to flogging. But he invokes it in verse 2!

[318] The logical progression here is not too clear. The previous verse had moved from warnings to exclusion. Now, however, we are back to warnings that are followed by beatings. RB 28, the model for this chapter, is also somewhat jumbled. Blows, of course, are abhorrent to us today but were a regular part of traditional discipline. Before the advent of psychology, people tended to approach discipline more directly than we do now.

[319] "Tumor of pride" (*in tumorem superbiae*). This is a striking image that Walbert has added to RB 28, which simply has "pride." Perhaps the medical terminology that follows is seen as applied to this tumor.

[320] "Defend the works and acts for which she is being corrected." The right to self-defense is an important element of the Rule of Law that governs all modern nations. It is probably not ruled out by the ancient monastic Rules, which refer only to a persistent, defiant self-defense in the face of salutary correction.

[321] "Expertise" (*sapientia*). This could also be translated by "wisdom," the usual rendition of the word. The key idea here is *practical* wisdom, which nowadays would certainly involve psychology. The purpose of Christian punishment is always restorative, not vindictive. Even a recalcitrant monk is never an enemy to be punished, but a sister to be saved.

[322] "Draining the abscess" (*saniei medendi*). *Sanies* means pus or other harmful fluid, so it is used here by metonymy. This graphic terminology follows "tumor of pride" in v. 2. Seilhac and Saïd, 89, have *à guérir l'abcès*.

5. If the deadly wound is not healed[323] by the fomentations[324] of tongue-lashings or the ointments of devotion and gentleness, at least[325] it should be cut out by knife strokes.[326]
6. But if the draining of the abscess does not remove the tumor,[327] then the sister will suffer the sentence of excommunication or the penalty of corporal punishment.
7. If neither the fear of excommunication nor the punishment of whipping succeeds in breaking her pride,[328] let the fuel

[323] "Healed" (*sospitati [non] redditur*). Although the sense is clear enough, the syntax is not. *Sospitas* is a rare word for healing, but why it is in the dative case is a mystery to me. Curiously, *Sospita* was a title of Juno, the Savior. *Sospitator* was later applied to Christ (Blaise, *Dictionnaire*, s.v.).

[324] "Fomentations" (*fomenta*), meaning the application of hot, wet compresses to an infected area to draw off poison. Whether tongue-lashing would have exactly this effect on a troubled monk is perhaps beside the point. Since this word forms a contrasting pair with *unguenta*, it probably refers to harsh treatment.

[325] "At least" (*saltem*). This does not seem like exactly the right word. Seilhac and Saïd, 89, have the following circumlocution: "it will be necessary to go so far as to. . . ." In other words, "at last." The corresponding text in RB 28.3 has *ultimum* (last) *ustionem* (cautery), which has probably guided Seilhac and Saïd.

[326] The use of medical terminology in RB 28 and the other monastic Rules based on it does not suggest that these authors had formal medical training. In ancient times, and indeed up to the discovery of antibiotics, etc., everybody had some knowledge of home medical remedies. No doubt religious superiors like Benedict and Walbert were especially keen to learn the ways and means of keeping their people alive.

[327] It does seem that Walbert has found an image he likes and cannot let go of. But the effective use of such images involves avoidance of overuse, especially since in this chapter the images are clearly meant spiritually and not physically.

[328] "Succeeds in breaking her pride" (*frangitur*). I have succumbed to the temptation of overtranslation here. The literal meaning is "she is broken," but the monastery is not a torture chamber. But if her body is not broken, then what is? My use of *succeed* is based on RB 28.4: "and if he sees that his efforts have accomplished nothing." Apparently Seilhac and Saïd, 90, take the same route: *n'en viennent à bout*. Yet I do not think we should reduce Walbert's colorful prose to such abstractions.

of piety[329] be increased: the whole community should assemble to pray for her to the Lord of all.[330]

8. This is done so that the sister who is held captive by the Devil's snare can be healed by the mercy and goodness[331] of the Lord.

9. If even then she refuses to be corrected, let her be segregated[332] from all, except the guardians,[333] within the walls of the monastery[334] as a penitent.

---

[329] "Fuel of piety" (*pietatis fomes*). Again, Seilhac and Saïd prefer an abstraction to Walbert's concrete image: *la dose de bonté*. Of course, my literal rendition makes it clear that Walbert is guilty of mixing metaphors.

[330] "Pray for her" (*pro ea . . . deprecetur*). This may suggest a special prayer service, like one of the old "storm novenas." It seems to me that Walbert, following Benedict, breaks the logical order of progression—we should expect expulsion here, not prayer. Maybe he wants to jolt us out of set patterns to deal with these hard cases. Moreover, it is well to interrupt this series of ascetical and disciplinary measures to remind us that conversion still depends on the grace of God.

[331] "Goodness" (*pietate*). Although the term was translated as "piety" in the previous verse, Blaise, *Dictionnaire*, s.v. *pietas*, notes that the word can mean either God's benevolence to man (v. 8) or man's good will toward God (v. 7).

[332] "Segregated" (*segregata*). This may or may not mean physical confinement. It probably did not for Saint Benedict or for Walbert, but jail cells in monasteries set in very early. Thus the Spanish *Rule of Fructuosus* 16 (in Lucas Holstenius, *Codex Regularum* 1 [rept. Graz, Austria: Akademische Druck-U. Verlagsanstalt, 1957], 146b) wants serious offenders bound with an iron chain in a prison cell for six months! This legislation appeared about a century after Wal, and it was for men. For a general survey of monastic prisons, see my article "People Storage."

[333] "Except the guardians" (*praeter custodibus*). This could also be translated "guards," but I doubt that their role was just surveillance. Perhaps they were more like Benedict's *senpectae* (RB 27.2), wise old monks sent in to console and admonish the excommunicated.

[334] "Within the walls of the monastery" (*intra septa monasterii*). This is internal excommunication, as opposed to expulsion or ecclesiastical withdrawal of the sacraments.

10. Let her be afflicted with various punishments[335] until her humility is patent to all on good evidence.[336]
11. For often[337] healing[338] is granted even to those who refuse it.
12. Therefore[339] she is to be expelled from the community lest she corrupt the innocent with her vice.
13. As for a sister of tender age who does not appreciate the force of excommunication,[340] she should be corrected by whipping.

---

[335] "Various punishments" (*diversis correctionibus*) could be either verbal or physical, but the latter seems more likely. "Diverse" is easier to construe as physical.

[336] "On good evidence" (*vera credulitate*). English *credulity* means naiveté, but *vera* (true) probably renders the word positive. Seilhac and Saïd talk about *preuves manifestes*, but I am not sure whether they are translating *vera credulitate* or not.

[337] "Often" (*saepe*). It is tempting to attach "often" to "refuse" since this is a chapter on recidivism. Unlike Benedict, Walbert seems to say that God will heal/save even those who do not wish it.

[338] "Healing" (*salus*) could also be translated "salvation," but I have chosen to stay with the medical terminology of the chapter. RB 28.5 says, "The Lord, who can do all things, will heal the troubled brother."

[339] "Therefore" (*nam ideo*). This connective is truly baffling. Just after the stubborn sister has been "healed," she is expelled! Could it be that *praestatur* in v. 11 does not mean "granted" but merely "offered"?

[340] "Appreciate" (*nescit*). Saint Benedict makes this point in RB 23.4, but he does not restrict it to the young. RB 30, however, does speak of the need to whip or spank children who cannot understand excommunication. The principle is general: only a person who values community can be hurt by excommunication. It might be added, however, that some cultures, such as the Indians of the North American Great Plains, disciplined children by shunning them, not whipping them. So apparently their children did value community!

Chapter 21. On Taking Back a Sister.[341]

1. If at any time a sister leaves[342] the monastic enclosure, a thing forbidden a Christian nun,[343] and flees outside but then returns because she recalls her former religious state and is struck with fear of eternal Judgment, she must promise the monastery a complete reform.[344]
2. Then if her penitence is deemed genuine,[345] let her be taken back into the walls of the monastery.
3. And if she does this two or three times, she should be cherished with similar tenderness.[346]

[341] "Taking back" (*receptio*). *Receptio* normally just means "receive," but the context makes it clear that this sister has previously defected. The OLD says *receptus* has the primary meaning of "take back." Since the prefix *re-* can mean "again" or "back," there is no theoretical reason why *receptio* could not mean "take back."

[342] "Leaves" (*discesserit*). Although this little chapter, like RB 29, follows directly on the mention of expulsion, it is not about expulsion but about voluntary departure. "Monastic enclosure" (*a septis monasterii*) is not to be taken literally. Monks and nuns sometimes have to leave the enclosure on business. "Leaving the monastery" normally means "without permission," which is a serious infraction.

[343] "Forbidden a Christian nun" (*absit a christiana religione*): Canon Law, not the moral law. Unauthorized departure is accepted today as sometimes necessary. Fifty years ago, it was almost unthinkable and the cause of terrible stigma.

[344] "Complete reform" (*omnem . . . emendationem*). These words are identical to RB 29.1, but Benedict makes them more specific than Walbert: "correct the fault that caused his departure."

[345] "Genuine" (*probabilis*), literally, convincing. Obviously the ones she must convince are her former sisters. For their part, they will be harder to convince after each departure.

[346] "Cherished with similar tenderness" (*simili pietate foveatur*). This may appear to be an unwarranted effusion of sentiment, but it is just what the Latin says. Walbert, following Benedict, recognizes that some instability is a result of weakness, not malice.

4. Then, however, she should be received into the last place among the penitents,[347] where her life should be monitored to see if she is reliable.

5. If, however, she is stained with the fault of flight[348] after having been taken back three times, she must know that all possibility of return is to be denied her thereafter.

Chapter 22. How the Sisters Ought to Practice Humility[349] toward One Another and Keep Their Rank.[350] How the Commandments Should Be Kept in the Smallest Acts.

1. The conferences of the holy fathers[351] lay down with what affection[352] and loving deeds sisters in the monastery ought to love each other.

---

[347] "Last place among the penitents" (*in extreme loco inter poenitentes*). Presumably this refers to their place at the liturgy, but it also means they are not yet restored to their rank in the community. Wal 6.24 indicates that penitents prayed the Divine Office apart from the main choir.

[348] "Stained with the fault of flight" (*fugae culpa maculata*) is a considerable elaboration of Benedict's language, and not necessarily an improvement. But Walbert hews close to RB 29.3 on the end of the possibility of return.

[349] "Practice humility" (*se humilient*). Strictly speaking, *se humiliare* means to bow or prostrate, but this chapter greatly expands the discussion. Humility is basically a Christian concept, with very little resonance in classical Latin vocabulary or practice.

[350] "Rank" (*ordines*). Walbert does not pay a lot of attention to rank, but he mentions it in Wal 2.13; 3.23; 19.2. Benedict, for his part, has a whole chapter (RB 63) devoted to rank.

[351] "Conferences of the holy Fathers" (*instituta sanctorum Patrum*). Many early monastic writers wrote *institutes*, so this is a very broad category. Of these, John Cassian was the most famous.

[352] "Affection" (*affectu*). Although monks probably cannot be expected to *like* all members of the community, it helps a great deal if mutual affection prevails among most of them. Christian charity cannot be reduced to affection, but without some degree of it, it tends to be a grotesque

2. Here, though, we must show in some detail by what acts and services humble love is to be shown.

3. What is more, the abundance of virtues forms a vast circle[353] in which the nun[354] can easily overcome the ancient enemy.

4. There are many things that seem insignificant[355] when we are doing them, and yet their performance or their neglect shows whether we are of a lukewarm or fervent spirit.[356]

5. So a nod of the head or a friendly verbal greeting will reveal the person's truest feelings, whether she is hard-hearted or peaceable, or even tender.[357]

6. Therefore, the male or female[358] servants of God should always be careful to promote within their minds those

---

thing. For a penetrating meditation on this, see Mary Gordon's novel *Final Payments* (New York: Anchor Books, 2006).

[353] "Vast circle" (*latissimum . . . ambitum*). The idea seems to be that loving deeds are the best way to shield oneself from Satan.

[354] "The nun" (*circumsepta*). Another translation would be the "circumscribed nun" as Seilhac and Saïd have it (91). This would be an obvious reference to "vast circle of virtues" in the last verse. But *septa* occurred in Wal chaps. 20 and 21 as "walls of the monastery."

[355] "Insignificant when we are doing them" (*in actu . . . exigua*). The point is that we are acting right, no matter how we are feeling.

[356] "Of a lukewarm or fervent spirit" (*aut tepescente aut fervente animi motu*). *Fervente* means "burning," although it is usually toned down in its spiritual usage.

[357] A rather difficult verse, both in form and content. "Truest feelings" (*purissimum . . . affectum*) is hardly the easiest meaning of *purus*, but it seems to be the one demanded here. Yet it has to be said that conventional gestures of politeness and courtesy can mask as well as reveal.

[358] "Male or female servants" (*famulis vel famulabus*). As in 5.23, Walbert refers to both monks and nuns. This could have several explanations: (1) He is used to talking to men and slips back into that groove. (2) There were some brothers serving the nuns of Eboriac, and he included them in his audience. (3) He sometimes incorporates material from Luxeuil, of which he was a monk and later abbot (629–670).

things that do not depart from true humility and charity,[359] which are the summit of the virtues.[360]

7. For just as true charity never exists without true humility, likewise true humility never exists without true charity.[361]

8. Let us grab the opportunity,[362] therefore, to lay a solid foundation so we might attain the pinnacle of virtue.[363]

9. So first one should show humility in both deed and feeling[364] so that then a plentiful supply of love may be built up.[365]

10. And when they meet on the path or any other place, they should ask for a blessing with all humility.[366]

---

[359] Seilhac and Saïd's note on 91 is a good summary: "Just as we had in chapter 5 a doctrine of charity, we find here a doctrine of humility in its connection with charity, with description of the acts that manifest it."

[360] Now we see the matter from the other side. If acts manifest what is in our minds, we had better make sure our minds are full of charity and humility!

[361] According to Seilhac and Saïd, 92 nn. 6–9, the association of charity and humility was "traditional," e.g. Caesarius, S 234.3 and *passim*. Although love is not a prominent theme in Benedict's long chapter on humility, *amor* does occur at 7.34 and 7.69. *Caritas* appears in 7.67.

[362] "Let us grab the opportunity" (*arripiamus*). I have taken the opportunity to use somewhat rough language to render the vivid term *arripio*. Seilhac and Saïd's *Efforçons-nous* ("let us strive") seems too pallid.

[363] RB 73.9, the last verse of that document, speaks of *virtutumque culmina*, which can only be reached by the monks who go beyond the rudiments of the Rule to follow higher spiritual doctrine. Walbert, however, thinks that loving humility is the basis of spiritual progress, not higher doctrine.

[364] "Both deed and feeling" (*tam actu quam affectu*) repeats the pair of deed and feeling from v. 1, thus creating a sort of leitmotif.

[365] "Built up" (*aedificetur*) continues this idea from the previous verse.

[366] "With all humility" (*cum omni humilitate*). *Humilitas* can be taken literally as a bow. So Seilhac and Saïd, 92, have *s'inclinant en toute humilité*.

11. And if one of them is the senior,[367] the junior should ask for the blessing first; then the senior should do the same.[368]

12. When they stand together for the Office, always depending on the abbess's ordering,[369] they should keep to their rank for singing a psalm,[370] for reading a lesson, or even for going to Communion.[371]

13. The abbess must make sure that their rank corresponds to their date of entry into the monastery. The exception is if one's exceptional way of life merits[372] a higher rank, or if grave fault demands that she be demoted.

---

[367] In traditional Benedictine cenobitism, one monk is always senior (or junior) to another monk by date of entry (RB 63).

[368] Although it could be cumbersome to be acknowledging seniority everywhere, it was observed in a few situations. Thus when a novice entered the room of the novice master, he said, *Benedicite*. The master answered, *Deus*. These terms were shorthand for a longer formula. The same routine was observed by the reader and the abbot at table and in choir. Some monasteries still carry on these formalities.

[369] "Abbess's ordering" (*ab abbatissa fuerint ordinatae*). The communal choir order is usually determined by the choir director under the supervision of the superior. It normally arranges people according to seniority, but the musical balance of the choir, etc., can require fine-tuning.

[370] "Singing a psalm" (*ad psalmum canendum*). Ancient psalmody often involved a single cantor, with congregational response. In the days of few books and candlelight, this was simply practical.

[371] "Even for going to Communion" (*etiam ad communicandum euntes*). The idea of going to Communion by order of rank may seem a bit odd. Yet it is quite natural, given that the brothers are seated by rank. At any rate, it was standard practice in monasteries up to Vatican II. Here Walbert is following RB 63.4.

[372] "Exceptional way of life merits" (*uberius conversatio religionis meruerit*), literally, "richly merits." In practice, monks are rarely advanced or demoted simply on the basis of behavior. Rank is usually altered by assignment to an office.

14. If, however, one of the sisters is known to aspire to a higher place, she should be blocked with a shameful rebuke.[373] For she presumed to claim a place of honor not due her. In trying to grab[374] an unmerited honor, she is not acting in a spirit of religion but of ambition.

15. In the assembly of the sisters, if another sister arrives, let those who are junior to her in rank rise and offer her their place.[375]

16. The juniors should never contradict their seniors in an arrogant way. When they are questioned or corrected, the juniors should respond with all humility.[376]

17. If a junior sees a senior falling into some fault, she should not rebuke her, but rather gently[377] suggest that she confess

---

[373] "Shameful rebuke" (*verecunda castigatione*). The rebuke is public, so the culprit is disgraced in the eyes of others. Indeed, this is a classic situation of "shame and honor," where one is shamed for claiming unmerited honor for herself. In a shame-and-honor culture, one is either moving upward toward more honor, or in the other direction.

[374] "Grab" (*arripere*). Again this pungent word is used as in v. 8. But now the nun is grasping for glory, not the opportunity to grow through humble charity.

[375] "In the assembly of sisters" (*In consessu Sororum*). Seilhac and Saïd, 93, have "When the Sisters are sitting together." At any rate, it is probably not a question of choir or table, where cenobites usually have assigned places.

[376] To our democratic and egalitarian eyes, this verse gives seniority too much authority. If it is based on RB 71.6-9, as Seilhac and Saïd suggest on p. 93, however, then Benedict's rather violent statement has been considerably toned down. In traditional societies, one does not contradict an elder.

[377] "Gently" (*dolendo*). *Doleo* generally means to suffer pain or sorrow, but here it must have a somewhat different connotation. The opposite of a rough rebuke is a gentle suggestion, not "sorrow" as Seilhac and Saïd, 93, have it. Of course, such a suggestion by a junior may require considerable courage!

her fault to the abbess or prioress. A senior should do the same for a junior.

18. When a nun comes to confess, she should first prostrate on the ground[378] and say she is guilty.[379] Then, after she is commanded to rise, she should make her confession.

19. When one seeks permission to do some work, first ask leave to speak,[380] and then ask permission to do the work.

20. When one comes to see the abbess, first approach her with all humility, asking leave to speak. Likewise, when departing, ask leave to go, and seek her blessing.[381]

21. No sister may bring her own needs directly to the abbess, but all should be careful to communicate their necessity to the abbess through the prioress.[382]

22. If a priest or some religious comes to visit, sisters may visit him only with the permission of the abbess. They should stand at a distance from him, asking his blessing on bended

---

[378] "Prostrate on the ground" (*prostratae super humum*). RB 71.8 also has the monk fall on the floor, but the vocabulary is different. Moreover, RB 71 wants the junior to placate an irate senior. Here a guilty nun is confessing her fault to her superior.

[379] "Say she is guilty" (*suam culpam esse dicat*). The syntax here is obscure, though the meaning is plain enough.

[380] "Ask leave to speak" (*venia prius petatur*). Seilhac and Saïd, 93, have *on s'excuse*, "asks pardon." But there is no fault here. Could this verse be under the influence of the Rule of the Master, chap. 9, where one must ask permission to ask a question? And permission may be withheld! Benedict avoids such nonsense.

[381] Formality in the presence of a superior was the general rule in the days before Vatican II. One generally stood before the abbot's desk, where he sat. Trappists always *knelt* before the abbot! So Thomas Merton, *Seven Storey Mountain*.

[382] Was Eboriac such a huge community that the abbess needed to filter requests through an intermediary? This kind of bureaucracy can make the superior seem an aloof, remote figure instead of an agent of God's love.

knee and in a low voice.[383] If the abbess orders it, some of the sisters may speak to him, always with humility and modesty and sobriety. The virtues of humility and sobriety should be evident in these matters.

Chapter 23. A Friend or Relative Is Not to Be Protected in the Monastery.[384]

1. We decree[385] that it is not permitted to protect in any way one's friend[386] or relative in the monastery.
2. Why should she who no longer lives for herself but for Christ protect another sister?[387] She remains crucified in order to imitate him.[388]

---

[383] The Rule of the Master, chap. 87, also displays a certain amount of nervousness about the visits of priests. No doubt they have to be controlled, but such regulations tend to skew normal human relations. Still, parlor violations became a hallmark of late medieval decadence in convents. Saint Teresa of Avila in her *Autobiography* tells how she spent her days in the parlor entertaining local hangers-on before her conversion to religious seriousness.

[384] "Protected" (*defendendum*). It is hard to find the exactly right word here. The real issue is *presumption*, which is mentioned explicitly in the title of RB 69, the model for Walbert's chapter. The problem is when someone besides the abbess takes a sister under her wing.

[385] "We decree" (*Censemus*). *Censeo* usually means to think or estimate, but in a juridical context it can be much more decisive. Monastic legislators such as Walbert give directives, not opinions.

[386] "Friend" (*proximam*). *Proxima* is generally rendered "neighbor," but here something closer is called for. The point is favoritism, which can plague monasteries as well as any other social body.

[387] "Not for herself but for Christ" (*sibi non vivit, sed Christo*). These words in the dative case are a direct quotation of Rom 14:7-8. There is no simple way of rendering Paul's dense, difficult idea in English. One thing is sure: the other Christian also belongs to Christ, and no bonds of human affection can override that fundamental relationship.

[388] "She remains crucified" (*manet crucifixa*). The idea seems to be that no one needs to rescue another Christian. If she is suffering, that is

3. For she first lost her life in order to join it more abundantly to salvation.[389]

4. She who has given up her own will in order to carry out the will of Christ in her, why should she defend the sins of others when she has crucified her own sins?[390]

5. And if she has truly crucified them and no longer lives for the world but for Christ, why does she protect on any grounds of familiarity those falling in the world by their faults?[391]

6. So then let her have equal love[392] for her relative as for any other sister who is not joined to her by ties of blood.

---

expected of a disciple of Christ. Clearly, this idea needs careful nuancing. The background is Gal 6:14. Columban himself quotes Gal 6:14 in *Coen* IV.1, but he uses the text to argue for monastic dispossession. In *Concordia Regularum* 74, Benedict of Aniane cites Wal 23 under the name of Columban.

[389] Another verse heavily based on Scripture. Now the source is Mark 8:35: "Whoever loses his life for my sake and that of the Gospel will save it." I do not quite understand the expression "join it to salvation." Perhaps Walbert wishes to avoid "will save it" as a bit jarring. Only God can save.

[390] The Pauline warrant here is Gal 5:24: "Now those who belong to Christ have crucified their flesh with its passions and desires." *Crucified* can be understood somewhat graphically: to nail one's sins to the cross. Walbert makes exceptionally extensive use of Scripture in this chapter. All of this is quite beyond RB 69.

[391] "Falling in the world by their faults" (*in mundo facinoribus labentes*). At this point it is clear that the context is penal: someone is trying to defend a nun who is in trouble because of misconduct. There is no hint of that in RB 69.

[392] "Equal love" (*aequus amor*). This seems like an unrealistic expectation, at least if one understands *amor* as natural affect. It is beyond the power of the will to feel equal affection for everyone. Yet Christian *caritas* is a different matter.

7. Therefore everybody should keep their affections to them-selves,[393] and no one should try to shield anyone placed under the regime of penance.[394]

8. This is to prevent the vice of defending from spreading.[395]

9. She whose charge it is to correct sisters should do so under the impulse of love. She should exercise discipline to cor-rect vice, not to fulfill her own will.

Chapter 24. The Education of Children.[396]

1. We learn from many documents[397] with what care and discipline children are to be educated in the monastery.

2. They ought to be raised with tender affection and also the application of discipline.[398]

---

[393] "Keep their affections to themselves" (*amor corde clausus*). This should not be taken too strictly to mean an atmosphere of cold grimness. Yet excessive displays of affection are out of place in a celibate community.

[394] This verse reminds one of RB 25, prohibiting monks from inter-vening in cases of excommunication.

[395] A monastery where everybody has a protector is a dysfunctional group of people.

[396] "Education" (*nutriendis*). *Nutrio* literally means "to feed," as its En-glish cognate indicates. Early medieval culture featured the education of noble children in monasteries. The Rule of Saint Benedict, for example, has several short chapters aimed directly at the topic of children in the mon-astery: RB 37 on feeding them, and RB 30 and RB 70 on disciplining them. The Cistercian movement (ca. 1150), however, decided that the monastery as such is no place for children. This carried the day: the Catholic Church no longer admits anyone but adults to monastic profession.

[397] At least two children are mentioned in the Miracles of Eboriac as coming to the monastery and leading holy lives: Ercantrude (II.13) and Deurechilde (II.15). Caesarius also witnesses to the presence of young girls in the monastery at Arles for which he wrote a Rule: Reg Virg 7.2–3.

[398] The next verse indicates that Walbert is more worried about laxity than harshness in the monastic treatment of children. In my experience, however, the opposite was true: heavy moral and spiritual pressure was often applied to teenage boys where tender mercy was called for.

3. Otherwise they will be blemished at a young age by the vices of laziness and indulgence. Then later on one will scarcely be able to correct them, or not at all.[399]
4. Thus make sure that they never lack a senior to keep them on the strait and narrow.[400]
5. They should be trained for the religious life[401] by the discipline they always receive from her and her teaching on the fear and love of God.[402]
6. Let them practice reading,[403] so they learn at a tender age what will profit them when they grow up.[404]

[399] Obviously children who are raised without discipline are being deprived of necessary lessons in how to lead a successful life. Yet this still leaves the question of what form discipline should take. RB 2, on the abbot, discusses this point in some depth. The gist: different personalities respond to different treatment: reasoning or blows?

[400] "On the strait and narrow" (*huc atque illuc liceat deviare*). Literally, "keeps them from wandering off here and there." The point is that children need and deserve adult supervision. The phrase "strait and narrow" may be too harsh, but discipline is an unavoidable aspect of child rearing. Clearly, the monks and nuns who boarded children in the early Middle Ages were *in loco parentis*.

[401] "For the religious life" (*ad cultum . . . religionis*). *Cultus religionis* also occurs in Wal 1.9, where it more clearly refers to the religious life itself. Since the phrase appears in the first and last chapters of Wal, it can be considered an *inclusio*. Children who were educated in the monastery often became lifelong monks. Indeed, the majority of medieval monks and nuns fell into that category. Adult vocations were the exception.

[402] "Discipline . . . teaching" (*disciplina . . . doctrina*). This refers to the whole pedagogical package, apparently dependent on the senior in charge of the children. Although such arrangements were more common in bygone days in this country, British monasteries may still have monastic housemasters living with young children.

[403] "Let them practice reading" (*Habeant lectionis usum*). Reading is not only essential to any worthwhile education but especially crucial to a profitable monastic life. For example, Saint Benedict wants his monks to do between two and three hours of *lectio divina* daily (RB 48).

[404] "When they grow up" (*ad perfectam deductis proficiat*). Literally, "profit those who have arrived at maturity." Perhaps this is an idiom: I

7. In the refectory they should have a table by themselves, placed near the table of the seniors.[405]

8. Two or more seniors, whose maturity[406] is not in doubt, should sit with them.

9. So they will always have fear before their eyes, let them be educated[407] in dread of the seniors.[408]

10. It is up to the judgment of the abbess as to when they will eat[409] and when they will sleep.

11. In all things, observe discretion,[410] which is the guardian of the virtues.

---

do not understand the precise sense of *deductis*. Caesarius of Arles also wants the *nutriti* to learn to read (Reg Virg 7.3 and 18.6).

[405] The placement of the children in the same dining room as the monastic community may seem strange. After all, there is no talking at those meals, so the discipline would be severe. No doubt this did not work if there was a large gang of kids, but ancient times did not baby children.

[406] "Maturity" (*religione*). The same phrase occurs in Wal 14.8. Seilhac and Saïd, 95, translate it "spirit of religion." Remember, too, that in v. 5 I rendered *cultus . . . religionis* as "religious life." The issue here, though, is maturity, not piety. Depending on how young the children were, the seniors might have to help them eat as well as discipline them. For Benedict, a major issue regarding the care of children was *anger*. RB 70 does not want people to fly off the handle against children.

[407] "Educated" (*nutriantur*). This term could also be translated as "fed," which would work here too.

[408] "Dread of the seniors" (*sub metu seniorum*). One wonders how to render *metus* properly. Is it a different kind of fear from *timor* in the same verse? What place has terror in education, not to mention in eating?

[409] "When they will eat" (*Quibus horis reficiant*). Since they seemed to eat with the main community in v. 7, this is a bit puzzling. RB 37.3 has the children eat before the regular time, which seems humane. The general norm of the Catholic Church now is that fasting begins at age eighteen. But of course monks and nuns fast more often than other people.

[410] Columban devotes Reg VIII to discretion (*discretio*). For him, discretion is mainly a matter of avoiding excess—though he himself was not a particularly moderate man. This half verse could be the close of the subject of care of children or of the entire Rule of Walbert.

Bibliography

Works of Columban

Columban. *Règles et pénitentiels monastiques*. Translated by Adalbert de Vogüé with Pierre Sangiani and Jean-Baptiste Juglar. Aux sources du monachisme columbanien, vol. 2. Vie monastique 20. Bégrolles-en-Mauges, France: Abbaye de Bellefontaine, 1989.

———. *Sancti Columbani Opera*. Edited by G. S. M. Walker. Scriptores Latini Hiberniae, vol. 2. Dublin: The Dublin Institute for Advanced Studies, 1970.

Other Primary Sources

Ancient Laws of Ireland. Ed. W. Neilson Hancock. 6 vols. Dublin: Alexander Thom; London: Longman, Green, Longman, Roberts and Green, 1865–1901.

Athanasius. *Life of Antony*. PG 26:835; PL 73.

———. *The Life of Antony, the Coptic Life and the Greek Life*. Translated by Tim Vivian and A. N. Athanasakis. CS 202. Kalamazoo, MI: Cistercian Publications, 2003.

———. *Vie d'Antoine*. Edited and translated by G. J. M. Bartelink. SCh 400. Paris: Éditions du Cerf, 1994.

Bangor Antiphonary. An Early Irish Manuscript in the Ambrosian Library at Milan. Ed. F. E. Warren. London: Harrison and Sons, 1895.

Basil of Caesarea. *Basili Regula a Rufino Latine Versa*. Ed. Klaus Zelzer. CSEL 86. Vienna: Hoelder-Pichler-Tempsky, 1986.

———. *The Rule of Saint Basil in Latin and English: A Revised Critical Edition*. Translated by Anna M. Silvas. Collegeville, MN: Liturgical Press, 2013.

Benedict of Aniane. *Codex Regularum*. Ed. M. Brockie. Vienna, 1759.

———. *Concordia regularum*. Ed. Pierre Bonnerue. CCCM 168A. Turnhout: Brepols, 1999.

225

Cassian, John. *The Conferences.* Trans. Boniface Ramsey. Ancient Christian Writers series 57. New York: Paulist Press, 1997.

———. *The Conferences.* Trans. Colm Luibheid. The Classics of Western Spirituality. New York and Mahwah: Paulist Press, 1985.

———. *Conlationes.* Ed. Michael Petschenig and Gottfried Kreuz. CSEL 13. Salzburg, Austria: Verlag der Österreichischen Akademie der Wissenschaften, 1886, 2004.

Donatus. "La Règle de Donat pour l'abbesse Gauthstrude. Texte critique et synopse des sources." Trans. Adalbert de Vogüé. *Benedictina* 25 (1978): 219–313.

———. "Rule for Virgins." In *Codex Regularum.* Ed. Lucas Holstenius. Rome, 1661; reprint Graz, Austria: Akademische Druck-U. Verlagsanstalt, 1957. 377–92.

———. "The Rule of Donatus of Besançon." Translated by Jo Ann McNamara and John E. Halborg. In Jo Ann McNamara, *The Ordeal of Community: Hagiography and Discipline in Merovingian Convents.* Toronto: Peregrina Publishers, 1990.

Excerpta Davidis. In *The Irish Penitentials,* edited by Ludwig Bieler. Scriptores Latini Hiberniae, vol. 5. Dublin: The Dublin Institute for Advanced Studies, 1963. 70–73.

Gennadius of Marseille. *De ecclesiasticis dogmatibus. Liber sive diffinitio ecclesiasticorum dogmatum.* In "The '*Liber Ecclesiasticorum Dogmatum,*'" edited by C. H. Turner. *Journal of Theological Studies* 7 (1906): 78–99; 8 (1907): 103–14.

Gildas. *Praefatio Gildae de Paenitentia.* In Ludwig Bieler, *The Irish Penitentials.* Dublin: The Dublin Institute for Advanced Studies, 1963. 60–65.

Gregory the Great. *Dialogues.* Edited by Adalbert de Vogüé. Translated by Paul Antin. 3 vols. SCh 251, 260, 265. Paris: Les Éditions du Cerf, 1978, 1979, 1980.

———. "Vie de saint Benoît." In *Dialogues II,* edited by Adalbert de Vogüé. Translated by Paul Antin. SCh 260. Paris: Les Éditions de Cerf, 1979.

Gregory of Tours. *Miracula et opera minora.* Ed. Bruno Krusch. MGH Scriptores Rerum Merovingicarum I.2. Hannover and Leipzig: Impensis Bibliopolii Hahniani, 1969.

Gwynn, E. J., and W. J. Purton, eds. *The Monastery of Tallaght.* Proceedings of the Royal Irish Academy, 29.C.5. Dublin: Hodges, Figgis & Co., 1911.

Jerome. *Epistulae 1–154*. Ed. I. Hilberg. 3 vols. CSEL 54, 55, 56/1. Salzburg, Austria: Verlag der Österreichischen Akademie der Wissenschaften, 1910–18.

———. *Select Letters of Saint Jerome*. Trans. F. A. Wright. Loeb Classical Library 262. London: William Heinemann; New York: G. P. Putnam's Sons, 1933.

John of Salerno. *Vita Sancti Odonis*. In *St. Odo of Cluny: Being the Life of St. Odo of Cluny by John of Salerno and the Life of St. Gerald of Aurillac by St. Odo*, translated by Gerard Sitwell. London: Sheed and Ward, 1958.

Jonas de Bobbio. "Life of St. Columban by Jonas, the Monk." Ed. Dana Carleton Munro. *Translations and Reprints from the Original Sources of European History*. Philadelphia: Dept. of History, University of Pennsylvania Press, 1900. Vol. 2, no. 7:1–36.

———. *Vie de Saint Colomban et de ses disciples*. Trans. Adalbert de Vogüé with Pierre Sangiani. Aux sources du monachisme colombanien, vol. 1. Vie monastique 19. Bégrolles-en-Mauges, France: Abbaye de Bellefontaine, 1988.

———. "Vitae Columbani abbatis discipulorumque eius libri." In *Ionae Vitae Sanctorum Columbani, Vedastis, Iohannis*, edited by Bruno Krusch. MGH Scriptores Rerum Germanicarum. Hannover and Leipzig: Impensis Bibliopolii Hahniani, 1905. 2:144–294.

———. *Vita Sancti Columbani Abbatis*. PL 87:1011–46.

———. "Vita Sancti Iohannis Monachi et Abbatis." In *Ionae Vitae Sanctorum Columbani, Vedastis, Iohannis*, edited by Bruno Krusch. MGH Scriptores Rerum Germanicarum. Hannover and Leipzig: Impensis Bibliopolii Hahniani, 1905. 2:321–44.

Pachomian Koinonia I. Armand Veilleux. CS 45. Kalamazoo, MI: Cistercian Publications, 1980.

"Paenitentiale quod dicitur Bigotianum." In *The Irish Penitentials*, edited by Ludwig Bieler. Scriptores Latini Hiberniae, vol. 5. Dublin: The Dublin Institute for Advanced Studies, 1963. 198–239.

Possidius. *Sancti Augustini Vita Scripta a Possidio Episcopo*. Ed. and trans. Herbert T. Weiskotten. Princeton: Princeton University Press, 1919.

———. *Vita S. Augustini*. In *Selecta opuscula SS. Patrum*, edited by Hugo Adalbert Ferdinand von Hurter. 54 vols. Innsbruck, Austria: Libraria Academica Wagneriana, 1868–1892.

"Règle de Walbert." In *Règles Monastiques au Féminin*. Trans. Lazare de Seilhac and M. Bernard Saïd, with M. Madeleine Braquet and Véronique Dupont. Dans la tradition de Benoît et Columban. Vie Monastique 33. Bégrolles-en-Mauges: Abbaye de Bellefontaine, 1996. 45–95.

"Rule of Fructuosus." In *Codex Regularum 1*, edited by Lucas Holstenius. Rept. Graz, Austria: Akademische Druck-U. Verlagsanstalt, 1957.

Strabo, Walahfrid. *The Life of St Gall*. Ed. Maud Joynt. London: SPCK, 1927.

Severus, Sulpicius. *Dialogi*. Ed. Karl Halm. CSEL 1. Vienna: Schulbuchverlag Hölder Picler Tempsky, 1866. 152–216.

———. *Vita Martini*. Ed. Karl Halm. CSEL 1. Vienna: Schulbuchverlag Hölder Picler Tempsky, 1866. 107–37.

Theodore of Tarsus. *Penitential*. In *The Old English Canons of Theodore*, edited by R. D. Fulk and Stefan Jurasinski. Early English Text Society, Supplementary Series 25. Oxford: Oxford University Press, 2012.

Vitae Sanctorum Hiberniae: partim hactenus ineditae. 2 vols. Ed. Charles Plummer. Oxford: Clarendon Press, 1910.

Walbert. "Cuiusdam Patris Regula ad Virgines." In *Codex Regularum monasticarum et canonicarum*, edited by Lucas Holstenius. Augsburg, 1759; reprint Graz, Austria: Akademische Druck-U. Verlagsanstalt, 1957. 393–404.

Wettinus. "Vita S. Galli." In *Passiones vitaeque sanctorum aevi Merovingici (II)*, edited by Bruno Krusch. Repertorium Fontium 11. MGH Scriptorum Rerum Merovingicarum IV. 256–80.

Secondary Sources

Bacht, Heinrich. *Das Vermächtnis des Ursprungs, II: Pachomius, der Mann und sein Werk*. Wurzburg, Germany: Echter Verlag, 1983.

Blaise, Albert. *Dictionnaire latin-français des auteurs chrétiens*. Strasbourg: Le Latin Chrétien, 1954.

Bullough, Donald. "The Career of Columbanus." *In Columbanus: Studies on the Latin Writings*, edited by Michael Lapidge. Woodbridge, England: Boydell, 1997. 1–28.

Clark, Francis. *The Pseudo-Gregorian Dialogues.* Studies in the History of Christian Thought, 1997. Leiden, The Netherlands: Brill Academic Publishers, 1987.

Daly, William M. "Clovis: How Barbaric, How Pagan?" *Speculum* 69, no. 3 (1994): 619–64.

Du Cange, Charles. *Glossarium Mediae et Infimae Latinitatis.* 10 vols. Paris: Didot, 1840.

Engelbert, Pius. "Zür Frühgeschichte des Bobbieser Skriptoriums." *Revue Bénédictine* 78 (1968): 220–60.

Facciolati, Jacobi, and Egidio Forcellini, eds. 4 vols. *Totius Latinitatis Lexicon.* Padova, 1771.

Gordon, Mary. *Final Payments.* New York: Anchor Books, 2006.

Guérout, J. "Fare." *Dictionnaire d'histoire et de géographie ecclésiastiques.* Turnhout: Brepols Publishers, 1967.

Hartley, L. P. *The Go-Between.* London: H. Hamilton, 1953.

Hašek, Jaroslav. *The Good Soldier Schweik.* New York: New American Library, 1930.

Heffernan, Thomas J. *Sacred Biography: Saints and their Biographers in the Middle Ages.* Oxford: Oxford University Press, 1992.

Kardong, Terrence. *Benedict's Rule.* Collegeville, MN: Liturgical Press, 1996.

———. "The Demonic in Benedict's *Rule.*" *Tjurunga* 37 (1989): 3–11.

———. "The Devil in the Rule of the Master." *Studia Monastica* 30 (1988): 41–62.

———. "The Healing of Shame in the Rule of Saint Benedict." *American Benedictine Review* 53, no. 4 (2002): 453–74.

———. "People Storage: Mabillon's Diatribe against Monastic Prisons." *CSQ* 26, no. 1 (1991): 40–57.

———. "Who Wrote the Dialogues of St. Gregory? A Report on a Controversy." *CSQ* 39, no. 1 (2004): 31–39.

———. "Who Wrote the Rule of Walbert?" In *A Not-So-Unexciting Life: Essays on Benedictine History and Spirituality in Honor of Michael Casey, OCSO,* edited by Carmel Posa. CS 269. Collegeville, MN: Cistercian Publications, 2017. 214–32.

Kreiner, Jamie. "Autopsies and Philosophies of a Merovingian Life: Death, Responsibility, Salvation." *Journal of Early Christian Studies* 22, no. 1 (2014): 113–52.

Laporte, Jean. "Saint Columban, son âme et sa vie." In *Mélanges de science religieuse* 6 (1949): 49–56.

Leclercq, Henri. "Luxeuil." *Dictionnaire d'archéologie chrétienne et de liturgie.* Paris: Letouzy et Ané, 1907.

Morey, Adrian. *David Knowles: A Memoir.* London: Darton, Longman and Todd, 1979.

Morin, Germain. "Mélanges d'érudition chrétienne." *Revue Bénédictine* 12 (1895): 193–203.

O'Carroll, James. "Sainte Fare et les origines." In *Sainte Fare et Faremoutiers. Treize siècles de vie monastique,* edited by Abbaye de Faremoutiers. 2 vols. Abbaye de Faremoutiers, 1956. 1:3–35.

Ó Fiaich, Tomás. *Columbanus in his Own Words.* Dublin: Veritas, 1974.

Oxford Dictionary of the Christian Church. Ed. F. L. Cross and E. A. Livingstone. Oxford: Oxford University Press, 2005.

Oxford Latin Dictionary. Ed. P. G. W. Glare. Oxford: Oxford University Press, 1968.

Peifer, Claude. "Appendix 2: The Abbot." In *RB 1980: The Rule of Saint Benedict,* edited by Timothy Fry. Collegeville, MN: Liturgical Press, 1981. 322–78.

———. "The Rule of St. Benedict." In *RB 1980: The Rule of Saint Benedict,* edited by Timothy Fry. Collegeville, MN: Liturgical Press, 1981. 65–112.

Sainte Fare et Faremoutiers. Treize siècles de vie monastique. Ed. Abbaye de Faremoutiers. 2 vols. Abbaye de Faremoutiers, 1956.

Swain, Lionel. "The Inspiration of Scripture." In *A New Catholic Commentary on Holy Scripture,* edited by Reginald C. Fuller, et al. London: Thomas Nelson and Sons, 1969. 1181–91.

Veilleux, Armand. *La Liturgie dans le cénobitisme Pachômien au quatrième siècle.* Studia Anselmiana 57. Rome: Herder, 1968.

Vogüé, Adalbert de. "Le 'Pénitentiel' de Columban et la Tradition Anterieure." In Adalbert de Vogüé, *Histoire Littéraire du Mouvement Monastique dans l'Antiquité.* 11 vols. Paris: Les Éditions du Cerf, 1991–2006. 10:253–66.

Wallace-Hadrill, J. M. *The Long-Haired Kings.* Toronto: University of Toronto Press, 1982.

Wood, Ian. *The Merovingian Kingdoms 450–751.* New York: Longman Press, 1993.

Index A
Biblical References

Chapter and verse references are found in the body of the four rules; references preceded by n. are found in the footnotes.

Inꝺex B
References to the Rule of Saint Benedict

Cited by footnotes.

RB 28.3	Wal 325	RB 41.1	Wal 190
RB 28.4	Wal 328	RB 41.5	Coen 192;
RB 28.5	Wal 338		Wal 225
RB 29	Wal 342	RB 41.9	Wal 195
RB 29.1	Wal 344	RB 42	Coen 182
RB 29.3	Wal 348	RB 42.8-11	Coen 140
RB 30	Wal 302, 340, 396	RB 42.8	Wal 154
RB 31	Wal 80	RB 42.10	Wal 154
RB 31.1	Wal 32, 73, 76	RB 43–46	Wal 294
RB 31.2	Wal 78	RB 43	Coen 190;
RB 31.3-4	Wal 79		Wal 129
RB 31.7	Wal 80	RB 43.3	Wal 132
RB 31.9	Wal 82	RB 43.4	Wal 134
RB 31.10	Wal 67	RB 43.8-9	Wal 137
RB 31.12	Wal 32, 84	RB 43.10	Reg 39
RB 31.13-14	Wal 88	RB 43.13-17	Coen 125
RB 31.18-19	Wal 235	RB 43.18-19	Coen 68
RB 32	Wal 229	RB 44.10	Coen 189
RB 33	Wal 84, 278, 286	RB 46.1-2	Wal 269
RB 33.1	Coen 179;	RB 46.1-4	Coen 187
	Wal 284	RB 46.4	Wal 274
RB 33.2	Coen 201	RB 48	Wal 204, 210, 403
RB 33.4	Wal 287	RB 48.6	Wal 192
RB 33.6	Coen 201	RB 49.5	Reg 135
RB 34	Wal 168	RB 49.7	Coen 195
RB 35	Paen 98; Wal 230	RB 50.4	Reg 135
RB 35.1	Coen 8	RB 51	Coen 119
RB 35.7-9	Wal 228	RB 53	Coen 31, 63;
RB 35.12	Wal 196		Paen 98
RB 35.17-18	Wal 226, 227	RB 53.13	Wal 228
RB 35.17	Wal 251	RB 53.18–20	Coen 117
RB 36	Coen 76; Wal 13,	RB 53.18	Wal 225
	260, 264	RB 53.23-24	Coen 116, 200
RB 37	Wal 264, 396	RB 54	Wal 187
RB 37.3	Wal 265, 409	RB 55.15-16	Wal 43
RB 38	Wal 156	RB 55.16	Coen 173
RB 38.5	Coen 176	RB 55.18	Wal 91
RB 38.9	Wal 156	RB 56	Wal 71
RB 39.2	Reg 133	RB 63	Reg 122;
RB 39.3	Wal 170		Wal 350, 367
RB 41	Coen 131;	RB 63.4	Coen 28; Wal 371
	Wal 176, 190	RB 63.13	Wal 96

Index C

Patristic and Monastic Sources

Cited by footnotes in the four rules.

Index D

Topics Discussed in Notes

Inдex E

Latin and Greek Words
and Phrases Discussed in Notes

Single-word entries are in the root form; phrases retain inflected forms.

Abbas	Reg 57;	Ambitio	Reg 67
	Coen 124, 170	Ambitus	Wal 353
Abbatissa	Wal 2, 369	Ambulansque	
Absolute	Reg 121; Paen 93	dormitet	Reg 138
Abstergere	Paen 66	Amicorum	
Accommodare	Wal 6, 58	saecularium	Coen 200
Adhaerens	Coen 94	Amor	Wal 96, 361, 392
Admittere	Coen 205; Paen 2	Amor corde	
Adulterium	Paen 53	clausus	Wal 393
Aedificare	Wal 365	Anima	Paen 102
Aedificatio	Coen 221	Animadversio	Paen 36
Aequalis	Wal 166	Animae	
Aequus	Wal 392	impunitate	Reg 99
Aequo animo	Coen 102	Animal	Paen 50
Aerumnosum	Wal 282	Aqua	Coen 109, 153
Aetas	Wal 264	Arcessire,	
Aeternae salutis		accerso	Coen 190
conpaginem	Paen 109	Archimandritus	Reg 57
Aeternus	Paen 43	Arguere	Coen 158
Affectus	Wal 267, 352,	Arripere	Wal 362, 374
	357, 364	Ars	Coen 56
Agnon	Reg 27	Assidue	Wal 103
Allegere	Coen 88	Ater	Coen 224
Altarium	Paen 41, 69	Auctor	Wal 252
Alternatim		Audire	Coen 129
per vices	Wal 219	Bilinguis	Coen 118
Altus	Coen 224	Blasfemare	Coen 210
Ambascia	Coen 169	Bonosiacus	Paen 87

Index F

Glossary of Columbanian Persons and Places